Irony and the Modern Theatre

Irony and theatre share intimate kinships, regarding not only dramatic conflict, dialectic, or wittiness, but also scenic structure and the verbal or situational ironies that typically mark theatrical speech and action. Yet irony today, in aesthetic, literary, and philosophical contexts especially, is often regarded with skepticism – as ungraspable, or elusive to the point of confounding. Countering this tendency, Storm advocates a capacious, wide-angle view of this master trope, exploring the ironic in major works by playwrights including Chekhov, Pirandello, and Brecht, and in notable relation to well-known representative characters in drama from Ibsen's Halvard Solness to Stoppard's Septimus Hodge and Wasserstein's Heidi Holland. To the degree that irony is existential, its presence in the theatre relates directly to the circumstances and the expressiveness of the characters on stage. This study investigates how these key figures enact, embody, represent, and personify the ironic in myriad situations in the modern and contemporary theatre.

WILLIAM STORM teaches dramatic literature, theory, and theatre history at New Mexico State University. He is the author of *After Dionysus: A Theory of the Tragic*, as well as numerous essays, articles, and plays. His scholarly specializations include dramatic theory and dramaturgy, the history and theory of the tragic form and sensibility, art in relation to literature and performance, and connections of science with theatre and narrative studies.

CAMBRIDGE STUDIES IN MODERN THEATRE

Series editor
David Bradby, *Royal Holloway, University of London*

Advisory board
Martin Banham, *University of Leeds*
Jacky Bratton, *Royal Holloway, University of London*
Tracy Davis, *Northwestern University*
Sir Richard Eyre
Michael Robinson, *University of East Anglia*
Sheila Stowell, *University of Birmingham*

Volumes for Cambridge Studies in Modern Theatre explore the political, social, and cultural functions of theatre while also paying careful attention to detailed performance analysis. The focus of the series is on political approaches to the modern theatre with attention also being paid to theatres of earlier periods and their influence on contemporary drama. Topics in the series are chosen to investigate this relationship and include both playwrights (their aims and intentions set against the effects of their work) and process (with emphasis on rehearsal and production methods, the political structure within theatre companies and their choice of audiences or performance venues). Further topics will include devised theatre, agitprop, community theatre, para-theatre, and performance art. In all cases the series will be alive to the special cultural and political factors operating in the theatres examined.

Books published
Maria DiCenzo, *The Politics of Alternative Theatre in Britain, 1968–1990: The Case of 7:84 (Scotland)*
Jo Riley, *Chinese Theatre and the Actor in Performance*
Jonathan Kalb, *The Theatre of Heiner Müller*
Richard Boon and Jane Plastow, eds., *Theatre Matters: Performance and Culture on the World Stage*
Claude Schumacher, ed., *Staging the Holocaust: The Shoah in Drama and Performance*
Philip Roberts, *The Royal Court Theatre and the Modern Stage*

Irony and the Modern Theatre

William Storm

New Mexico State University

CAMBRIDGE
UNIVERSITY PRESS

CAMBRIDGE UNIVERSITY PRESS
Cambridge, New York, Melbourne, Madrid, Cape Town,
Singapore, São Paulo, Delhi, Tokyo, Mexico City

Cambridge University Press
The Edinburgh Building, Cambridge CB2 8RU, UK

Published in the United States of America by Cambridge University Press, New York

www.cambridge.org
Information on this title: www.cambridge.org/9781107007925

First published 2011

Printed in the United Kingdom at the University Press, Cambridge

A catalogue record for this publication is available from the British Library

Library of Congress Cataloging in Publication data
Storm, William, 1949–
Irony and the modern theatre / by William Storm.
    p.   cm. – (Cambridge studies in modern theatre)
Includes bibliographical references.
ISBN 978-1-107-00792-5 (hardback)
1. Irony in literature.   2. Drama – History and criticism.
3. Drama – Psychological aspects.   I. Title.
PN1929.I7S76   2011
809.2'918–dc22

                                                        2010043726

ISBN 978-1-107-00792-5 Hardback

133304

For Deborah

Contents

Acknowledgements

I am indebted to those who have contributed extensively to understandings of irony and theatre, especially Bert O. States and Kenneth Burke, and to others who have written on irony and the ironic more inclusively, including D. C. Muecke and Claire Colebrook, and, in relation to postmodernism, Linda Hutcheon, and to language, Eric Gans. I am grateful to Robert Brustein, Richard Gilman, and Eric Bentley, whose landmark writings on the modern and contemporary theatre were formative and have been a continuing resource of information and insight. My thanks also to colleagues who read early versions of these chapters: H. Porter Abbott, Christopher Innes, W. Davies King, Peter Rabinowitz, Brian Richardson, and Simon Williams. I am deeply appreciative of Cambridge editors Victoria L. Cooper, Christina Sarigiannidou, and Rebecca Taylor, and my copy-editor Caroline Howlett for the guidance and support they have given this book, and of readers for the Press for invaluable scholarly and editorial acumen.

Introduction

Irony, in its contrariness, has gained a reputation for indeterminacy, for being all but ungraspable except perhaps in the most traditional contexts of wittiness, paradox, the assumption of an opposite, or a perspective of stylish but world-weary commentary. Irony in the more complicated view can now be confounding, a perspective that has become more pervasive, or at least more presumed, in connection with postmodernist or deconstructive assumptions regarding the disassociative properties of language in particular. Irony does, in fact, imply opposition, a consistent if at times hidden presence of the alternate view; and when such alternation is reiterated or compounded, the contrary properties of the ironic become correspondingly more manifest, leading potentially to progressive negation or even self-cancellation. This, in brief, is an attribute belonging innately to a trope with philosophical as well as verbal and aesthetic properties, a trait that may at times contribute to a perception of capriciousness and contradiction.

Yet irony is also capacious, with an ability to imply or embrace a universalized as well as localized or delimited perspective. The existential or ontological implications of the ironic are plenteous, even when coupled with (or, at times, because of) the self-nullifying traits that arise from a fundamental basis in antagonism and conflict. Moreover, the ironic mode is, as Northrop Frye would say, "naturally sophisticated," one that "takes life exactly as it finds it" (*Anatomy* 41). Indeed, and as a ratio, the more sophisticated the irony, the broader its scope and potential range of implications – even, once again, when a verbal or philosophical complexity goes hand-in-hand with an internal propensity toward negation, ironic self-reference, or tautology. Irony is, in other words, fully capable of being ironic in relation to itself. Still, the capaciousness of the ironic manner relates directly to its revelatory capabilities and to its interrelation among conversational, theatrical, literary, and philosophical discourses.

How, then, to proceed analytically with a term that is so innately multifarious? Or, put differently, how to employ by way of reference a single word for so extensive a menu of identities and capabilities? If irony is applicable across a spectrum that extends from stylish badinage to the paradoxical and dialectical, including at given extremes a sweeping existential purview, might it be the case that no single word can contain so much, at least without substantial contextual qualification? Even with that question in mind, and justifiably so, the ambition of this book is to adopt a wide-angle view of this versatile and changeable trope, with an eye toward giving its capabilities a due recognition in the theatrical context. This is not to say that irony cannot be elusive to the point of confounding (a part of its allure, perhaps) but rather that the fullness of the ironic perspective merits as thorough and rounded a set of viewpoints as can be identified and integrated.

Moreover, and since irony evinces such close associations with drama, the aim of the discussion here is to expand rather than constrict its range of possible understandings in specific connection with the theatre. Irony is contradictory, to be sure, yet that very quality is what aligns it so fundamentally with dramatic conflict and dialectic. Irony can be performative as well as verbal, and as such can be communicated through theatrical spectacle as well as in dialogue or thematic implication. While the particular focus of this study is on the recent theatre – beginning with the late nineteenth century – the lengthy ancestry of irony in drama is taken into account. In the nearer historical setting, and pertaining mostly to modern European drama, the discussion in these chapters includes perspectives ranging from New Critical to deconstructive, modernist to postmodern. The approach is phenomenological insofar as emphasis is sustained on the nature and behaviors of the trope per se, but inclusive with respect to critical stances and philosophies of irony. Here again, the effort is to enlarge rather than marginalize the capabilities of the ironic even while acknowledging that a single term is being called upon to denote

2

disparate uses and understandings. Even though comprehensiveness may, of necessity, be impossible with respect to ironic iteration, the goal nonetheless is to pursue a rounded perspective, and one that can be useful in applying the myriad incarnations of the ironic to a full range of dramatic expressiveness.

Irony arises in juxtaposition – this in relation to that, with a point of view that is generally implied rather than stated, particularly in Frye's "sophisticated" mode. In drama, this juxtaposition is wed naturally to conflict – this in opposition to that, with an implicit dramaturgical development arising among the antagonistic parties. Since dramatic conflict is embodied as well as enacted, irony in the theatre is situated typically in character (through verbal expression, representation of personality and deeds, or the dramatic situation itself) or, as a totality, in the assembly of characters or dramatis personae. Indeed, the cast of any given play must necessarily contain the conflict – or, by association, the ironic pattern or dialectic. This is the Burkean "philosophic sense in which agon, protagonist, and antagonist can each be said to exist implicitly in the others" (*Philosophy* 77). Dramatic irony is in this sense partnered – not only in the juxtapositions and conflicts but as these elements are personified through characterization. Along these lines, and especially in the theatrical contexts of enactment, embodiment, and dramatic opposition, the nature of irony can be aligned directly to the aesthetic properties of drama itself. Here, too, an inclusive perspective is pertinent, to the extent that fundamental behaviors in theatre relate so typically to irony's mechanisms. To summarize: the single term, irony, is innately contradictory and can manifest considerable slippage in its definitions and connotations; at the same time, its natural propensities as well as elemental relations to the theatre call for a capacious rather than restrictive perspective for analysis. Further, the fact that historical, cultural, or philosophical trends associated with the modernist and contemporary theatre have added to irony's multidimensionality might, in fact, be understood as enlarging rather than diminishing the trope's purview.

Theatre, in recent decades as in past centuries, contains the ironic in ways that are intrinsically and markedly different from narrative fiction, poetry, or other literary art. The reasons for these differences are situated in the drama's performative as well as structural or scenic qualities. Irony gains an additional dimension through the theatre's ability to demonstrate an ironic instance or pattern through dramatic action and spectacle. Also, irony in the theatre can be dramatized over the totality of a play's action as well as encapsulated within a single moment of stage imagery. Here too, the essential trait of juxtaposition can, in the theatrical context, be enhanced greatly by what is visual as well as what is verbal.

For the purposes of inquiry here, emphasis is placed on the experiences of dramatic characters – so as to stress the repercussions of the ironic as it is experienced by figures that, in effect, stand for and personify irony under widely varying circumstances. To embody or to enact are related and yet different functions of theatrical character, with enactment pertaining more to the dramatic action while personification and embodiment apply more to what is represented through the depiction of personality or a set of characteristics and predispositions. With respect to character, irony can be conscious – as in the observations of a deliberate ironist – or unconscious, as in situations where an irony catches a stage figure unawares. In addition, theatrical irony can be authorial – in the sense of a mastered or overarching irony that marks the dramatic representation overall – as against an ironic flavor that may be more individually situated in characterization.

In the case of Henrik Ibsen, each of these variations applies. For one example, the action of *Hedda Gabler* as an overall dramatic pattern completes the title character's progress from an ill-advised marriage to George Tesman through the consequent and related encounters with Eilert Loevborg and Judge Brack to a suicide that is the direct and ironic result of these interrelations. As an individual personification, Hedda continually embodies an irony that is, to a large degree, her birthright – hence the choice of self-destruction by gunshot, using one of her military father's ornamental pistols. That Hedda is shown as impassioned, sensual, egoistic, and vengeful – yet at once desperately fearful of shame or scandal – is for Ibsen the portrait of an ironic double bind that once again connects directly with the tragic outcome.

Indeed, similar instances of ironic personification or embodiment in characterization comprise a recurring motif in modernist

4

playwriting. Konstantin Treplev, in Anton Chekhov's *The Seagull*, himself a suicide by gunshot, embodies and enacts the ironies of his artistic and filial involvements within a triangle made up of the older writer Trigorin, the dominant figure of the mother Irina, and the young actress Nina as romantic love object. In typical Chekhovian fashion, in which ironies must include a thwarting of desire and mismatching of romantic partners, Constantine is especially victimized. For Bernard Shaw, although certainly not in a tragic vein, the title figure of Mrs. Warren is made to recognize and endure the painful irony of what she herself has created – that is, the defiant personality of her daughter Vivie, who Mrs. Warren has unwittingly fashioned as her own comeuppance.

The personification of irony can apply to duets as well as individual portrayals. The pairing of Halvard Solness and Hilda Wangel in Ibsen's *The Master Builder* makes for a profoundly ironic match that generates a resonance well beyond the limits of either figure's depiction individually. The supreme irony of Lopakhin's purchase of the family estate at auction in Chekhov's *The Cherry Orchard* can only achieve maximum impact in connection with Madame Ranevskaya's investment in the cherry orchard and also with her past, which Lopakhin once shared in the relation of serf to nobility. In Shaw's *Candida*, the effect of Eugene Marchbanks's intrusion in the household of Reverend James Morell attains its full ironic import through a pairing of the intruder with the hapless Morell, not to mention the title figure of the preacher's enigmatic wife. Each of these cases, though individual, exemplifies a typical pattern in the modern and contemporary theatre: the tendency for the ironic to be situated in, and made personal through, the natures and the experiences of dramatic characters, alone or possibly in tandem.

There are categories of irony in theatre that may, in a broad sense, be termed philosophic, due in large part to an extent of application beyond the circumstances of any single play. Such philosophic irony has a long history in the theatre, extending to the tragic, or Sophoclean, perspective on ironic disparity or discrepancy of knowledge. When Oedipus refers to himself as "luck's child," his prideful comment accentuates the degree of dissonance between what the audience may see and the limitations of the character's own self-awareness. By the time that *Oedipus the King* was performed, however, Aeschylus had already fashioned the majestic scene in the *Agamemnon* in which the king, stepping down from his chariot and walking on purple tapestries to appease the soon-to-be-murderous Clytemnestra, states: "My will is mine." He is, in this moment, oblivious to his fate; the Greek audience, however, would be witness to his obvious blindness to an omnipotent order of daimon and divinity, not to mention the dissembling of the queen. In the ancient setting at least, such ironic disparities may exist not only among characters but between characters and cosmic powers, notably the gods whose dealings remain ever beyond the divination of the powerful yet mortally delimited.

The modern theatre has employed irony of the philosophic variety in several key ways, including at times dramatic situations with notable affiliations with their ancient predecessors, especially in the context of tragic drama. Halvard Solness, even more so than Oedipus, is aware of a "luck" that has marked his life to such a pronounced degree that he wonders what power in or outside of himself might be participatory in a guiding of events. Ibsen draws attention to Solness's luck by having the master builder himself as well as other characters (Aline, Dr. Herdal) refer to it on several occasions, but he illustrates it most vividly and scenically through Hilda Wangel's intrusion into the Solness household – an arrival laden with ironic implications. In *The Master Builder*, the interventions of chance, happenstance, and meaningful "luck" are so mysteriously appropriate that a strong impression of an overarching and supersensory order ensues – for Solness and perhaps for the observer in the theatre as well.

In the case of Chekhovian drama, an ironic tone emerges typically and familiarly from the foibles and miscalculations among characters in their everyday and often misguided pursuits, but in this instance, too, irony in the philosophic mode can achieve a connotative power well beyond the immediate circumstances. In his major plays, and often with reference to factors of time, Chekhov transforms an ironic (and at times comedic) world-view into a universalized statement. With Chekhov, as with Ibsen, the use of irony can transcend the quotidian and imply a destiny, thus entertaining a philosophic question of what may be transcendent or cosmically sensical, albeit mysterious, by contrast with the commonplace or apparently random.

While the ironic may be associated in such rare instances with something perpetual, or with some veiled quality of transcendence, the realms of aesthetics and dialectic provide the more typical theatrical settings for irony's philosophical capabilities. In the former, irony is understood as a property closely related to dramaturgical principles having to do with the structure of action; in this context observations can follow that align the trope with the art of drama itself. Regarding dialectic, the strategy of Bernard Shaw (as prime example) is to juxtapose thematic components in ways that highlight rather than resolve an array of ironic oppositions. The dialectical debate that is carried out, for instance, in *Mrs. Warren's Profession* is designed to set forth and then elaborately complicate the terms of argument – in this case having to do with a capitalistic versus a survival impulse, together with what Shaw might suggest is for sale in human affairs more generally. In the absence of a "well-made" dialectical synthesis, Shaw's tactic is to leave any concluding impressions of Mrs. Warren's or her daughter Vivie's "way of life" for an audience to decide. The kinship of irony and dialectic, so strongly evident in Shavian drama, is in fact a partnership that is characteristic of a much broader spectrum of dramatic action, perhaps especially in the Burkean sense of an equation between these two terms and – in the context of irony as one of "Four Master Tropes" – with the "dramatic" as well (*Grammar* 503, 511).

A key affiliation between irony and drama lies in the ways in which opposition has a developmental or progressive aspect. That is, while irony is always based in comparison, juxtaposition, and opposition, dramatic action tends to advance and also interrogate the opposing elements. This, in brief, is the ironic pattern in drama that is proposed as an innate property by Kenneth Burke and elaborated by Bert O. States, notably in the latter's *Irony and Drama*. Here once more the philosophic aspect is allied directly with the dramaturgical, but here also the negative propensity of the ironic can be pronounced. With respect to Pirandello's theatre, and in *Six Characters in Search of an Author* particularly, a flummoxing set of intersections concerning what is true, illusory, or "theatrical" turns the ironic dialectic into

7

a progressive and accelerating co-negation among the antagonistic terms. In this scenario, and unlike the Shavian dialectic that aims for a provocative equipoise among terms, the dramatic development evinces a *sentimento del contraria* leading ultimately to cancellation. This, in effect, is dramatic irony as ne plus ultra – or, from a different angle, as nihilism. Irony in drama may have, as Burke would say, an "internal fatality" (*Grammar* 517), but it also contains the implicit wild card of non-containment that arises when opposition goes unchecked and can run the full course of its ironic potentials, ontologically as well as dramaturgically.

Absurdist irony, in one respect a hyperextension of this negative proclivity, can bring with it a cancellation of logic, sensible cause and effect, and – as in Eugene Ionesco's conception of the "anti-play" – a radical devaluation of the communicative capabilities of language. And yet, the ironic development need not be taken to the extremes of, say, *The Bald Soprano*, for irony's negative propensities to be strenuously felt. Rather, Ionesco's drama can be understood simply as a deliberate exaggeration of what is already built into the ironic mode, most particularly in relation to language. As Hayden White observes, the ironic trope "provides a linguistic paradigm of a mode of thought which is radically self-critical with respect not only to a given characterization of the world of experience but also to the very effort to capture adequately the truth of things in language." More broadly, White identifies irony's "apprehension of the essential folly or absurdity of the human condition" with a tendency to "engender belief in the 'madness' of civilization itself" (37–38). It should be noted here, and perhaps ironically, that at these extremes the ironic trope in the theatre can move interchangeably to comic or tragic polarities, as the degree of negation can be similar in either instance of genre.

Irony in the comic context has an ancestral tie to comedy of manners that dates to the origins of this sub-genre in the Restoration and extending through the comedies of (most notably) Oscar Wilde, Noel Coward, and more recently, Tom Stoppard. The Restoration truewit is often an ironist in the observation of, typically, the hypocritical culture in which he or she flourishes. Figures such as Mr. Dorimant (*The Man of Mode*) or Mr. Horner (*The Country Wife*) demonstrate their verbal as well as sartorial superiority through wittiness to a degree so exacting as to set them definitively apart from less showy or nimble minds. Simply in irony's verbal context, opposition and deliberate contrast or contradiction remain key factors, often to accentuate in an arch or wry manner the acumen or acuity of perception that distinguishes the speaker. When Oscar Wilde observes famously (through his character Gwendolen in *The Importance of Being Earnest*) that, "In matters of grave importance, style, not sincerity is the vital thing" (174), he is simply reversing an expectation to produce the sardonic effect. Such a tactic is reiterated by Tom Stoppard, in *Arcadia*, when Septimus Hodge wittily parries his protégé Thomasina's curiosity concerning "carnal embrace" – which, for the deft Septimus, is "the practice of throwing one's arms around a side of beef" (1). Irony's own embrace may extend to the vastness of a cosmic joke, as in Chekhov, but a less rarified theatrical usage is through comedic wit, typically reliant on paradox, inversion, or simply a telling antagonism between terms, ideas, or expectations. With comedy of manners, and in the hands of Stoppard or Shaw as well as Wilde, performative irony is likely to be part of the theatrical milieu, as a visual disparity is brought into bold relief through stage spectacle. At the close of *Arcadia*, for instance, a waltzing couple provides a potent image of what the audience, but not the two characters, would recognize as an ironic duet with a terrible consequence; the gleeful Thomasina Coverly will soon die in a fire that could have been prevented had the gallant Septimus Hodge been willing to accept the invitation to her room following the dance.

Ironic wit pertains commonly to sarcasm – as Cleanth Brooks would say, the "most familiar form of irony" (Zabel 730) – but even within that typicality, the scope of ironic implication is potentially extensive. In *The Well-Wrought Urn*, and with particular relevance to poetry, Brooks underscores the "importance assigned to the resolution of apparently antithetical attitudes," with respect to factors including "wit, as an awareness of the multiplicity of possible attitudes to be taken toward a given situation" and "irony, as a device for definition of attitudes by qualification" – also noting "paradox, as a device for contrasting the conventional views of a situation" (257). Extrapolating Brooks's arrangement from its deliberately poetic and literary

9

contexts, such associations might apply also to spoken or performative wit, and to variations on the sarcastic or sardonic in dialogue.

The ironist is adept in the art of the antithetical, but needs to be dependent upon others, or at least one other, who is also in the know – an affinity that may exist among characters in a play or between given characters and the audience. The dependency of irony upon mutuality – quite simply, the need for another party to get the joke or the implication of meaning – is associated with the trope's connection with the referential, perhaps especially with respect to cultural phenomena or the temper of a particular moment in time. Moreover, irony has been seen as sharing this propensity with a postmodernist inclination toward artistic or linguistic referentiality – or, to say it differently, toward the quoting of something that is known in the context of something that is "new" (with the quotation itself qualifying the conception of newness). In this context at least, the affiliation would seem to open up a further range of ironic resonance and help also perhaps to liberate the ironic from historically binding categorizations – that is, from an understanding of irony as something that is delimited per se by historical period.

Yet there is also an important sense in which irony's predilections toward cultural referencing can be restrictive, perhaps especially so in the postmodern relationship. From this perspective, and precisely to the extent that the ironic is a tone of choice for enlightened disillusionment or *weltschmerz*, the necessity for mutuality (getting the joke) has been adaptive to levels of an immediate cultural discourse, often with a prompt from the transitive (and likewise adaptive) voices of media and the languages of popular culture. In this situation, the potential for transcendent, not to say universalized, associations of the ironic is curtailed by the need for broadband communicative conduits for the moods and tones of a given present day. Irony in these circumstances tends to be more situational, ephemeral, or "virtual" by contrast with what might be perceived as more embracing or continuous, even if mysteriously so. Irony's gravitation, under such circumstantial conditions, is away from mystery or the inclusive cosmic joke and more toward what may be, for a time at least, most wryly penetrating or culturally on target. For the theatre, alone with its ancient heritage among other dramatic arts and entertainments, the contrast between present and past ironic voices can, consequently, be especially marked. Indeed, variations in the ironic component's incisiveness and resonance in drama may, within this framework at least, be understood as historically indicative (and highly mutable) with respect to cultural temper.

Irony for one dramatist, or even for one century or decade, is not the same as for another, and different cultures locate possibilities in the ironic mode that are, to a large extent, reflective of the capabilities or inclinations of theatrical art in various eras. From this perspective, historical, cultural, and aesthetic variations can further complicate the connotations of a trope that is already elusive by definition. So again the question: how (if at all) to employ a single word for so extensive a range of identities, applications, and settings? Here it may be advantageous to underscore a simplicity that also belongs to the nature of irony, whether the expression of the ironic be verbal, dramaturgical, or philosophical; to wit, that the trope's identity always lies fundamentally in meaningful opposition and juxtaposition, and that from this basic equation much can result. Again, irony's oppositional mechanisms contain not only a relationship but a ratio among contesting terms, with this innate characteristic signifying a range of possible implications that can fluctuate from an immediate circumstance to an all-embracing condition. Under these oppositional and flexible conditions, theatre, with its own innate tendencies regarding conflict and dialectic, becomes irony's natural partner; and in this affiliation, too, there is a fundamental simplicity from which intricacy and complexity can issue, as well as a common denominator that can help to unify an approach to irony's elusive identities and multiple manifestations.

As a means of correlating and contrasting the behaviors of irony in the theatre of the past century, and by way of anchoring the analysis in relation to drama, the chapters that follow return to such concepts as personification, embodiment, enactment, and the universal potentials (or lack of same) of the ironic sensibility and its practice on the stage. With irony understood as a phenomenon that is historical as well as aesthetic and ontological, the discussion emphasizes the fact that in spite of the many familiar associations of the ironic in recent times, irony as a component in drama has fluctuated notably in potency and range of application since the early twentieth century. While its flavors and nuances may yet be displayed vividly or subtly in the theatre, the potentially universalized implications of the ironic can be markedly delimited in both scope and impact. Indeed, and to the extent that irony in its simpler forms has become familiarized as a linguistic coin of the realm, there is benefit in rescue from its more facile understandings and usages, perhaps especially with respect to the theatre

Irony may be regarded in the abstract, or as a "master" behavior – as in the simple Burkean correspondence between what arises in time and what must (ironically) fall in time (*Grammar* 516) – or dramaturgically, in the sense of theatrical interaction that must proceed structurally along oppositional lines of development. And yet, the tendency of the theatre is to insure that irony is felt personally, even in the context of the more abstracted or philosophic conceptions. Irony is fundamentally existential; its signifying oppositions and contradictions pertain most frequently to circumstances of being and to strategies of existence. For this reason also, irony in the theatre relates pointedly, and often intimately, to the depicted personalities, sensibilities, and experiences of stage characters. The discussion here, which attends to irony in relation to illustrative plays and dramatists, does so with extensive attention to representative characters, to the figures that, in effect, bear the ironic freight. The ambition is to relate a spectrum of ironic techniques, capabilities, and world-views directly to figures that are shown in individuated theatrical situations, relationships, historical periods, and locations – from Ibsen's Halvard Solness to Stoppard's Thomasina Coverly or Wasserstein's Heidi Holland. Perspectives on irony are anchored, therefore, in the experiences of modern and contemporary dramatic characters – or, put differently, in select embodiments of the ironic mode that only the theatre can offer in so personal a fashion.

1 Irony personified: Ibsen and *The Master Builder*

Henrik Ibsen is masterful in his translation of an ironic world-view into the traits and behaviors of his characters, their interrelations, and the organizing structure of his dramatic action. In *Hedda Gabler*, when the title character marries George Tesman and not Eilert Loevborg, becomes vulnerable to the manipulations of Judge Brack and shoots herself with her father's pistols, she is enacting, among other behaviors, an inclusive ironic pattern. When Nora Helmer, in *A Doll House*, performs an elaborate show of domestic dutifulness, all the while sneaking macaroons and engaging in other, more helpful duplicities, she too is embodying the very ironic pattern that brings about the ultimate, and indeed logical, reversal – shutting the door on all that was apparently affirmed on her part in favor of another, more personal duty. And when, in *The Master Builder*, Halvard Solness refers with ironic self-awareness to his "luck," he is intensely aware that the fabric of his life has been transformed – and continues to be fashioned – by a power of fortune that is not only double-edged but contradictory, bringing with it both blessing and catastrophe. Such "luck" is for Solness a manifestation not so much of providential good or ill but of an overarching pattern in its visitation upon individual fate. Luck of this signifying variety is also, of course, related by its very nature to the ironic. In the case of *The Master Builder* in particular, Ibsen's arrangement and juxtaposition of events is planned so that, as in the case of Solness himself, apparent happenstance is invested with degrees of meaningfulness, and a cosmos is created where mystery and sense exist side by side, each reflecting and commenting upon the other.

To be sure, the ironic magnitudes and complexities that are achieved in *The Master Builder* are constructed upon a foundation of clear and simple interrelations. Is it not supremely ironic, after all, that a man who suffers from vertigo must climb nonetheless to the top of a spire in order to meet and fulfill his destiny? Or that a man who turns from building churches in favor of houses for people to live in can no longer establish a home or family of his own? Or that a man who believes, and even hopes, that a destructive house fire may begin with a crack in a chimney is faced with both the beneficial and disastrous effects of that fire, along with the realization that it wasn't ignited in the chimney at all? These are but a few of the more obvious ironic relations that are simply there, that Ibsen includes as part of the fabric of his play. However, even as Northrop Frye would distinguish between "naïve" and "sophis-ticated" irony in the context of authorial voice – saying in effect that the former announces and calls attention to its presence while the latter is merely stated – the case of Ibsen is more subtle, and also more complex, than this distinction would imply.[1] By no means does this dramatist comment overtly on his meaningful juxtapositions, yet at the same time they announce themselves too strenuously to be regarded merely as unadorned ironic statements.

Indeed, the ironic magnitudes that are achieved in this play are prepared for on the most unassuming levels. Even in terms of this foundation, however, there is indication of a pervasive world-view that emerges through an overall orchestration of character rela-tions, patterns of behavior, and dramatic events. In effect, Ibsen depends upon a forthright announcement of irony as a basic language in order for the play's grander thematic reaches to be discernible on those same terms. In this regard, Solness, who recognizes and calls attention to his own ironic proclivities, provides the symptoms for a larger and more significant pattern than even the ambiguous crack in the chimney can signal. *The Master Builder* is a play in which appa-rently natural and seemingly ordinary concepts – youth, marriage, age, fortune – are made to assume broader ranges of implication, and this is accomplished largely through the ironic and contradictory dynamics among such ostensibly common terms. "Youth," for example, is what Solness both fears and craves; it is what he cannot have again yet desperately needs in order to accomplish his deliverance; it is at once ungraspable and yet physically manifest in Hilda Wangel, Kaja

Fosli, and Ragnar Brovik. The Solness marriage, which once brought twin baby sons into the world, is now a hollow vestige of the union that was, with remorse and duty taking the place of any potential for joy. Here too, however, the ironies can serve as components of Ibsen's larger picture, establishing a language and finally enabling the encompassing agon, the ironic vision of a cosmos and the personal relationship to a deity, to "Him," that brings Solness to his fall and overarching tragedy.

As tragic drama, *The Master Builder* conducts an elaborate argument between its title character and the forces that would intrude into, and even define, his psyche and destiny. Solness is tortured by guilt and yet, as purely tragic irony would have it, he is also innocent, absolved, or at least not completely implicated in the actions and events for which he feels such remorse.

> SOLNESS: Put it this way. Suppose it was my fault, in some sense.
> HILDA: You! For the fire?
> SOLNESS: For everything, the whole business. And yet,
> perhaps – completely innocent all the same.
>
> (*Complete* 827)

To a large degree, in fact, it is the depth of Solness's passion and the intricacy of his psychic mood that provide this play with its breadth of vision. *The Master Builder* is, in Robert Brustein's description, "a great cathedral of a play, with dark, mystical strains which boom like the chords of an organ" (*Revolt* 77). Magnitude, in terms such as these, is accomplished through an essentially tragic sensibility and vocabulary – but here that sensibility entails a corresponding ironic philosophy and procedural method. In order for Solness to scale a spire at the end of the play, in a vertiginous mirroring of the earlier climb at Lysanger that was witnessed by the younger Hilda, Ibsen must fashion a character who is, in effect, irony personified, one for whom life's incidents turn into evidence of an inclusive pattern of self-reflexive commentary. From the beginning of the play, attention is called to Solness's "luck," which all of those who know him appear to recognize – Knut Brovik, Doctor Herdal, and Aline all acknowledge or make reference to it in one context or another. It is only Solness, however, who knows the depth of its repercussions. "Well – I had luck on my side," Solness admits to Knut Brovik early in the action (788). Yet in spite of the apparent off-handedness in this moment, this is the same man who knows exactly what his wife means when she comments on Kaja Fosli's presence in the house: "You've certainly been in luck, Halvard, to have gotten hold of that girl" (794). And then, there is the following exchange with Dr. Herdal:

> HERDAL: I must say, to *me* it seems that you've had luck with you to an incredible degree.
> SOLNESS (*masking a wan smile*): So I have. Can't complain of that.
> HERDAL: First, that hideous old robbers' den burned down for you. And that was really a stroke of luck.
> SOLNESS (*seriously*): It was Aline's family home that burned – don't forget.
> HERDAL: Yes, for *her* it must have been a heavy loss.
> SOLNESS: She hasn't recovered right to this day. Not in all these twelve-thirteen years.
> HERDAL: What followed after, that must have been the worst blow for her.
> SOLNESS: The two together.
> HERDAL: But you yourself – you rose from those ashes. You began as a poor boy from the country – and now you stand the top man in your field. Ah, yes, Mr. Solness, you've surely had luck on your side.
>
> (799)

"Luck," even at this early point in the play, is characterized not as happenstance or innocent fortune but as an abstract, aleatory force that attends to this one individual, a quality that is at large in Solness's life, that can intrude or attach itself to his personal relationships, associations, and career opportunities – but never innocently. The same luck that brings building opportunities also brings destruction of the Solness family – the deaths of the baby boys and the end of what Solness calls Aline's talent for building the "souls of little children" (827). Later, when Solness acknowledges to Hilda the true burden and severity of his fortune, luck has been fully and manifestly transformed into a daimonic presence.

> HILDA (*animated*): Yes, but isn't it really a joy for you then, to create these beautiful homes?
> SOLNESS: The price, Hilda. The awful price I've had to pay for that chance.
> HILDA: But can you never get over that?
> SOLNESS: No. For this chance to build homes for others, I've had to give up – absolutely give up any home of my own – a real home, I mean, with children.
> HILDA (*delicately*): But did you have to? Absolutely, that is?
> SOLNESS (slowly nodding): That was the price for my famous luck. Luck – hm. This good luck, Hilda – it couldn't be bought for less.
>
> (825)

Solness is excruciatingly aware, not only of the contradictions in his circumstances but also of what is, for him, their meaning. Continuing, in the same scene, when he tells Hilda in detail about the cause of the fire and its aftermath, he is not merely recalling events but is demarking the contours of a world, and a world-view, that is defined in essence by an ironic sensibility.

The personification of irony within character extends, however, beyond the figure of Solness, even though he is its primary incarnation. Dr. Herdal, too, is an ironist, as is Aline Solness. The devastation of the Solness marriage is such that the two partners can scarcely endure being in a room together, let alone engage in forthright conversation. As a result, they communicate through a coded subtext, and for Aline this means chiding, deflecting, and upbraiding Solness along the lines of her remark concerning his "luck" with Kaja Fosli. When Solness voices concern about his mental condition to Dr. Herdal – who, in his turn, speaks with Aline – his inquiry is conducted, in effect, within an ironic circle that sustains its own self-commentary. Again, though, the pattern here is but the foundation for a larger manifestation, which is Solness's conviction that what has happened is of a piece, that the interrelations he recognizes are in line with punishment, with "retribution," with his argument with divinity.

The world that Ibsen has built around Solness is mysterious, even unfathomable. Yet at the same time it is highly ordered, with an omnipresent and palpable impression of sense. The past, which weighs so grievously upon both of the Solnesses, is in one sense open to question, as in the report of Hilda Wangel concerning the early events at Lysanger, yet it is also clear and delineated, as with the facts concerning the fire, Aline's illness, the loss of the little boys, and the destruction of her "nine beautiful dolls." Even Solness's "luck" is without the capriciousness that typically adheres to such a quality, and the very retribution that he imagines is being exercised against him carries with it a reciprocity and an order – this in exchange for or in response to that. Irony, in such a context, can aid in the creation of what appears orderly, conveying a sense of reason even though it might be inscrutable. Irony of this type is suggestive of that which is apt, makes sense, and belongs, yet accomplishes such impressions mysteriously; the ironic appears, in this view, to be utterly fitting and yet with indistinct reason – at the same time. Indeed, Solness conducts his life according to such a system: he believes in the mystery but also the appropriateness and underlying sense within events – the fire, his success, the summoning of "helpers and servers," the hiring of Kaja Fosli, even Hilda's arrival at his door – and he also believes in, even as he wonders about, the power of his own psychic abilities in these respects.

Even within a mysterious world, then, events can be perceived as occurring with reason, and in this case that reason is delivered through ironic means and sensibility. Solness would not fear youth so much if he did not fear another onslaught of "retribution." He would not suffer so much in Aline's presence were it not for his conviction that he deserves the anguish for what has befallen her, even as he suspects his own absolution. He would not climb the building's new tower without a belief that the earlier climb might be duplicated – would *need* to be duplicated – at this exact point, ten years from the original event at Lysanger. In *The Master Builder*, Ibsen constructs a multilayered cosmos of intricate and, at times, only faintly readable metaphysical associations and daimonic stresses – but at the very same time it is a cosmos with balance, with a precise system of causes and effects. And, as Solness knows better than anyone, this cosmos is neither impersonal nor impervious; it has impressed itself too severely on his mind, his marriage, and his building career for that to be the case.

Solness has arrived at a point of marked instability as regards all three of these areas: his psychological condition, relationship with Aline, and future as a designer and builder of houses. The situation is, for him, volatile on all sides, and he is exceptionally vulnerable to any sort of catalyst that could prompt such latent areas of tension into full-blown personal and dramatic crises. Ibsen's achievement in this play is such that he can dramatize the sheer explosiveness of this situation, together with its supersensible and transcendent aspects, yet still convey an impression of orderliness threatened by the chaotic – or, inversely, a world of mystery within a broader context of sense. As Bernard Shaw puts it in *The Quintessence of Ibsenism*, Solness is "daimonic" (120), an assignation that in the context of ancient, rather than modernist, tragedy would refer to a connection to some boundary zone of divine activity, not the gods specifically but a level of abstract divinity which exists apart from, but within the sphere of consciousness of, humankind.[2] And, of course, Solness is intensely and self-consciously aware of other beings – devils, trolls, "helpers and servers," perhaps even Hilda herself – that are a necessary part of the "daimonic" realm that he can sense and, possibly, direct. Richard Schechner, in his Jungian reading of Ibsen's late works, writes that, "as each play unfolds, the daemonic is integrated into the personality of the hero – 'introjected into human nature' – with a subsequent 'power which extends the bounds of personality ad infinitum, in the most perilous way.' Knowledge of the daemonic, possession of it, or by it, kills" ("Visitor" 161–162).

To lend a visible order to such a multivalent environment, Ibsen employs irony not only in characterization but also in his dramaturgical strategies. Even as he personifies irony in character, he builds it into the fabric of the dramatic construction, and into a pattern of enactment that includes the stage spectacle. Characters such as

Solness, Aline, and Dr. Herdal maintain and express their own, individuated ironic views and beliefs, but their collective interrelations,
movements, and behaviors are also the perceivable symptoms of a
sensible, if ironically conceived, order. The universe that Solness
inhabits is exquisitely in equipoise: causes will have directly related
effects, the young will arrive in "retribution," Hilda Wangel will stand
in for Kaja Fosli, the suffering of one partner in marriage will provoke a
commensurate penance in another, an exact decade is book-ended by
Solness's ascents up the spires.[3] And even the master builder, who at
times fears for his sanity and talks of trolls, is not irrational; he's too
aware of how in balance and readable his circumstances are, too aware
of how his own ironic philosophy plays out and is verified in the world
around him.

To make such a world-view tangible – that is, to show and enact
it – Ibsen advances the action through an orchestration of ironically
appropriate entrances and exits, arrivals and departures that contain
their own implicit commentary on the immediate action. Throughout
the play, Solness and Aline act out a dance of negative attraction, as if
the power than once drew them together had been reversed, and the
magnetism repels rather than unites them. Ibsen arranges for Solness
and Hilda to be together on stage for lengthy encounters, allowing a
world to be created in the duet between them, with any intrusion into
that world seen as a violation of something that belongs, increasingly,
only to the two of them. But Ibsen's plan is even more precise than such
an arrangement would suggest, and his ironic pattern of arrival and
departure is more exacting, with more innate meaningfulness implied.
In effect, the playwright fashions a succession, not simply of entrances
and exits that demark these encounters, but hinge moments that tellingly shift the ironic balance and, in turn, supply a commentary on the
developing action. There is, for example, this encounter, early in act
one:

> SOLNESS: Then try to rid Ragnar of these stupid ideas. Marry him
> as much as you like – (*Changing his tone.*) Well, I mean – don't let
> him throw over a good job here with me. Because – then I can keep
> *you* too, Kaja dear.

KAJA: Oh yes, how lovely that would be, if only we could manage it!

SOLNESS (*caressing her head with both hands and whispering*): Because I can't be without you. You understand? I've got to have you close to me every day.

KAJA (*shivering with excitement*): Oh, God! God!

SOLNESS (*kissing her hair*): Kaja – Kaja!

KAJA (*sinks down before him*): Oh, how good you are to me! How incredibly good you are!

SOLNESS (*intensely*): Get up! Get up now, I – I hear someone coming!

(791–792)

Here is a theatrical moment of jarring intensity as Solness's relationship with Kaja is brought into immediate visual relief against the one with his wife. Aline has her first entrance in the play, sees the two of them, and remarks: "I'm afraid I'm intruding." And it is not long after her "intrusion" that Aline makes the remark, referred to earlier, on how "in luck" Solness has been to have Kaja in the house working for him, a comment that, in turn, leads to a further ironic exchange on how Solness has grown "used to doing without" (791–792). In addition, of course, Aline's perfectly opportune entrance at this point foreshadows the more significant "intrusion" – that of Hilda Wangel – which takes place soon after, and will prompt most of the ensuing action in the drama.

Later in the first act, Ibsen brings together in deliberate succession the characters who witness the tangible appearance of "youth" at the door (Solness, Dr. Herdal), the character who stands for that quality (Hilda), and then Aline, who has just finished creating a space (one of the nurseries in the house) for that person to stay with them overnight. Here once more, the arrivals are timed so as to accentuate their ironic potentials and underscore them visually:

SOLNESS: Oh, of course I can! Because I feel that you've come, too, almost – under some new flag. And then it's youth against youth–!

(*Dr. Herdal comes in by the hall door.*)

HERDAL: So? You and Miss Wangel still here?

SOLNESS: Yes. We've had a great many things to talk about.

HILDA: Both old and new.

HERDAL: Oh, have you?

HILDA: Really, it's been such fun. Because Mr. Solness – he's got such a fantastic memory. He remembers the tiniest little details in a flash.

(*Mrs. Solness enters by the door to the right.*)

MRS. SOLNESS: All right, Miss Wangel, your room's all ready for you now.

(812)

Such moments are splendidly crafted and layered with successive ironic tonalities. Dr. Herdal is unabashedly arch in calling attention to Hilda's continued presence, and Hilda herself is playfully, wickedly ironic in praising Solness's memory, since his recollections of Lysanger have, from her point of view, been so very fallible. Adding to this tone is the fact that if there is one thing Solness remembers all too well it is what he has helped to bring about in Aline's life – and here, just at this moment, Aline walks in, as if she has been conveniently brought to mind and summoned. Moreover, she appears with the mission of announcing that the room (the "nursery") is prepared for Hilda, thereby giving voice to exactly what Solness most hates to remember – that is, the *other* nursery, the one that once held his little sons. In instances such as this, the ironic planes and tonalities in the action fold in upon each other, creating a collective field of resonant comparisons and effects.

Act two begins with a confrontation between Solness and Aline –"You can build as much as you ever want, Halvard – but for me you can never build up a real home again" (816) – that culminates in his confession of "debt" to her and, again, an exquisitely timed arrival by Hilda Wangel:

MRS. SOLNESS (*rising slowly*): What's back of all this? Might as well tell me right now.

SOLNESS: But nothing's back of it. I've never done anything against you – not that I've ever known. And yet – there's this

22

sense of some enormous guilt hanging over me, crushing me down.

MRS. SOLNESS: A guilt toward *me?*

SOLNESS: Toward you most of all.

MRS. SOLNESS: Then you are – ill, after all, Halvard.

SOLNESS (*wearily*): I suppose so – something like that. (*Looks toward the door to the right, as it opens.*) Ah! But it's brightening up.

(*Hilda Wangel comes in. She has made some changes in her clothes and let down her skirt.*)

HILDA: Good morning, Mr. Solness!

(818)

In this instance, Hilda brings a change so immediate and powerful that Solness's whole demeanor shifts to its opposite mood, from the source of his greatest guilt, embodied in Aline, to his best chance for deliverance.

Ibsen's dramaturgy of ironic entrance is, however, best exemplified in its most intensified form – that is, in Hilda's initial appearance at the Solness home, an occasion that represents, in fact, the arrival of an embodied catalytic power. Here again it is worth noting the condition that Solness is in at the onset of the play's action with respect to his mental and marital states and also his career status. These conditions, if understood as latent potentials for drama, await the sort of provocation that can bring forth, to the fullest possible extent, the crisis that is promised by Solness's status as the play begins. Seen along these lines, Hilda's arrival brings a catalytic agency to the latent and extremely volatile personal situation in which Solness finds himself.[4] Hilda, with her unique qualities, desires, and recollections – and, not least, her ability to hear Solness, to join him on his particular wavelengths – is able to affect matters on all levels: psychological, marital, and in relation to his vocation as master builder. She is, indeed, the ideal reflector for Solness, in that her personality is so complementary and also so contrapuntal to his own. There are many points of entrance in the play that supply their own ironic and self-reflexive demonstrations; there are a number of such instances that serve as important hinges in the developing action; but there is none so potent as this one, the arrival that, in effect, enables the entire tragedy to unfold as it does.

Hilda's first appearance in *The Master Builder* is made dense with an explosive power awaiting release. Ibsen, in creating this volatility and its associated ironic potentials, directs deliberate attention to the perfected irony and, implicitly, the related components of sense or predictability in Hilda's arrival. In one way, certainly, her entrance can be perceived as happenstance – that is, "luck" – the appearance of a young woman who, in search of Solness, simply happens to arrive at the house at a fortuitous moment. But once her story is told, it is clear that she is, rather, a messenger of cosmic symmetry; it is ten years to the day since the earlier events at the spire at Lysanger. Even before she appears, however, Ibsen deliberately announces and underscores the ironic charge that will be concentrated and thus magnified in this moment:

> SOLNESS: The change is coming. I can sense it. And I feel that it's coming closer. Someone or other will set up the cry: Step back for *me*! And all the others will storm in after, shaking their fists and shouting: Make room – make room – make room! Yes, Doctor, you'd better look out. Someday youth will come here, knocking at the door –
> HERDAL (*laughing*): Well, good Lord, what if they do?
> SOLNESS: What if they do? Well, then it's the end of Solness, the master builder.
> (*A knock at the door to the left.*)

The ensuing moment is, certainly, a "*coup de théâtre*," providing a singular impression of stage spectacle along with the heightened coincidence of timing.[5] Hilda has arrived in immediate fulfillment of Solness's prophecy; "youth" has come knocking, and soon thereafter Herdal, ever the ironist, points the fact out to Solness:

> HERDAL: You read the future, all right, Mr. Solness!
> SOLNESS: How so?
> HERDAL: Youth *did* come along, knocking at your door.

SOLNESS (*buoyantly*): Yes, but that was something else completely.
HERDAL: Oh yes, yes. Definitely!

(800–802)

Even Doctor Herdal, however, cannot possibly fathom the extent of what is implied by Hilda's knock at Solness's door, and certainly not the full ramifications of the cry that Solness had imagined – "Step back for *me!*" – in relation to this young woman. As Joan Templeton describes the arrival: "Not since *Ghosts* has there been such a sense of fatality in an Ibsen play. Hilda enters bringing Solness' death with her as though she were carrying it in her knapsack" (266). Hilda's appearance is, in Ibsen's construction, more than a primary hinge in the action, and more even than the instigation of the play's central dialectic. It is a point of mastered interrelations, an ironic contraction, in which all of the dramatic force that is yet to come is focused into one isolated instance of potentiality, embodied in this singular character's reunion with her master builder. The remainder of the play's action does, indeed, issue almost solely from this meeting, and from the density of its ironic associations. Here is the character who can fulfill Solness's desires yet at the same time bring him to destruction – and on the same path of dramatic action. As Henry James writes, Solness "encounters his fate all in the opening of a door." James, too, calls implicit attention to Hilda's catalytic power; as he puts it, she is "only the indirect form, the animated clock-face, as it were, of Halvard Solness's destiny; but the action, in spite of obscurities and ironies, takes its course by steps none the less irresistible" (268).[6]

Hilda's entrance also has a direct and immediate effect on how the play's particular realms – realistic, psychic or prescient, metaphysical and supersensory – might be perceived. It is clear from the beginning that Solness is troubled, mercurial, and wrathful in his insistence on his own course: "I'm not giving up! I never give ground. Not voluntarily. Never in this world, never!" (790). Once Hilda is present, however, and then when she recounts her story and begins her lobby for a "Kingdom of Orangia," the extent of the play's domain and, correspondingly, its tragic magnitudes are widened enormously. Regarding

25

Hilda's entrance, Inga-Stina Ewbank writes that in his late plays, "Ibsen thrusts such coincidences and pointers at us, as if to challenge the very principle of verisimilitude" (130–131). Yet "coincidence," in a play such as this, must be regarded with suspicion, particularly in its relation to irony, to "luck," and to what may be quite sensible but only in the context of the play's more abstract or inscrutable realms. Brian Johnston speaks directly to this proclivity, to Ibsen's "audacity" in the design of this ironic moment:

> The militant army of the young, in Solness's alarmed vision, will, he believes, come "knocking at the door," and there follows that audacious stage direction of the knock on the door that, at first seeming a too blatant irony, is, on further reflection, seen to have exactly the right shock value for the audience, for we are now seeing onstage the mysterious power Solness has described: his uncanny ability to will into existence his wishes . . . The knock at the door thus is as effective as that of *Macbeth*: it suddenly lifts the whole drama from the psychological plane upon which, up to now, it has existed, and suggests a direct intervention from the spirit world. It brings onto the stage the presence of the wonderful and awesome over which Solness's mind, in solitude, has been brooding, and the reactions of the two men to the knocking emphasize this dual nature of the reality being presented.
>
> (314)

Strictly in the ironic context, however, the relationship between Solness and Hilda can be understood as standing for, or embodying, a dialectic that, while suggestive of the play's varied realms, also reflects the sense and symmetry of its cosmos. Hilda is not only the ideal catalyst for Solness in his present travails, but also his necessary partner in the mastered irony that Ibsen fashions, forming the relationship that Kenneth Burke refers to, in his "Four Master Tropes," as "kinship" with a character's necessary antagonist. "True irony, humble irony, is based upon a sense of fundamental kinship with the enemy, as one *needs* him, is *indebted* to him, is not merely outside him as an observer but contains him *within*, being consubstantial with him" (*Grammar* 514). In terms such as these, Hilda and Solness belong to one another on both dialectical and ironic terms. Solness *must* have Hilda – to hear him, to share "the impossible," to recognize and know his trolls – and yet her partnership is exactly what brings about both his ascendancy and his fall.

"She is of medium height, supple, and well-formed. Slight sunburn. Dressed in hiking clothes" (800). Here the visual image is, in one sense, unprepossessing, at least in Ibsen's brief description. Yet Hilda's entry, in its perfection, is exemplary of what Roland Barthes would term *le comble*, an acme, an event which, while apparently a happenstance, nonetheless achieves meaning – that is, which signifies – and does so through ironic means. The acme is the moment of fateful perfection in drama, ideal in its symmetries and concentrated range of implications. In Barthes's illustration, "it is precisely when Agamemnon condemns his daughter to death that she praises his kindness; it is precisely when Aman believes himself to have triumphed that he is ruined" (192–193). Or, as dictated by the law of the acme and with reference to another theatrical father and daughter, it is inevitable that Lear's favorite child is the only one who can say "Nothing, my lord" – and thus provide another instance in which a tersely mastered expression contains within it a play's instigating power, in this instance the catalytic prompting for Lear's fury and ultimate tragedy. In the case of Hilda and Solness, however, the acme (which by its nature is connected to the aleatory as well as the ironic) must be seen in direct relation to the latter's "luck." As Barthes inquires:

> What does this predilection signify? The acme is the expression of a situation of mischance. Yet just as repetition "limits" the anarchic (or innocent) nature of the aleatory, so luck and mischance are not neutral, they invincibly call up a certain signification – and the moment chance signifies, it is no longer chance; the acme's precise function is this conversion of chance into sign, for the exactitude of a reversal cannot be conceived outside of an intelligence which performs it; in mythic terms, Nature (Life) is not an exact force; wherever a symmetry is manifested (and the acme is the very figure of symmetry), there has to be a hand to guide it.
>
> (192)

Solness's "luck," of course, adheres to his destiny on all fronts, affecting virtually all aspects of his experience. When seen in terms of Barthes's acme, however, the quality of this luck takes on another, even more inclusive connotation. The clarifying mission of the acme is, as Barthes points out, to change happenstance into significance, to convert "chance into sign," to endow fortune with sense and inevitability. Whereas Johnston points to the "spirit world" that Hilda's entrance opens up, the acme provides, through symmetry and its related ironic balance, the indication of another sort of exertive force at work in the drama. It is this exertion, in Barthes's terms a performative intelligence, that also is manifest in Hilda's knock at Solness's door. The "audacious" mastering of that scenic moment provides so ironic an impression of symmetry, in other words, that there must be a "hand to guide it."

It is under these circumstances, in fact, that the full impact of Hilda's timely appearance in the Solness household may be understood. If her entry is catalytic, containing its own incipient and unreleased power, then such a potential dynamism can be seen in terms not only of possibilities but of direct consequences and results. Hilda's arrival in Solness's life points directly toward the final confrontation between the builder and his deity – "Him" – and then to the master builder's death. What is suggested in such a pattern is not only a dramatic development but, in ironic terms, a ratio – seen here as a specific relation of potential, catalytic, and released power that creates another type of symmetry between forces that are latent and ones that are realized. Solness, in the volatile state in which he begins the action, meets in Hilda the ideal catalytic agent, designed by Ibsen in a way that is suited precisely to his title character's condition. In their initial meeting, a synergy takes shape but cannot yet be fully expressed or enacted. Yet all of the subsequent action of *The Master Builder*, including Solness's developing passion and its consequences, is contained within the singularity, the symmetry, and the ultimate order and sense behind this one character's appearance.

To fully comprehend the impact of Hilda Wangel's intrusion in the Solness house, in all of its dynamism and resonance, it is necessary to consider Ibsen's own relationships with certain inspiring figures in his own life, and Emilie Bardach in particular. Although much has been written (and with several points in dispute) on which of the young women known by Ibsen may have provided inspiration for the character of Hilda Wangel, the discussion does not often pertain to dramaturgical or theoretical matters having to do with the playwright's use of irony. And yet, the fact that Ibsen created a fictional character such as Hilda, who wields so profound an influence on the stage figure that is generally believed to be a direct reflection of Ibsen himself, indicates a strong correlation with the effect that these inspirational figures were able to exert. If Solness and Hilda are "consubstantial," to borrow Burke's term, and if they enact a trope of supremely ironic interrelations through inter-personal need and indebtedness in this context, then the affinity of Ibsen and Bardach might be consulted for an analogous relation, not with "the enemy" per se, as Burke would have it, but rather with the "fundamental kinship" and its implications.

The core issue here is the nature and extent of the effect that Hilda has on Solness, in its direct relation to Ibsen's most likely point of reference for such an influence. If Ibsen's strategy in *The Master Builder* is to personify through characterization a pervasive ironic substrate, and one that it is manifested in relationships and behaviors as well as in the dramatic pattern, the degree to which such conditions may have a tangible personification in his own life bears investigation. In brief, the reference here is to Ibsen's first encounter with Bardach, a meeting that took place at Gossensass, in the Austrian (now Italian) Tyrol, in 1889, when the playwright was sixty-one and the young woman eighteen. Although the relationship appears to have continued from that summer primarily through letters, the depth of their revealed feelings for one another has led to generally shared opinions concerning her influence on given plays, including *Hedda Gabler* but, in partic-ular, *The Master Builder*.[7] In the view of Ibsen's biographer Michael Meyer, in fact, it is against the background of these letters and this particular relationship that one must apprehend *The Master Builder* ("Introduction" 124).

Regarding the connection of Ibsen and Bardach's relationship to that of Solness and Hilda, biographer Halvdan Koht reports that, "An open declaration of their feelings seems to have taken place on

September 19, as the summer drew to an end, for that is the date in *The Master Builder* of the encounter that Hilde reminds Solness of: 'You seized me in your arms and held me back and kissed me … many times.' Whether this actually happened in Gossensass cannot be certain, but Emilie's diary clearly indicates they had experienced some great upheaval" (391). In further alignment of the character of Hilda with Ibsen's experiences with Emilie, Koht says: "The Hilde who comes to the master builder derives many traits from Ibsen's relationship with Emilie Bardach; she is the 'princess' in Solness' dreams, and her kingdom is called 'Orangia.' He likens her to an untamed beast of prey in the forest wanting to capture him. He yields to her saying, as Ibsen had said to both Emilie and Helene [Raff], that he needs and longs for her youth" (434).

Emilie Bardach was, in fact, only one of three young women who may have been suggestive in Ibsen's depiction of Hilda Wangel, and it bears noting, too, that a younger Hilda appears in Ibsen's *The Lady from the Sea*.[8] Helene Raff and Hildur Andersen were also admired by the playwright, and as Templeton suggests, "Hilda Wangel is to some extent, and in different ways, a mixture of Bardach, Raff, and Andersen" (262). Still, it is Bardach who appears to have provided the most persuasive and enduring influence. Based on Ibsen's letters to her – "whose authenticity is not in question" – Templeton believes that the playwright "felt a strong romantic attachment to her" (237), and despite the fact that there was no sexual relationship with any of his "three princesses" (257), that he was in love with her.[9] What is more significant for the discussion here, however, is the degree to which the feelings of Ibsen are reflected in those of Solness, and on this point we have the testimony of both Emilie Bardach and the playwright himself. Ibsen acknowledged that *The Master Builder* "contained more of his own self than any other" (Koht 433). And, as Meyer recounts: "In 1908, in Munich, Emilie Bardach saw *The Master Builder* for the first time. After the performance, she commented: 'I didn't see myself, but I saw him. There is something of me in Hilde; but in Solness, there is little that is not Ibsen'" ("Introduction" 128).[10]

For Ibsen, the emotional depth of his relationships with Emilie Bardach and other young women has not only an autobiographical correlation but a corresponding intensity in the dramatic arrangements

30

of *The Master Builder,* particularly in regard to the personality of Hilda
Wangel and its effect upon Halvard Solness. Indeed, Ibsen's own associations in this respect provide yet another instance of meaningful
personification in the play, in this instance a transference of the playwright's own feelings and experiences and the manner in which these
are translated into the play's action. As David Grene argues: "The love
affair with Emilie Bardach and the later relationship to the Norwegian
pianist [Hildur] Andersen, both women very much younger than himself, and Ibsen's intense emotional involvement with both, are certainly echoed in *The Master Builder* and *When We Dead Awaken*" (2).

The effect that Hilda has upon Solness is felt most strongly as a
psychic affinity, an experience that he has not, presumably, encountered
in this way before. Solness suspects that he is prescient, able perhaps
to prompt events through an exertion of will. It is early in the play when
he first suggests evidence of this proclivity for Dr. Herdal, with reference to his hiring of Kaja and the desired retention of employee Ragnar
Brovik. Solness reports that he was struck by a thought: "suppose that
I could get her here in the office, then maybe Ragnar would stay put too."

> HERDAL: That was reasonable enough.
> SOLNESS: But I didn't breathe a word of any of this then – just
> stood looking at her – every ounce of me wishing that I had her
> here. I made a little friendly conversation about one thing or
> another. And then she went away.
> HERDAL: So?
> SOLNESS: But the next day, in the late evening, after old Brovik
> and Ragnar had gone, she came by to see me again, acting as if
> we'd already struck a bargain.
> HERDAL: Bargain? What about?
> SOLNESS: About precisely what I'd been standing there wishing
> before – even though I hadn't uttered a word of it.
> HERDAL: That *is* strange.
>
> (796–797)

It is this sense of a power over events, and people, that later in the first
act prompts Solness to confess something similar to Hilda, this in
response to her story about the events at Lysanger and the promise for a

"Kingdom of Orangia." She says: "You caught me up and kissed me, Mr. Solness." And then: "You held me in both your arms and bent me back and kissed me – many times." At first, Solness is disbelieving, and offers that she must have dreamt such memories. Then he is "struck by a sudden thought": "I must have willed it. Wished it. Desired it" (807). It is this power of wishing and desiring, this power of will that Solness believes he may possess, that not only finds repeated expressions in the second act – including Solness's report of the fire and the crack in the chimney – but also leads to a key transitional moment in the play's overall iteration of an ironic reversal of circumstances, in this instance a suggestion of the power shift from Solness to Hilda:

> SOLNESS (confidingly): Don't you believe with me, Hilda, that there are certain special, chosen people who have a gift and power and capacity to *wish* something, *desire* something, *will* something – so insistently and so – so inevitably – that at last it *has* to be theirs? Don't you believe that?
> HILDA (with an inscrutablel look in her eyes): If that's true, then we'll see someday – if I'm one of the chosen.
> SOLNESS: It's not one's self alone that makes great things. Oh no – the helpers and servers – they've got to be with you if you're going to succeed. But they never come by themselves. One has to call on them, incessantly – within oneself, I mean.
>
> (830)

Here Solness is so consumed with his own command of desire, and the extent of his personal will, that he only glancingly perceives the potential power of the young woman – "youth" – that he is confronting. The depth of their psychic rapport, however, is by now clearly established, providing the groundwork for a duet that can include the "helpers and servers" and also a mutual awareness of "trolls" and of "the impossible," reifying the terms of a shared spiritual world. Ewbank refers to the special and cumulative range of associations that creates their rapport: "Jointly, completing each other's sentences, they build their identification with these images, across a sub-text of sexual and spiritual affinity, charging every word with significance and creating a mythical world of their own" (143).

If Hilda Wangel's presence in the Solness house provides the catalytic prompting for the title character's ensuing passion, igniting what was abiding and latent in his circumstances, it is the shift of power dynamics within a shared psychic arena that provokes the play's later movements toward its tragic end. In this case, too, the synergy between the characters has, in relation to the overarching shape of the play's action, a basis in irony. In this instance, however, it is the irony of peripety rather than of the mastered moment or of a dramaturgical pattern in which one character's qualities are precisely and, in this instance, devastatingly appropriate for another's. The ironic peripety adds, in effect, a new dimension to such appropriateness, extending the implications from the individual characters into the dramatized turn of events. Kenneth Burke describes this phenomenon as the progressive pattern of reversal that, precisely because of its innate qualities, achieves a fateful, determinate, and thus unavoidable quality. If one imagines Solness, in this view, as the "prior" character, the peripety follows from the addition of Hilda as the "new" character: "The point at which different casuistries appear . . . is the point where one tries to decide exactly what new characters, born of a given prior character, will be the 'inevitable' vessels of the prior character's disposition. As an over-all ironic formula here, and one that has the quality of 'inevitability,' we could lay it down that 'what goes forth as A returns as non-A.' This is the basic pattern that places the essence of drama and dialectic in the irony of the 'peripety,' the strategic moment of reversal" (*Grammar* 517).

Irony of this sort, pertinent to both situation and dramaturgical process, is related directly to what Bert O. States points to, in *Irony and Drama*, as a play's "principle of curvature," a cumulative tendency in the drama that, in effect, unites the various instances of the ironic into an overmastering ironic progression (27).[11] "As ironies proliferate in a play," he writes, "we may begin to anticipate the inevitability of a master irony" (26). Confronted with "impossible" situations in his home as the play begins, Solness advances toward a renewed confrontation with "the impossible"; beginning the play with a terror of youth, he ends with a dependency upon it; in each instance, the reversal of field is contingent upon the "master irony," the arrival and then the progressively increasing influence of Hilda Wangel.

HILDA: Tell me, Mr. Solness – are you quite sure that you've never called for me? Within yourself, I mean.

SOLNESS (*slowly and softly*): I almost think I must have.

HILDA: What did you want with me?

SOLNESS: You, Hilda, are youth.

HILDA (*smiles*): Youth that you're so afraid of?

SOLNESS (*nodding slowly*): And that, deep within me, I'm so much hungering for.

(833)

Solness needs Hilda, must have her, if for no other reason than to attempt, one last time, "the impossible." She is the only one who can sanction, or even comprehend, such an attempt. And yet, by the end of the play, it is he who belongs to her, rather than vice versa. In his heroic ruination, Solness is for Hilda "*My – my* master builder!" (860). Or, in David Grene's words, Hilda is "the retributive agent who will do to Solness what he has done to others – make him an instrument for the achievement of her desires and fantasies." Solness himself has, of course, experienced his share of personal reversal, as a corollary aspect of his "luck," with respect to his plans to establish home and family, and – especially – in his relationship to the deity that he refers to and argues with. With reference to "Him," following the death of his twins: "From the day I lost them, I never wanted to build another church" (824). And yet, the change brought about by Hilda's arrival can only be seen, for Solness, as the most profound turnabout yet. Hilda becomes, in Grene's phrasing, "the ironic symbol of the retributive power of youth" (11).

The play moves in two directions simultaneously, toward an enhanced understanding and identification between Solness and Hilda, and also toward an increasingly abstract conception of what is truly "possible," either between them or as a consequence of the master builder's efforts in particular. At first, the concept of the "impossible" is simply a discovered common ground, a shared experience and language:

SOLNESS (*seriously*): Have you ever noticed, Hilda, how the impossible – how it seems to whisper and call to you?

34

HILDA (*reflecting*): The impossible? (*Vivaciously.*) Oh yes! *You* know it too?

SOLNESS: Yes.

(826)

Here once more is a briefly defined exchange between the two characters that becomes a significant hinge in the action, containing as it does a deeply ironic strain, a sense of change that is, if not foretold, then more and more implicit in the ensuing action. For Johnston, this single moment is "a turning point in the play"; in his view, "the word 'impossible' (*umulig*) now will be used with extraordinary frequency, reaching a climax of iteration when Solness, in the last act, climbs his tower. We notice that Hilde receives Solness's concept of 'the impossible,' *reflects* upon it, thus taking it into her mind, then 'vivaciously' (*livfull*) assents to it – another of the many moments in the play when either Solness or Hilde receives a concept from the other, takes it over, and thus spiritually 'grows' onstage, like a master and a devoted disciple" (330).

For Solness, though, the "impossible" is contradictory; it can have no tangible or reified manifestation despite its immediate corroboration in the figure of Hilda. For him, in fact, it becomes the representation of an ultimate, abstract irony. There is no way, in spite of his assurances to Hilda, to build their castle in the air "on a solid foundation" (856). Indeed, by the end of the play Solness's building plans are, in themselves, impossible, and can only come to what Shaw terms "dead men's architecture" (*Quintessence* 118). The master builder's argument with divinity is surely impossible to win, in spite of what Solness reports to Hilda about what occurred at Lysanger: "Then I did the impossible. I no less than He." Solness was able to climb the tower there, to hang the wreath atop the spire, and even to announce: "Hear me, Thou Almighty! From this day on, I'll be a free creator – free in my own realm, as you are in yours" (854). Now, however, Solness is neither free nor actively creative, in spite of his avowal to "Almighty God" to "build only what's most beautiful in all the world," a castle for his princess "on a solid foundation" (856). It is just prior to his death, in fact, that Solness continues his "impossible" argument – at least in Hilda's ecstatic vision:

HILDA: Yes, it's the impossible, now, that he's doing! (*With the inscrutable look in her eyes.*) Do you see anyone up there with him?
RAGNAR: There's nobody else.
HILDA: Yes, there's somebody he's struggling with.
RAGNAR: You're mistaken.
HILDA: You don't hear singing in the air, either?
RAGNAR: It must be the wind in the treetops.

(858–859)

The scene at Lysanger, from exactly ten years earlier, is thus recreated and enacted with a deliberately symmetrical irony at the play's end, with Hilda hearing a "tremendous music" and returning Solness's last wave of his hat with her own waving of a shawl in place of the younger girl's banner.

To achieve this magnitude – that is, the extraordinary degree of tragic and metaphysical import – Ibsen has built a play that unites a realistic plane of action with levels of supersensory activity and implication. In Johnston's phrasing, he has fashioned a "mediation" between realms of "everyday appearances" and "universals" (350). To accomplish this intricate interplay among realms, the dramatist uses irony in several key ways, including the investment of an ironic world-view in his characters, creating a dramaturgical structure with ironic turns and hinges, emphasizing the appropriateness of the acme in Barthes's sense of the term, and engaging a continual, unfolding process of ironic reversals of circumstance. In doing this, Ibsen successively constructs a complex and interactive field of irony on several levels. More importantly, the playwright is able to condense this field, to concentrate its intensities in such a way that a potential dramatic power is compressed into singular and definitive moments in the action and then powerfully released. This compression is given its most clarified and representative form in the arrival of Hilda Wangel at Solness's house, and from that point on the ratio between her appearance and its effect is used to broaden Solness's sphere of psychic awareness even while delimiting his range of possible action. In one sense, certainly, *The Master Builder* is concerned with the terrible double bind of Solness's fortune, what Gosse calls the "tyranny" of his luck (192). Even more significantly, though, the drama highlights another double-edge, the builder's construction of his own destiny and doom, with this very contradiction ironically personified in Hilda Wangel. Each of these two characters is, in fact, a personification of ironic exertions in the drama; irony is instilled into the persona of each figure and into what they do, especially with respect to one another – in this sense, again, they are "consubstantial." As Schechner suggests, Solness gradually arrives at the knowledge that he has "summoned" Hilda, that she is the "daemon," his "helper and servant" ("Visitor" 165). It is this recognition, perhaps, that provides Solness with the most ironic luck of all:

> SOLNESS (*looks at her with bowed head*): How did you ever become what you are, Hilda?
> HILDA: How have you made me into what I am?

2 The character of irony in Chekhov

In *The Master Builder*, Henrik Ibsen uses the catalytic power of one character's opportune entrance to insure a forceful concentration of dramatic potential and ironic timeliness. The occasion of Hilda Wangel's appearance holds within it all the latent magnitudes of the drama that is to come, and Ibsen consciously employs the irony of this scenic moment to signal the many implications of youth's arrival in the master builder's domain. And, within the broader pattern of the play's dramaturgical arrangements, the playwright emphasizes timely entrances as an ongoing motif, not only in the case of Hilda but for Aline Solness as well. Ibsen is not alone with respect to such emphasis. Anton Chekhov is exacting, too, concerning the potentials that exist in the drama of entrances or arrivals – and, indeed, in the orchestration of his characters' comings and goings generally – but the effects that he derives from such arrangements are markedly different from what is encountered with Ibsen. Chekhov's own strategy of juxtaposition is such that irony is incorporated perpetually into the dramaturgical structure as well as, correspondingly, the tenor and tone of events and the interrelations among characters.

As *The Cherry Orchard* begins, for example, Yermolai Alekseyevich Lopakhin is one of the first two characters to appear on stage. The nursery at the estate house of Lyubov Andreyevna Ranevskaya is lit by a May dawn, and Lopakhin comes into the room with Dunyasha. Announcing that Madame's train has arrived, he inquires characteristically: "What time is it?" (315).[1] Not only will Lopakhin have a consistent interest in the precise time – or an exact date such as August 22 when the estate will be put up at auction – but his appearances in the action gain significance in markedly timely

38

ways. Indeed, the occasion of his entrance in the third act, following immediately upon the sale of the orchard, is given as much preparation, centrality, and weight of implicit resonance as any arrival in Chekhovian drama. His brief yet momentous answer to Lyubov's query about the sale ("I bought it.") provides what David Magarshack has called "perhaps the most perfect climax in any of Chekhov's plays" (*Dramatist* 281). And Lopakhin's exits can also provide vivid examples of the playwright's overall weaving of arrival and departure, as when, near the play's end, he hurries away from Varya as their last opportunity for marriage is passed by as if unknowingly.

In *Three Sisters*, the reappearance of Lieutenant Colonel Aleksandr Ignatyevich Vershinin (the former "lovelorn major") into the lives of the Prozorov sisters provides the instigation for movements that continue in the play. His arrival signals not only the incipient romance with Masha but also the possible deliverance the soldiers bring more collectively to the Prozorov household and to the town, and what is lost forever when their regiment departs. When *The Cherry Orchard* ends and Lopakhin leaves the estate house prior to its vacancy and imminent destruction, he goes off hurriedly to catch a train to Kharkov, apparently oblivious to what is being sacrificed regarding Varya. At the close of *Three Sisters*, when Vershinin kisses Masha good-bye, holds her tightly and then departs, he is taking away all that she has left to value and hope for. Along these lines, the arrivals and departures of both Lopakhin and Vershinin can be understood in microcosmic terms and in direct relation to the moment-to-moment dramaturgical structures of their respective plays. And yet, in the case of each character there is also the macrocosmic signification. The manner in which Chekhov has plotted their comings and goings, primarily through a technique of ironic juxtaposition, provides for a magnitude that is different from Ibsen's, and with a decidedly distinct sort of affective power.

To observe that Chekhovian drama evokes particular resonances through ironic turns is an idea so familiar as to constitute a truism. As Bert O. States suggests in *Irony and Drama*, it is in the works of Chekhov that we find the *"locus classicus* of the ironic play," with Chekhov as the "first master" of this type of drama (88, 102). Yet still, the ways in which this dramatist's vision of irony takes on the form of dramatic action or event, and the manner in which it is embodied and enacted through the dramatis personae, are matters that deserve a sustained scrutiny. Lopakhin, for example, might be characterized readily as a personification of Chekhovian irony in the sense that he embodies *The Cherry Orchard*'s core ironic twist: the son of serfs becomes the owner of the estate. Lopakhin might be described also as having an ironic world-view, or at least a wry and often humorous perspective on events, and he is the first to appreciate the ironies in his newfound circumstances as estate owner. However, when the factor of enactment is added to, but also distinguished from, that of embodiment, the ironies associated with his character acquire a more performative dimension and take on, correspondingly, a more defined agency in the action. So, too, with Vershinin, a figure who does not offer a consciously ironic viewpoint on his circumstances yet strongly epitomizes the shared situations of the characters in *Three Sisters* – that is, the mutually held tensions that are played out continuously in the time-related, past and future contradictions of "I wish" or "I remember" in opposition to the present tense "I am." From this perspective, Vershinin becomes irony's unwitting spokesman but also its performative agent in the action.

Here a distinction can be drawn between the ways in which an individual character may or may not perceive the world in ironic ways and the manner in which he or she may function nonetheless in the ironic pattern of a play's action: irony in strictly dramaturgical by contrast to expressly philosophical or thematic terms. Irony for the stage is, after all, as performative as it is literary or textually based, and the characters, perhaps especially in Chekhov's hands, are charged with its demonstrative purposes. Even as Chekhov is celebrated for the lifelikeness of his situations and for his avowed determination to present life in its quotidian haphazardness, the actual stipulations of his dramaturgy reflect a self-conscious and calibrated view of life's circumstances as a finely orchestrated dance of ironic appearances and disappearances. If plot in the Aristotelian sense is the arrangement of stage events, such an ordering for Chekhov is a continual insuring of meaningful appositions, with significance supplied just as much through the arrangement itself – pairings, comings and goings, coincidences, missed chances, and so on – as through whatever happens to be felt or expressed by characters in given moments.

Here, as in the case of Ibsen, there is a difference between authorial irony and the standpoint or situation of a given dramatic character. So, by extension, can the quality of an ironic vision that is reflected in the immediate and delimited realm of character behaviors be contrasted with an inclusive, or even cosmic, impression of a broadly resonant order. In either case, the particular flavor and character of Chekhovian irony must pertain to the dramatis personae, to the playwright's dramaturgical arrangements and intricacies, and also to his representation of a cosmos: irony in relation not only to time but also to a space-time in which the characters are affixed as to a web, no matter their struggles or degree of awareness of circumstances. It would be a mistake, however, to charac-terize a single or unified Chekhovian cosmos, if only because the vaster realms of his plays (the discussion here features *The Cherry Orchard* and *Three Sisters*) are in fact quite distinct from one another, in spite of clear similarities, with respect to both the nature and the performance of irony.

Lopakhin and *The Cherry Orchard*

Together with Lyubov Andreyevna, Lopakhin occupies the dramatic center of *The Cherry Orchard*. His persistent yet self-contradictory motives – first to convince Lyubov to sell the estate for parcels and cottages, and then to buy the land himself – provide a full demons-tration, not only of the blind helplessness and inertia that afflict the estate owners but also of the sheer power of social change that will oust them from the ancestral property. Lopakhin's traits and qualities are such that he comes across as well-intentioned as against opportunistic, sensitive and alert to circumstances as opposed to coarse or bumbling. Lopakhin, in short, is no Natasha, the usurper of the Prozorov house-hold in *Three Sisters*. He is not especially intrusive or even acquisitive, and rather than manipulate those around him he often looks first to the welfare of others. As Chekhov writes to Stanislavsky (October 30, 1903): "It is true that Lopakhin is a merchant, but he is a decent fellow in every respect, and he must behave with the utmost decorum like a cultured person and without any vulgarity or tricks." On the same day, Chekhov writes to Olga Knipper, referring to Lopakhin as "a gentle person," one who must not be played "as a typical merchant," and a few days later the playwright indicates to Stanislavsky that "Lopakhin's role is central in the play."[2] Indeed, as Maurice Valency reports in *The Breaking String*, Chekhov "disapproved strongly of Stanislavksy's intention of casting himself as Gaev. He wanted him for Lopakhin" (264).

Chekhov endows Lopakhin with select behavioral mannerisms, such as the waving of his arms and the checking of his watch, and he incorporates scenic moments for the character that are so distinct, such potent encapsulations of the play's tones and directions, that each one becomes a finely wrought gestus of the drama's wider currents and ironic arrangements. The first of these, early in the first act, comprises a nearly instantaneous entrance and exit on Lopakhin's part. It occurs so quickly and unassumingly that it might almost pass without appreciable notice were it not for the context and immediate effect. Varya and Anya are in conversation about the future of the estate, when Lopakhin swiftly pokes his head into the room and "moos."

> ANYA: Well, how are things? Have you paid the interest?
> VARYA: How could we?
> ANYA: Oh, my God, my God!
> VARYA: In August the estate will be put up for sale.
> ANYA: My God!
> (*Lopakhin peeps in at the door and moos like a cow.*)
> LOPAKHIN: Moo-o-o! (*Disappears.*)
> VARYA (*through her tears*): What I couldn't do to him! (*Shakes her fist.*)
> ANYA (*embracing Varya, softly*): Varya, has he proposed to you? (*Varya shakes her head.*) But he loves you … Why don't you come to an understanding, what are you waiting for?
>
> (320–321)

This sequence, which follows soon after the arrival of Lyubov and the others, provides a telegraphic encapsulation of Lopakhin's larger involvement with the house and family (his failure to persuade, followed by his own purchase of the estate) and serves also to foreshadow the fleeting, final scene with Varya, which is meant by Lyubov to include a proposal of marriage. Thus, when Lopakhin "disappears" in

42

this early sequence, something is conveyed of the man he will prove to be, perhaps especially so in this moment that is also filled with his elation over Lyubov's arrival.

The audience is alerted right away to Lopakhin's regard for Lyubov by an incident that he recalls for Dunyasha as the play begins, an event that took place when he was only fifteen years old. His father, drunk, had punched his face and drawn blood. Lyubov, the young mistress of the estate then, helped him to a washstand, saying, "Don't cry, little peasant ... It will heal in time for your wedding" (316). Much of what Lopakhin says and does in *The Cherry Orchard*, including his dogged persuasiveness regarding the sale of the land but possibly also his ultimate reticence with Varya, can be attributed to this lingering memory and to his loyal admiration for the lady of the estate. Prosperous as he may be, Lopakhin is still the "little peasant" in this house and among these people. His "moo" is a completely spontaneous and unplanned utterance of the moment, and as such it lends a sudden and undisguised voice to the son of serfs who can never feel quite natural or at home in this environment.[3]

The "moo" also brings about an abrupt collision of comedy and pathos. Lopakhin's interruption is meant by him to be funny, or at least to mock or undercut the somber tones of Anya and Varya. And yet, his utterance is framed by the young women's discussion of quite serious matters – to wit, the estate sale and the question of the latter's marriage prospects. David Magarshack attributes Lopakhin's behavior to the excitement that he is feeling here, due in part to Lyubov's arrival but also to his conviction that he has found a solution to her financial worries and can barely stand to wait until he can make that discovery known. Lopakhin's ardent wish, in Magarshack's view, is to repay Lyubov for "having treated him like a human being and thus having awakened in him a sense of self-respect which proved so important to him in his climb from poverty to riches" (*Dramatist* x). Elaborating on this fundamental motivation in *The Real Chekhov*, Magarshack speculates on Lopakhin's state of mind:

> He had a plan which would not only save her estate from being sold, but would make her a rich woman. It seemed so simple and reasonable to him that he had no doubt that she would not

hesitate to accept it. That was why he had come specially to the old house so as to be in time to meet the train, help her with the luggage, see whether she had greatly changed, and, above all, tell her that she need not worry any more.

In Magarshack's vision, then, Lopakhin's monosyllabic interruption of Varya and Anya results from a joyousness, an overflow of feeling: "Overhearing the girls talking, he could not contain his excitement any longer: it was he, he alone, who knew how the estate could be saved!" (198–199).

In truth, Chekhov's pattern of ironic apposition is suggestive of a number of ways in which Lopakhin's spontaneous gestus might be understood and how it might connect with other moments in the play. There can be little doubt, as Richard Gilman writes, that Lopakhin's interjection "says something about his nature and position in the play" and that Varya's response to it sets up her "dealings with Lopakhin at the end" (*Plays* 217, 218). At the same time, there is the relation of Lopakhin's present elation to his former status as "little peasant," and by extension to his feelings, past and present, for Lyubov. "He worships Lyubov," says Valency, "and can refuse her nothing, though he has given her up for lost. It is clear that she is the secret love of his life, his ideal of womanhood, and perhaps the true reason why he will not compromise by marrying Varya" (*String* 273). Within such an inclusive perspective, then, the ironies are compounded, and the love of the transformed peasant for Lyubov is exactly what stands in the way of him marrying the person that she, Lyubov, would have him wed.

The import of this type of irony, in the stage image as well as dialogue, issues in part from the brevity and visual clarity of the enactment itself. Lopakhin is an ironist in terms of intellect, dryly aware of his circumstances, but he is also a performative ironist who defines a standpoint in physical, gestural, and behavioral vocabularies. Along these lines, a patently comical intrusion – "moo" – modestly crude and mocking, delivers the multilayered content of the sequence in terms more succinct than an elaborated verbal irony might accomplish. The juxtapositions here are finely wrought, with only the bookends of an estate sale and possible marriage to lend Lopakhin's quick appearance and monosyllabic bleat an unexpected magnitude. Gilman argues persuasively for Chekhovian scenic construction to be understood as a "dramatic field" as opposed to a "dramatic line," and cites the playwright's letter to his brother in which Chekhov says, "the more mosaic-like the results, the better" (*Plays* 217). The playwright's dramaturgical strategy derives, to borrow his own image, from exactly how the mosaic pieces fit and relate to one another. In this sense, the question of "what goes with what" pertains directly to the ironic meanings that arise from exacting and often minute positionings. Here it is only a "bleat," in connection with a prospective estate sale and a marriage that will never be, that accomplishes the task.

Later on in the play, when Lopakhin appears following the sale of the orchard, the extraordinary impact of his proclamation ("I bought it.") also derives in large measure from his long-held feelings toward Lyubov together with his boyhood status as the son of serfs. Yet the galvanizing power of this moment in act three issues also from Lopakhin's unrestrained glee at what has transpired and from his perception of how ironic the turn of events has been, in spite of his own determination to bring about an opposite result. That effort begins early in the action when Lopakhin initiates and then steadfastly pursues his campaign to convince Lyubov of his plan for saving the estate. "As you know, the cherry orchard is to be sold to pay your debts. The auction is set for August 22, but you need not worry, my dear, you can sleep in peace, there is a way out. This is my plan. Now, please, listen!" But Lyubov and Gaev are incapable of listening or, certainly, comprehending what Lopakhin is telling them. She cannot imagine cutting down the orchard, "the one thing in the whole province that is interesting, not to say remarkable," and her brother can only protest that the orchard is "mentioned in the Encyclopedia." Here once again Lopakhin checks his watch, a gesture that in this particular instant captures his impatience with Gaev (and probably Lyubov), the awareness that he must hurry on his way, and his knowledge of how swiftly August 22 will be upon them. As Lopakhin repeats this ordinary mannerism throughout the play, what begins as a simple motif in characterization becomes a reiterated instance of performative irony, in this case an expressed awareness of dissonance between the approaching sale and the intransigence of those he would persuade – and, quite likely, a developing awareness of how little time is left before he will need to take action himself.

> LOPAKHIN (*glancing at his watch*): If we don't think of something and come to a decision, on the twenty-second of August the cherry orchard, and the entire estate, will be sold at auction. Make up your minds! There is no other way out, I swear to you. None whatsoever.
>
> (325–327)

Chekhov underscores the inability of Lyubov and Gaev to absorb Lopakhin's warning by having her tear up two telegrams from Paris, unread, and by placing Gaev's paean to the ancestral bookcase in immediate juxtaposition to Lopakhin's prophecy. If, as Valency suggests in another context, "Chekhov is almost always ironic at the expense of the activist" (*String* 275), such an attitude is certainly prevalent in this sequence which counterpoises Lopakhin's logic and determination against those who will not understand yet mock him nonetheless.

Lopakhin may be, as Brustein puts it, "the most positive character in the play." Unlike the others, Lopakhin "labors, with ever-increasing frustration, to bring the befuddled family to its senses" and is the only one who "seems to possess energy, purpose, and dedication." Comparing Lopakhin to the student Trofimov, Brustein argues that "one of the many ironies of *The Cherry Orchard*, in fact, is that while Trofimov theorizes about work ... Lopakhin quietly, and untheoretically, performs it" (*Revolt* 172). Gaev may, in his homage to the bookcase, mention such "unflagging" qualities as "fruitful endeavor" and "courage and faith in a better future." In this setting, however, Richard Risso finds the relation of Lopakhin and Gaev to be especially ironic, noting with regard to the latter that "the comic irony is compounded by the fact that he addresses his self-serving speech to the family bookcase and in the presence of Lopakhin who, more than any other character in the play, exemplifies those qualities that Gayev ascribes to himself" (186). When Gaev, who has the behavioral tic of continually miming or referring to the game of billiards, alludes in this sequence not only to the bookcase but to "carom" shots, Chekhov insures that a full range of interconnections are brought into relation, albeit through indirection, with one point of reference glancing off of another. Thus, when Lopakhin finally departs the room, after promising Lyubov "a loan of fifty thousand or so," Gaev's single word – "Boor" – is all the ironic punctuation that is necessary (327–329).

Lopakhin does not give up easily, nor is he dissuaded by attitudes with which he has been long familiar. He persists in his solution for saving the orchard, even as the response of the other characters remains obtuse. In the second act, the scene shifts to the outdoors – a meadow at twilight – and in this atmosphere the contradiction among the characters' points of view is felt even more starkly than earlier. Time has passed, as Lopakhin need hardly have prophesied ("Time, I say, passes"), and his arguments have taken on more urgency as the date in August draws nearer. Correspondingly, the response of Lyubov and Gaev is ever more abstract:

> LOPAKHIN: You must make up your mind once and for all – time won't stand still. The question, after all, is quite simple. Do you agree to lease the land for summer cottages or not? Answer in one word: yes or no? Only one word!
> LYUBOV ANDREYEVNA: Who is it that smokes these disgusting cigars out here?
>
> (339)

Chekhovian drama evokes the vagaries of time in many ways, but Lopakhin enacts and animates it here as though it were something tangible, definite, and available to be pressed upon the others as a persuasive force. Indeed, the time that is elapsing even as they speak seems to quicken Lopakhin's urgency. This is, of course, also the sequence in the play when the mysterious breaking string is heard first, itself perhaps another of time's voices. For Lopakhin, though, destinies are determined not so much cosmically as by a steady passage of days:

> LYUBOV ANDREYEVNA: But what are we to do? Tell us what to do.
> LOPAKHIN: I tell you every day. Every day I say the same thing. Both the cherry orchard and the land must be leased for summer cottages, and it must be done now, as quickly as possible – the auction is close at hand. Try to understand! Once you definitely

decide on the cottages, you can raise as much money as you like,
and then you are saved.

LYUBOV ANDREYEVNA: Cottages, summer people – forgive me,
but it's so vulgar.

GAEV: I agree with you, absolutely.

(341)

Lopakhin's final line in the second act is also his last stand against
the inertia: "Let me remind you, ladies and gentlemen: on the twenty-
second of August the cherry orchard is to be sold. Think about that –
Think!" (350). And yet it is Lopakhin who does the thinking, and by
the very next time he is seen on stage, he has purchased the orchard
himself.

Risso mentions "Chekhov's fondness for the ironic discrepancies between what a character says and what a character does" in *The
Cherry Orchard* (186), an observation that can apply certainly to Gaev
and his paean to the bookcase or to Trofimov's vocation as perennial
student, but it's one that relates along different lines to Lopakhin. The
instance of supreme and concentrated irony, and of ironic peripety, in
The Cherry Orchard – "I bought it" – is powerful climactically exactly
because Lopakhin has been so energetic in his effort for this result
not to come about. The "discrepancy" between what he says, arguing
futilely against Lyubov and Gaev, and what he finally does, which is to
take time into his own hands, contains in this instance a forceful ironic
torque. Time itself is brought into the ironic equation, in Risso's view,
as the dissonance that is dramatized between Lopakhin's careful meas-
urements and the abstractions of Lyubov and Gaev. "The sense of time
that Lopakhin urgently measures in terms of days, hours, and minutes"
is brought into "ironic contrast" with a time frame that "is occupied
principally by Lyubov and Gayev and is in direct contrast to the accel-
erated time frame governed by Lopakhin" (187).

Significantly, the sharply accentuated moment of peripety that
is exemplified by Lopakhin in the third act ("I bought it.") is largely the
result of these operative stresses themselves – including the perception
of time – as opposed to more directly felt or conventional antagonisms
among the characters. The dissonance itself is ironic or, as States puts

48

it: "Though there are no antagonists in a Chekhov play, the form itself is antagonistic: the play is, one might say, a carefully supervised irony" (*Irony* 91). August 22 arrives, and the build-up to Lopakhin's arrival at the estate is intensified by the characters' attempts to sustain a party mood that is both contrary and complementary to their anxiety over the auction. They alternate between making merry and lashing out at one another, as when Lyubov castigates Trofimov for his being "above love," or when Varya explodes at Yepikhodov over the issue of "discernment." Indeed, all of the emotional intensities in the household, taken together with all that Lopakhin has argued concerning the estate, are now concentrated as if to coalesce in Lopakhin's moment of return. Appropriately, he is nearly knocked flat by a billiard stick, swung by Varya, as he comes into the room.

> LYUBOV ANDREYEVNA: Is the cherry orchard sold?
> LOPAKHIN: It's sold.
> LYUBOV ANDREYEVNA: Who bought it?
> LOPAKHIN: I bought it.
>
> (365)

Here, as in the initial entrance of Hilda Wangel in *The Master Builder*, is an instance of supreme theatrical irony that comes across through striking visual spectacle as well as aurally and in the juxtaposition of events. First there is a pause, then a brief intrusion of silence, and then the full weight of the completed ironic turnabout crushes in. Lyubov is overcome, and must steady herself against a table. Varya throws her keys to the ground. Lopakhin speaks, exultantly and a bit drunkenly, celebrating not only the sale but what for him is the unexpected beauty of the reversed circumstances. Once more, this is irony enacted, irony embodied in performance and, even more acutely, in Lopakhin's expressive self-awareness: "If my father and my grandfather could only rise from their graves," he exults, "and see all that has happened, how their Yermolai, their beaten, half-literate Yermolai, who used to run about barefoot in winter, how that same Yermolai has bought an estate, the most beautiful estate in the whole world. I bought the estate where my father and grandfather were slaves, where they weren't even allowed in the kitchen" (366).

Lyubov weeps as the orchestra plays. Yet even as Lopakhin glories in the turnabout of "Yermolai" purchasing the orchard, his attitude is not one of superiority. No one knows better than he how astounding a reversal of fortune has come about, and no one has more admiration for Lyubov, despite her inability to act on his warnings or perceive her situation. And, in this moment in which severely contradictory currents are abruptly brought to bear on one another, Lopakhin himself is torn. As Gilman puts it, "the closer a Chekhov character is to the dramatic center, the more contrarieties or at least dissonances he or she is likely to contain. So it is with Lopakhin." For Gilman, this character's "victory is in no sense over Liubov, who sits weeping, but over his own past, over past time itself" (*Plays* 236). Indeed, the "dissonances" that Lopakhin embodies here do not arise only from what Gilman calls "internal clashes" (*Plays* 236), but include the more sweeping contradictions inherent in the irony of the reversed circumstances. Even Lopakhin, when he calls out, "Here comes the new master, owner of the cherry orchard," must do so "ironically" in Chekhov's stage direction (366).[4]

"Chekhov hides his ironies more expertly than any other writer of the ironic theatre," claims States (*Irony* 90). This may be the case, to be sure, in many instances, and Chekhov's web of juxtapositions can be subtle in the extreme. Lopakhin's announcement, however, is an irony so pronounced, so heralded, that clearly no attempt has been made to hide it. It is so obvious, and so accentuated, that it bears comparison to the "audacity" of Ibsen's design for Hilda's arrival in *The Master Builder*. What Chekhov has hidden, or at least kept offstage, is Lopakhin's moment of decision. He reports in detail on the bidding, but when exactly did he decide it would be he who would own the orchard? The fact that there is so little build-up to the climactic announcement through Lopakhin himself, but only through those who are there at the beginning of the act, serves to make the instant of reversal even more surprising, and therefore more powerful. Lopakhin's total pattern of ironic enactment in the play is, in fact, a classic instance of Burke's formulation: drama as a process of inherent trajectories turning through dialectical agency into their opposites, with a possibly gradual turnabout focused into an event of reversal. Again, Burke's dictum is that "'what goes forth as A returns as non-A.' This is the basic pattern that places the essence of drama and dialectic in the irony of the 'peripety,' the strategic moment of reversal" (*Grammar* 517). In this scenario, Lopakhin can be understood not only as irony's performative agent, but also as the messenger of its primary dialectical purpose.

Lopakhin's embodiment of the play's ironic stresses does not end, however, with his announcement of the sale. Toward the end of *The Cherry Orchard*, in fact, Lopakhin's discussion of business matters with Trofimov is accompanied by the sound of the trees being cut down. In this sequence, too, Chekhov includes the meeting with Varya, the missed opportunity for proposal and marriage that in itself connects Lopakhin yet again to the adored Lyubov. As the two of them set up the encounter with Varya, Lopakhin and Lyubov seem to understand one another perfectly and to agree on what is to happen. Lyubov doesn't comprehend why Lopakhin and Varya seem to "avoid each other":

> LOPAKHIN: To tell you the truth, I don't understand it myself. The whole thing is strange, somehow . . . If there's still time, I'm ready right now . . . Let's finish it up – and *basta*, but without you I feel I'll never be able to propose to her.
> LYUBOV ANDREYEVNA: Splendid! After all, it only takes a minute. I'll call her in at once . . .
> LOPAKHIN: And we even have the champagne.
>
> (375)

Lopakhin's reference to remaining "time" is, clearly, an alert that there might not be enough, or that the timing may not be propitious for other reasons. Francis Fergusson speaks to the proclivity on the part of Chekhov's characters for the missed moment, "as the moods shift and the time for decision comes and goes." Here in the fourth act of *The Cherry Orchard* there is a fleeting chance for union on the parts of Lopakhin and Varya, the fragile moment between the two of them existing as a synecdoche for the play's larger drama of missed commitments. And, in the play's complex weaving of arrivals and departures, Lopakhin's final exit stands also as a succinct representation of the play's larger cross-currents. In Fergusson's phrasing, "the wish to save the cherry orchard has amounted in fact to destroying it; the gathering of its denizens to separation; the homecoming to departure" ("Theater-Poem" 149).

> LOPAKHIN: I'm off to Kharkov ... by the next train. I have a lot to do. I'm leaving Yepikhodov here ... I've taken him on.
> VARYA: Really!
> LOPAKHIN: Last year at this time it was already snowing, if you remember, but now it's still and sunny. It's cold though ... About three degrees of frost.
> VARYA: I haven't looked. (*Pause*) And besides, our thermometer's broken. (*Pause*)
> (*A voice from the yard calls: "Yermolai Alekseich!"*)
> LOPAKHIN (*as if he had been waiting for a long time for the call*): Coming! (*Goes out quickly.*) (*Varya sits on the floor, lays her head on a bundle of clothes, and quietly sobs. The door opens and Lyubov Andreyevna enters cautiously.*)
>
> (376–377)

"Why doesn't Lopakhin ask Varya to marry him?" wonders Gilman. A complicated question, to be sure, but Gilman connects the answer to Lyubov. "Might it be that Lopakhin will never propose as long as Liubov is there?" Or "Is it that to marry Varya, adopted daughter though she may be, is to come too close, aspire too high, perhaps even violate a taboo?" (*Plays* 241–242). In either case, the action is brought full circle, reinstating the way in which the play began with Lopakhin's adulation of Lyubov and, indeed, bringing to mind Lopakhin's interruptive comment – "Moo!" – that first bespoke his attitude toward Varya and perhaps at the same time announced his exultation over a plan for saving the estate and its mistress.

In Chekhov's ironic pattern, it is Lyubov and not Varya who is Lopakhin's necessary partner. In *The Master Builder*, it is not only through individual characters but also in a core relationship or duet that irony is fully personified and enacted, and that type of figuration applies also, along these different lines, to *The Cherry Orchard*. Lopakhin may embody the mastering irony of an ancestral estate passing to the son of a serf, but in order for this reversal to achieve its full impact, there must be a personification of the contradictory situation through another character who will complete the partnership. What may be realized individually through Lopakhin is, in other words, accentuated markedly because of his particular background with, and depth of feeling toward, Lyubov. To reference Burke once again, it is the "fundamental kinship with the enemy" that provides the basis for the ironic (*Grammar* 514), the same shared necessity that is so apparent in *The Master Builder* in the pairing of Solness and Hilda. In the case of *The Cherry Orchard*, both Lopakhin and Lyubov are needed to stand for, as well as to enact, the play's ironic opposition. And, in addition to the passing of the estate from one to the other, the two share a complementary, yet ironically fateful, sense of time. Lyubov is drawn to certain memories that are pleasurable, but is also haunted by past events – her "sins" – especially having to do with the death of her son on the estate. She is so absorbed, in fact, with the past, including what has happened in Paris, that she cannot make a future tangible. Lopakhin, by contrast, is of the moment, is able to understand the present circumstances, and can anticipate the future. The past for him is a heritage that is clearly in the process of alteration beyond familiar recognition. Lopakhin may love Lyubov, yet he is the agent of her greatest loss; she and the orchard can be saved by Lopakhin, but only if she will hear and believe his message – and she can do neither.

Gilman, sounding the play's mysterious encounter between Lopakhin and Varya, suggests that within the interrelations of these characters there is an element of "sheer chance" that figures in their missed opportunity and in the "way things unpredictably unfold" (*Plays* 242). Judging by the offhandedness of their behavior in the final scene – Varya looking for a lost item, talk of the weather, Lopakhin's thinking about the next train – Gilman's notion is certainly legitimate. At the same time, as Barthes would say, "chance signifies." The nature of Chekhovian dramaturgy is such that his plays unite a show of artlessness with the most meticulous attention to juxtaposition, to minutiae, to phenomena presented in elaborate arrangement and through a weave of interrelationships. It is not "luck" of the sort Halvard Solness would recognize that afflicts this scene, yet it is still a species of ironic happenstance – that is, something more than accident. If Chekhov's theatre is ultimately one of heartbreak, Lopakhin's departure from Varya is surely demonstrative of all that might have been possible – and yet is not. Here again it is the potency of a Chekhovian irony that, in effect, stands in for the more typical antagonisms in dramatic conflict. Or, as Skaftymov writes: "No one is to blame. Then since no one is to blame, there are no real adversaries; and since there are no real adversaries, there are not and cannot be struggles. The fault lies with the complex of circumstances which seems to lie beyond the influence of the people in the play. The unfortunate situation is shaped without their willing it, and suffering arrives on its own" (82). Chekhov knew, during the composition of *The Cherry Orchard*, that his illness was going to kill him, a knowledge that is perhaps felt most poignantly in the drama of what Gilman calls the "minute particulars," and through the "extreme momentariness of our experience" (*Plays* 243).[5]

Vershinin and *Three Sisters*

That "momentariness," the fragile and evanescent quality of the passing instant, is dramatized in *Three Sisters* in ways unequaled by any other of Chekhov's plays. The story of the Prozorov sisters, in their transient relations with the military men who are stationed in their town for a while, is centrally a story of an impossible present moment – a "now" that is the consistent yet transitory point of intersection and collision between a recollected past and the anticipated future. Present time in *Three Sisters*, sufficiently abstract anyway, can never be pinpointed simply on its own terms: it is necessarily in debt to what has come before and what is hoped or feared will come later. Because the temporal directions of the play extend well into the past and, at once, deep into the future, time is given by the author a cosmic as well as an immediate application, with the characters responsive to both.[6] In precisely this way, an irony of the present moment emerges, like so much in Chekhov's drama, from a pairing or a juxtaposition – in this instance the cosmic and the quotidian compressed together into an intersection in time, with the characters who exist within this compression presented as mystified witnesses to its nature.

Chekhovian irony here, as in *The Cherry Orchard*, is performative. It is localized in character and dramatized through enactment and stage imagery as well as in conversation or the scenic content per

54

se. Here it will be advantageous to differentiate further between the performance of irony and some of the more familiar conceptions of the ironic that are associated with Chekhovian drama. For example, it is well known that Chekhov's ironic expressiveness is often tonal in nature. In this regard, Brustein calls attention to the playwright's accentuation of the atmospheric aspect by "carefully balancing pathos with irony" (*Revolt* 153). Along closely related lines, Chekhovian irony can be linked to the playwright's frequently contested sense of the comic, or, as Brustein puts it, the tendency of the plays to alternate "between moods of wistful pathos and flashes of ironic humor which disqualify them from being mere slices of life" (139). Irony may exist, too, in the interrelation of the manifest action with that which is subtextual, a distinction between the Chekhovian surface action and a substratum that Brustein describes as "a constant ironic tension" (*Revolt* 137), and Gilman refers to as the "ironic contrast" among varying strands of plot (*Plays* 152). Still, and in spite of such formulations that are by now familiar, it must be the characters themselves who deliver, as it were, the ironic goods, and they must do so through specific embodiments and behaviors.

Both plays, *Three Sisters* as well as *The Cherry Orchard*, are built upon a dramatic pattern of progressively reversed circumstances. The Prozorovs are inexorably disenfranchised, not by someone who surprises them by buying their land but by somebody who stealthily but steadily takes over their house. The sisters, especially Irina, expect deliverance, but the benevolent future that is hoped for never assumes a graspable shape. With reference to one of Chekhov's more familiar oppositions, Risso remarks that "the intrinsic irony in the play is revealed in the disparity between what the characters hope to achieve and what, in fact, is achieved" (185), a contrast as applicable to Varya as to Irina, Masha, or Olga. The two plays bear a structural relation, too, in what Robert Corrigan terms "a variation of an arrival-departure pattern" (80) which, as already noted, is connected in Chekhovian dramaturgy to an ironized pattern of apposition among entrances and exits, including the implicit commentary that issues from who arrives or departs at specific moments.

When Lieutenant Colonel Vershinin arrives at the Prozorov house and encounters the sisters after so many years away, he certainly does not know that he is an authorial messenger of irony, although his occasional tendency is to grasp eagerly for whatever cosmic import may be inferred from a situation. In truth, Vershinin himself is not much of an ironist. He does not consciously maintain an ironic vision as world-view, as Solness does, nor is he particularly aware of the supreme irony of his circumstances or behaviors, as Lopakhin is, even though he can be benignly wry in sharing his observations with others. Vershinin is Chekhov's representative, and here the ways in which an ironic vision can be authorial as opposed to situated in character alone can be distinguished further. Gilman recalls Chekhov's conviction that "the truth (about life) is by nature ironical" (*Making* 118), but as Lopakhin and Vershinin demonstrate in their different ways, this perspective can be represented through characters who in themselves appreciate the irony of their own actions or circumstances or by those who, unknowingly, simply embody its terms.

Chekhov's ironic vision, perhaps especially in *Three Sisters*, extends to a cosmic perspective in which the characters are framed at once in immediate circumstances and eternal ones, with irony supplied in their insolvable coexistence. Thus, the interactions that take place in the foreground of Chekhov's drama continually bespeak a background that is sensed vaguely by his people but only on the most mysterious and intuitive terms, at once recognizable and fathomless. It is, in fact, upon this contradiction that Chekhov can build such a breadth of scope and magnitude, with the ironic viewpoint itself bringing with it a considerable potential for signification. Valency contends, along these lines, that *Three Sisters* "marks an important stage in the evolution of the type of drama which depends for its magnitude on the association of its characters with a cosmic process external to themselves." Such a suggestion, of course, aligns the play most closely with a tragic tradition of long standing, but Valency is concerned particularly with comparing Chekhov's sensibility with that of Ibsen. Contrasting *Three Sisters* with an Ibsen play (*Rosmersholm*, in this case), Valency notes that:

> ... while Ibsen is often ironic at the expense of his characters, he is completely serious with respect to the order of change in which

they are involved, while Chekhov takes nothing for granted. Chekhov concedes the possibility of the social process which Vershinin expounds, but he cannot accept the idea whole-heartedly, and the suggestion is inescapable that perhaps all these hopes, these dreams, and these efforts are in the end equally meaningless and equally absurd.

(*String* 244)

Chekhov, in this view, is not so much being ironic "at the expense of" his characters; rather, he is simply allowing Vershinin, in the charac-ter's own fashion, to conjure up a future that may be quite at odds with an "order of change" that the play is dramatizing alongside a concurrent but greatly expanded standpoint. Or, in Valency's concep-tion, "the play itself is symbolic of a greater drama, the cosmic drama which it suggests, and with which it corresponds" (*String* 245).

Vershinin, whom Richard Peace characterizes as the play's "chief philosophiser of the future" (101), is fashioned by Chekhov as a particularly effective match for, but also as a notably marked coun-terpoint to, the Prozorov sisters who have, both individually and together, their own perspectives concerning what is yet to come. The family name itself, as Peace points out, may be aligned meaningfully with this future, and also with this fateful orientation: Prozorov, from the Russian "*prozorlivyy* – 'perspicacious,' 'able to see into the future.'" Peace's suggestion, in fact, is that Chekhov's title is meant to evoke the three Parcae of classical myth, and here again there may be indication, not only of the nature of Chekhov's ironic outlook but of the extent of its reach: "Yet the suggested identification of the three sisters with the Parcae can only be made with heavy irony: Chekhov's sisters are not in control of fate – they are rather its vic-tims" (85–86).

> VERSHININ (*gaily*): How glad I am, how glad I am! But there were three sisters. I remember – three little girls. The faces I no longer remember, but that your father, Colonel Prozorov, had three little girls. I remember perfectly, I saw them with my own eyes. How time passes! Oh, oh, how time passes!
>
> (243)

By the time Vershinin arrives at the Prozorov home and Masha has remarked on "how much older" he looks, the phenomenon of time passing has already been given centrality in the drama. *Three Sisters* begins on this note and, indeed, never strays far from it. Chekhov immediately situates his characters in relation to recognizable, shared standards of time: it is Sunday, May 5, at midday. It is Irina's name day, which is the year anniversary of their father's death. As Olga calls attention to these matters, a clock strikes the hour. In the course of the remaining action, however, time is not always so exacting as this. In fact, a key component in Chekhov's presentation of an ironized present moment is his opposition of time as measured by human markers with time as an eternal and unquantifiable phenomenon within which the characters exist and upon which they speculate. Even as Vershinin may stand, as many of Chekhov's characters do, for a simple form of dramatic irony, what Risso calls the "knowledge of a disparity between what a character does and anticipates and what actually occurs" (181), he also represents this much deeper ironic situation, that of time as experienced in its cosmic yet day-to-day aspects – and in this role he becomes Chekhov's ideal emissary.[7]

With a nod to Henry James, Gilman brings eloquent expression to the ways in which Chekhov in *Three Sisters* is more concerned with depicting a "condition" or "state of existence" than a sequence of action:

> To put it as swiftly and unceremoniously as I can, I think the
> condition which *Three Sisters* portrays (to once again use James's
> sweetly unfashionable term) is that of living within time. I mean
> being caught in it, resident in it, experiencing it as chronology or
> duration only in its most superficial or apprehensible manifest-
> ations but more deeply as a place, a habitation; being rocked in
> it as the cradle of all we do; knowing it as wholeness,
> indivisibility, but more often in fragments; trafficking with
> it as myth; projecting everything ahead to await its presumably
> transforming arrival as future and simultaneously seeing
> everything disappear into its wake as past; time, the

"double-headed monster of damnation and salvation," as
Beckett, whose *Waiting for Godot* has such profound affinities
with *Three Sisters*, called it in his essay on Proust; time, which
flattens out all distinctions, refutes and covers over all meanings
except its own; time, which leaves us like the sisters at the end of
the play, with only one possible response to its inscrutability: "If
only we knew!"

(*Plays* 148)

Vershinin is, after his own fashion, obsessed with time, although not
in the way that Lopakhin is. Whereas Lopakhin glances fretfully at
his watch and is mindful of when his train will be leaving, Vershinin
continually consults the temporal reference points of a distant, abstract
future by comparison with a transitory present, often with the past linked
not so much to a recorded history as to memory. In the first act, as Masha
tries to recall her mother's face, Vershinin is prompted to one such
speculation:

> MASHA: Imagine, I'm already beginning to forget her face. And we
> won't be remembered either. We'll be forgotten.
> VERSHININ: Yes, we'll be forgotten. Such is our fate, we can do
> nothing about it. What to us seems serious, significant, highly
> important – a time will come when it will be forgotten, or seem
> unimportant. (*Pause*) And it's interesting that now we absolutely
> cannot know just what will be considered great, important, and
> what pitiful, absurd.
>
> (245)

Later on, when Masha remarks on how much of what they know is
"useless," it is the cue for another of Vershinin's arias, a speech that
prompts Masha, who had been all set to return to her own home, to
change her mind about leaving:

> VERSHININ: In two or three hundred years life on this earth will be
> unimaginably beautiful, wonderful. Man needs such a life, and so
> long as it is not here, he must foresee it, expect it, dream about it,
> prepare for it; and for this he will have to see and know more than

his grandfather and father knew. (*Laughs.*) And you complain of
knowing a great deal that is useless.

MASHA (*takes off her hat*): I am staying for lunch.

(249)

Vershinin, who is all too aware of how his own circumstances (particularly his marriage) might compare with such idealized projections,
offers the speculative possibility for redrafting one's life – once a person
has recognized the mistakes that have been made during an imagined
trial run. What he offers, however, is not merely the idea of starting
life over again, armed with better knowledge. Instead, his vision is of a
parallel life, a life that is conscious of the other one, existing apart but
in a continuum of time or space that includes both at once:

> I often think: what if one were to begin life over again, but
> consciously? If one life, which has already been lived, were only a
> rough draft, so to say, and the other the final copy! Then each of
> us, I think, would try above everything not to repeat himself, at
> least he would create a different setting for his life, he would
> arrange an apartment like this for himself, with flowers and
> plenty of light . . . I have a wife and two little girls, but then, my
> wife is not in good health, and so forth and so on, and . . . well, if I
> were to begin life over again, I wouldn't marry . . . No, no!
>
> (250)

And now, just as Vershinin makes this declaration, Masha's husband
Kulygin enters the room. Vershinin is naturally unaware that he is now
placed, in Chekhov's stage image, in signifying juxtaposition, not only
with a woman who admires him but also with the husband who bores
her so terribly.

This, of course, is Chekhov's deliberate positioning and not his
character's, but the intrinsic range of commentary extends beyond a
romantic triangle to all that Vershinin has said about the life to come
in comparison to the life that Masha has been living with her school-
teacher husband. It is the well-meaning Kulygin who presents Irina
with a name day gift that betrays his own painfully constrained understanding of time and the past – a printed history of all those who have

graduated from the local high school over the past fifty years – and, as a further commentary on his lack of perspicacity, it is the same book that he gave her already at Easter. Reminded of this, he attempts to pass the book off on Vershinin – "Take it, Colonel. Read it some day when you're bored" – but instead of doing that, the colonel welcomes the opportunity to make a hasty exit (250–251).

Chekhov's perspective on romantic interrelations is such that an ironic perspective is virtually assured, often pertaining to a character who loves someone without reciprocation, somebody who is in a relationship with the wrong partner, or a situation in which two characters who might reasonably enjoy a successful union somehow miss out on the opportunity. Ronald Hingley observes that, "Among the sources of frustration in Chekhov's plays love occupies pride of place. Broadly speaking no one is allowed to be in love with anyone who is in love with them, and on the rare occasions when this rule is broken some external circumstances can be relied upon to create an effective obstacle" (241). In *The Seagull*, probably the most exemplary case of this tendency, Nina is caught between the attentions of Konstantin and Trigorin, a situation which, in turn, frustrates Irina Arkadina's intentions concerning the latter. Masha, matched with the sorry Medvedenko, admires Konstantin who, with eyes only for Nina, has no interest in Masha whatsoever. In *The Cherry Orchard*, Lopakhin and Varya manage to miss their chance to be together in spite of Lyubov's energetic efforts to the contrary, and in *Three Sisters*, Andrei marries Natasha only to have her turn her attentions to Protopopov, while Masha and Vershinin carry on a courtship that is impossible because of his marriage and hers.

> VERSHININ: I love you, love you, love you . . . I love your eyes, your gestures, I dream about them . . . Splendid, wonderful woman!
> MASHA: When you talk to me like that, for some reason, I laugh, though I am frightened. Don't do it any more, I beg you . . . (*in a low voice*) But, say it anyway, I don't mind . . . (*Covers her face with her hands.*) I don't mind. Someone is coming, talk about something else . . .
>
> (262)

Within Chekhov's web of exacting juxtapositions, the pairing of Vershinin and Masha is followed here by the entrance of Tuzenbach and Irina (another of the play's impossible romantic combinations), and the encounter that follows includes both men expanding on their respective philosophies – including Tuzenbach's prediction that "men will fly in balloons, change the style of their coats, discover a sixth sense."

> VERSHININ (*after a moment's thought*): How shall I put it? It seems to me that everything on earth must change little by little, and is already changing before our eyes. In two or three hundred years, let's say a thousand years – the time doesn't matter – a new, happy life will dawn. We'll have no part in that life, of course, but we are living for it now, working, yes, suffering, and creating it – in that alone lies the purpose of our existence, and, if you like, our happiness.
>
> (265)

By this point, of course, it is clear that speculation such as this is Vershinin's trademark, and it's a characteristic that entertains and fascinates Masha. It is also the chief means through which Chekhov limns Vershinin as the play's primary embodiment of a core ironic situation having to do with the several characters' relationships with time.

Vershinin himself is unaware that he is enacting so broad a perspective, and yet it is his nature to reiterate a set of contradictory relations, expressed generically as the difference between what he foresees and where he stands at the moment, or a difference between what he wishes for and what he presently has. His talk of the future may amuse or enchant Masha, yet it comments implicitly on the dreariness of her situation generally and with her husband more specifically. Correspondingly, Vershinin's vision of a life to come, another "draft" of what he might have chosen given the chance, contains of necessity the contrast with his unhappy family life. The degree to which Vershinin appears in a comic light could, in this view anyway, be reflective of Brustein's conviction that a good deal of Chekhov's humor "proceeds from the ironical contrast between a character's opinions and his behavior, as if the political animal and the human being were somehow mutually incompatible" (*Revolt* 146). As punctuation for the ironic inter-plays that he has arranged in the course of act two, particularly regarding the married couples, Chekhov has Vershinin return from his own home to the Prozorov house only to learn that Masha is not there and the maskers have not come after all – and so he heads off alone with none other than Kulygin.

Vershinin's characteristic linkage of a present moment to both past and future time is made substantially more acute during the fire that occurs in the middle of the night during act three. It is in this part of the play, in fact, that Vershinin mentions that the brigade may be transferred, and soon after this he recalls his feelings upon finding his daughters during the fire. His lengthy speech describes an immediate reaction to their "faces full of alarm, terror, entreaty," an impression that leads directly to anxious speculation on what they will confront and endure later in life, in some unknown future circumstance. Then, as if conditioned to think in terms of one tense in the same time frame as another, the speculation on the future leads directly, and almost seamlessly, to recollection – and then immediately to present and future again:

> When my little girls were standing in the doorway in their underwear, the street red with the blaze, and the noise terrible, I thought that something of the sort must have happened many years ago, when the enemy made a sudden raid, plundering, burning ... And yet, what a difference between things as they are and as they were. When a little more time has passed, say, two or three hundred years, then people will look at our present-day life with horror and contempt, and all this will seem awkward, difficult, very uncertain and strange. Oh, what a life that is going to be, what a life!
>
> (285–286)

Vershinin's rhapsody concludes with a lyric from the opera *Eugene Onegin* – "To love at every age we yield, and fruitful are its pangs" – and then, as if to demonstrate the sentiment, he and Masha hum the tune to one another in counterpoint, then laugh aloud together. Then later, as the act ends, Chekhov brings this theme back again, adding it into the weave of entrances and exits made by the married couples, which now includes Andrei and Natasha. Vershinin sings the tune as a signal to Masha, who leaves in order to be with him. Kulygin arrives, in search of Masha, and departs not knowing where she has gone. The sequence is played almost as a dance, accompanied by Andrei's futile justifications concerning his wife Natasha, who is now in a barely disguised relationship with Protopopov. The undertone is consistently ironic, as the characters gravitate toward those with whom they would belong – except, that is, through marriage.

Chekhov delays Vershinin's final entrance until the play is nearly over and the brigade is about to leave the town. Time has passed, as Lopakhin would say, and Olga is headmistress at the school. It is expected that Irina will marry Tuzenbach and move to another town (though, certainly, not Moscow), but it is known that "something happened yesterday," having to do with the dispute between Tuzenbach and Solyony. Vershinin and Olga share a brief exchange, where he says they will likely not meet again – and then comes the farewell to Masha. Before Masha's entrance, however, Vershinin has one more statement to make regarding past and future. During this particular speech, he is more directly concerned with time in its immediate, rather than distant, impression. Like Lopakhin, he keeps looking at his watch, knowing the hour has come:

> Time for me to go, it's time! Formerly mankind was occupied with wars, filling its entire existence with campaigns, invasions, conquests, but now all that has become obsolete, leaving a great void, with nothing to fill it; humanity is passionately seeking something, and, of course, will find it. Ah, if only it would come soon! (*Pause*) If, don't you know, we could add culture to the love of work, and love of work to culture. (*Looks at his watch.*) I really must go . . .
> OLGA: Here she comes.

> (308)

Here again Chekhov is masterful, as in *The Cherry Orchard*, in the use of theatrical spectacle to underscore the ironic import of a scene.

Masha appears, and she and Vershinin must face their good-bye at last. There is a prolonged kiss. Then, in concert with the playwright's perfected interweaving of opportune arrivals, Kulygin walks in upon the departure scene to find his wife sobbing violently.

The ironies of the isolated present moment are, in all of Chekhov's dramaturgy, nowhere more acute than in the final sequences of this play. In the *Anatomy of Criticism*, Northrop Frye asserts: "In those parts of Chekhov, notably the last act of *The Three Sisters*, where the characters one by one withdraw from each other into their subjective prison-cells, we are coming about as close to pure irony as the stage can get" (285). Yet there is another, related sense in which *Three Sisters* gravitates toward the tragic as well as ironic direction. In Frye's study, which proposes an overarching progression among artistic modes or genres, the tragic and the ironic – as a "mythos" of autumn and of winter, respectively – are presented not in terms of variation or evolution but rather as similarity. Frye's claim is that in the "nineteenth century drama the tragic vision is often identical with the ironic one" (285). In another setting, however, Frye addresses the question of a tragic vision specifically, and in a way that also has application to *Three Sisters* and its temporal renderings especially. Frye's contention in *Fools of Time* is that "the basis of the tragic vision is being in time," and his emphasis is placed on "the one-directional quality of life, where everything happens once and for all, where every act brings unavoidable and fateful consequences, and where all experience vanishes, not simply into the past, but into nothingness, annihilation" (3).

This condition – and the echo of Henry James's usage is appropriate – of "being in time" lingers close to the heart of what Chekhov dramatizes in *Three Sisters*, including the relation of his characters to a quotidian concept of time that is measurable in human terms and, concurrently, an abstract, universalized time of which they may also be aware but do not comprehend. To advocate on the side of the tragic in Chekhovian drama may, of course, evoke the dramatist's own casting of his stories in a comedic light – although he does subtitle *Three Sisters* a "drama." And again, if one entertains the more standardized comic associations of irony, it is not unusual to find in Chekhovian portrayals some variation of the cosmic joke, which often entails varying orders of haplessness in the face of mysterious or eternal patterns. Even so, it is difficult not to relate the situations and relationships in *Three Sisters*, especially given the inextricable interconnections with temporal factors, to the sort of tragic context that Frye identifies. Irony as a cosmic joke, applicable certainly in *The Cherry Orchard*, does not find a comparably conducive setting in Chekhov's earlier play. As Valency argues: "Even if we concede that all its characters lend themselves to irony, it is impossible to give a comic bias to *The Three Sisters*."[8] Valency's contention is, in fact, that audience "identification" itself is sufficiently strong to prevent that from being the case (*String* 247). The emotional tone of the play's ending is surely one of heartbreak, elicited nowhere more strongly than by Masha's anguished sobs and the sound of the military band playing as the soldiers leave the Prozorov sisters forever. This is a present instant in time defined in shades of overwhelming sadness and loss, as past dreams of a finer life merge into a future that, for the moment at least, can only seem bereft.

Such a sequence in present time is not, it should be noted, ironic in itself. Time is abstract, innocent, dispassionate – or, as Gilman puts it, "Time has no logic, no reasons or rationale; it doesn't proceed smoothly, it doesn't *proceed* at all but simply is. And it doesn't have a plot" (*Plays* 158). To add in the ironic element, there must be "plot," a sequential development of interaction. There must be characters who, in their individuated behaviors and attitudes, their memories and predictions, can bring this particular sort of meaningfulness to a depicted present, even unintentionally. Thus, it is through personification that time's progression becomes ironized: what Chekhovian characters hope for in the future becomes, inevitably, a memory – and the memory is always at odds with what had been anticipated. Present time in Chekhovian drama may appear inert, unpurposeful, yet it cannot be held still, no matter how recalcitrant the people on stage may be when faced with choosing a future or even with performing an action. As Frye would say, the movement is "one-directional." In this sense, indeed, Chekhov's irony can be understood as continually manifest with respect to the characters' standpoints on temporality. One moment is replaced by the next, with each one being unclaimable, and the characters are seen to age as the play advances in time, scene by scene. Yet there is also a built-in dissonance in Chekhovian drama between a character's age in years and "age" as a synonym for an era. Chekhov's people are distinguished by a tendency (and Vershinin is the epitome of this) to cast themselves unintentionally in ironic light by the very ways in which they remark upon their ages or their aging by comparison with the epoch in which they exist. This behavior has both near and macrocosmic associations, as the characters attempt to situate themselves in current circumstances and in accord with their respective social worlds, yet at the same time unwittingly delineate themselves against a timeless, cosmic skein of interrelations.

Again, it is essential for Chekhov's conception in *Three Sisters* that Vershinin not be an ironist himself, but rather an energetic personification of an ironic tendency or, indeed, vision. Vershinin is, to be sure, a visionary, but the fact that he does not himself have an ironic world-view is a key to his ability to project the situation that Chekhov means to delineate. Chekhovian drama typically sets a character's own view of self or circumstances in apposition to that of another – as in the case of Vershinin and Tuzenbach – or places it in implicit comparison with a collective portrait that is at odds with an individual's self-conception or perspective on events. As Corrigan puts it, this is "one more ironic device," which, one might say, can be understood also as characteristic of the dramatist's pattern of juxtaposition. Corrigan observes that, "by contrasting the way the characters see themselves with what they do and with the way the other characters view them, Chekhov, again by indirection, is able to reveal the way life really is" (91).[9]

This idea does, however, have a broader basis in irony than might be reckoned at first, and once again the figure of Vershinin is for Chekhov an ideal personification of ironic agency. As States would have it, irony "requires three people: the ironist, someone who gets the irony, and someone (at least implicitly) who doesn't, or wouldn't, get it. In ironic drama there is, so to speak, something to recognize, and in Chekhov this something is exactly the characters' nonrecognition – or at least the gulf between the display of behavior and its possible inner consequence." In truth, Chekhov makes the import of this contradiction doubly acute, in that he depicts Vershinin as a philosopher, a visionary, but as one who is still the necessary figure who "doesn't, or wouldn't, get it." If Chekhov is the ironist, then the person or persons who would, ideally, get the message are those who comprise the audience – or, as States puts it, the "radical irony" in Chekhov is to be found in the presence of the observer, that "'second person' whose presence is presumed in the conduct of the mimesis" (*Pleasure* 96–97).

Ironies in Chekhov come in all shapes and sizes, from Chebutykin's breaking of "Mama's clock" to Olga's final apostrophe ("If we only knew!"), but within the connective fabric of a particular work the varying types do not necessarily exist independently of one another. Rather, the steady accumulation of meaningful oppositions suggests a broader vision on the playwright's part – or, put differently, the lesser ironies, in their variety but also their accrual, reflect and imply larger ones. The trope of irony is in this way tied directly to those of metonymy and synecdoche, and in a way that puts a spin, often an inclusive one, on the convention of the part/whole ratio. In the Chekhovian theatre, where the effect is to derive a universal impression from immediate, albeit timeless, circumstances, such a linkage is requisite to the playwright's purpose. In States's formulation: "If metonymy and synecdoche are means of reducing and transporting whole worlds by substituting parts for whole, or parts for the qualities of wholes, irony is a means of expanding our perspective beyond the part-whole entity" (*Reckonings* 75–76). Irony has not only the ability to enlarge the field, but to do so in given ways, and with specific effects. States would say that irony has the ability to "infect" the other tropes with "self-skepticism" (76), but in fact its spectrum can be assessed more embracingly, depending on the authorial vision. In the case of Chekhov, the interrelation and accrual of ironies large and small creates a universal impression of haphazard sense, but one that is only dimly perceived by the characters – that is, by those who must act out the severity of its terms.

The universalized, or cosmic, viewpoint in Chekhovian drama is achieved by several means, the ironic impression being one. It was not long after the first performances of *Three Sisters* and *The Cherry Orchard* that Leonid Andreev (in 1912) described the totality of Chekhovian dramaturgy and spectacle as "panpsychism," and included the many elements of representation in the compass of "one vast soul." For Andreev, this includes the component of time as a psychological factor, together with the particulars of Chekhov's characters, properties, and landscapes. Objects, people, and time itself are, in this view, "animated," not as discrete factors but in unison:

> Chekhov animated *everything* that meets the eye: his landscape is no less psychological than his characters; his characters are no more psychological than the clouds, stones, chairs, drinking glasses and rooms. All the things in the visible and invisible world take part only as components of one vast soul; and if his stories are only chapters of one vast novel, his things are only *thoughts and sensations* scattered through space, a single soul in action and spectacle.

Andreev also emphasizes a performative aspect that, precisely because of this degree of co-participation, is intrinsic in the dramaturgy – that is, within this "animation." "On the stage," he writes, "Chekhov must be performed not only by human beings, but by drinking glasses and chairs and crickets and military overcoats and engagement rings." Andreev does not highlight the ironic aspect in Chekhov's arrangements, but calls attention instead to the importance and the style of the playwright's juxtaposition of elements, pointing to the end of *Three Sisters*, when "all of the protagonists of the play are *thinking and feeling to the rhythm of the military march* which, as if by chance, is being played in the street by the departing soldiers" (239–241). The ending of *Three Sisters* is, indeed, exemplary of what States calls "the arrangement of the counterpoint" (*Pleasure* 98), with sound and spectacle that includes Chebutykin's tune along with the military music, the image of Andrei and the baby carriage along with the cheerful Kulygin, and the sisters themselves in their respectively isolated situations.

Three Sisters, as Andreev might have said, is panchronological as well as panpsychological. This play stands, as Gilman puts it, as "a replica of time itself," particularly so in its success at conveying, simultaneously, a sense of time passing and of time standing still (*Plays* 150). It is, however, one matter to consider the vision of the play as representing, in Frye's terms, "being in time" or the "one-directional" aspect of that situation; it is another project altogether to apprehend the nature of time as it is shown theatrically, in the details of its particular representations, and to ascertain how "being" is portrayed as existing within time's hold and duress. The appositions among the characters, situations, pasts and futures, and the elusive linkages of cause and effect are transformed by Chekhov into a skein of inter-dependent circumstances that reflect in on one another – or in Gilman's telling oxymoron, into Chekhov's "eventful immobility." Such oppositions turn quickly ironic, but when time is depicted as a fundamental connective substance, irony assumes the fullest possible range of implications. Gilman describes a Chekhovian drama with effects but not causes, one that delivers "as pure a state of noncontin-gency as it's possible to find in a play until Beckett" (*Plays* 158–159). The phenomenon of time, says Gilman, how we pass through it, "what we do during the only real time granted to us, the present, that confluence of what is no more and what is not yet, is the play's story." Chekhov's play renders, in this way, "presence and duration: what is, has been, and unfathomably is still to come" (*Plays* 194, 196). At the same time, though, Chekhov dramatizes a continual interrelation among past, present, and future, and does so in a way that assigns the present, and those who live in it, a sharply ironic aspect with respect to both the past and the future. Once again, it is the characters' future hopes that become, within the play's compass, past memories, with the present always bearing witness to this dissonance – and to just what is being altered in the transition.

The relation of time and space in *Three Sisters* is such that the familiar and immediate environs of the Prozorov home share the stage with the more abstract dimensions in which the characters are also situated. Valency points to the "Chekhovian 'Beyond,' the strangely unreal atmosphere in which the realities of his later plays are suspended" (*String* 198). Andrey Bely writes of a Chekhov who "draws back the folds of life," revealing "an aperture into Eternity" (92). Simply in terms of Chekhov's basic dramaturgy, however, the concept of a "dramatic field" of interrelation is again pertinent. Gilman describes the way in which Chekhov "prevents a linear, destination-bound plot from taking shape, as he steadily fills the stage with a multiplicity of shifting presences, with their differing densities and angles of vision. A revolving dramatic field, we might think of it, which as it turns gives us glimpses of successive arrangements of feeling and idea, connectedness and disconnection, participations near the center of the imaginative frame or farther away" (*Plays* 216).

Yet again, though, the factor of time adds not only chronology but also a dimensional magnitude. States refers to the view of life that Chekhov represents as "the time-space arrangement of events" (*Irony* 102), and it is, in fact, just this factor of dimensionality that provides the plays, and *Three Sisters* in particular, with the feeling of a greater realm, or cosmos, that transcends their immediacies. In this regard, Gilman's phrase, "drifting plot clusters" (*Plays* 159), neatly suggests the departure from linearity, but the sense of an action separated from chronologically measured time is also implicit. Chekhov's characters may reveal their awareness of time and geography in immediate and recognizable terms: Lyubov arrives from Paris; Lopakhin must catch the train to Kharkov; the brigade will be transferred to another town. Concurrently, though, his characters strive to situate themselves against a much more expansive and abstract panorama. Irina may envision Moscow as an idealized destination, but the shared and more generalized effort on the part of Chekhov's characters is toward a location of self, and to this end they attempt to define the coordinates of space and time, as though to find an identity, or at least a congruency, in the connections of geography and chronology. The effect of Chekhov's "panchronology" is, from this standpoint, the impression of a vast web of interconnectedness that comes across not as location per se but rather as dimension. In both *Three Sisters* and *The Cherry Orchard*, the continual references on the part of the characters to times and places – in present, past, and future tenses – becomes, ultimately, the fabric and weave of this immense and intricate web. The characters strive continually to orient themselves within its bounds, to chart, graph, and define their coordinates within it, thus situating their lives and relationships – but in spite of all the efforts, the sought-after congruency cannot be realized. In Gilman's words, the characters "live within time and time lives within place" (*Plays* 167–168). But in the actual, living circumstances of Chekhov's people, time refuses to be aligned with space in terms that are truly comprehensible, a situation that brings with it (even as the characters share as much unity as can be possible in the interconnections of the web itself) a continual state of disjuncture – or, as Chebutykin might say, there's finally more "nonsense" than "consensus."[10]

Chekhov's dramaturgy, in its organizing principles, is directly reflective of this underlying fabric of space and time – what Gilman refers to as "a series of discrete phenomena bound together with invisible wires" (*Plays* 161). In terms of structure and revealed atmosphere, Chekhov accomplishes this effect not only through "panpsychism" but through a continually shifting pattern of entrances and exits, scenic compositions, and finely detailed juxtapositions of sound and spectacle, what Slonim calls the "successive changes of impressions to arouse the emotions" of the audience (76), or what Reid refers to, with respect to *The Seagull*, as the "musical logic of the whole ironic structure" (614). In Chekhov's drama, the character of irony belongs finally to the playwright, his people, and to his dramaturgy, concurrently. Such a character exists within a world-view, in the dramatic conflicts, in the arrangement of events, in the web of time and location. For Lopakhin, an encompassing irony is caught and performed in one concentrated moment of self-awareness – "I bought it." For Vershinin, irony's moment is neither recognized nor isolated in time. It is, rather, perpetual, existing in the relentlessly mysterious present condition of his past recollections and future predictions. For Chekhov's dramatis personae collectively, it is the faintly perceived cosmic weave itself – the vast and impenetrable interplay of vectors, past and future, here and away – that brings with it the ultimate irony: an awareness or recognition that comes hand in hand – "If we only knew!" – with bafflement.

3   Irony and dialectic: Shaw's *Candida*

Eugene Marchbanks is among the youngest of the magnificent odd-balls of drama. He is fashioned by Bernard Shaw as an eighteen-year-old quixotic and contradictory spirit, shy by his own description yet consciously and intrusively assertive, poetic in sensibility but of undetermined talents. Marchbanks intrudes into the home of James and Candida Morell and in doing so forms a household triangle that is only quasi-romantic and yet distinctly dialectical in matters of conjugal, sexual, courtly, and familial relations. In essence, Marchbanks is a complicated dialectic unto himself. He is at once acutely perceptive and painfully jejune, an ardent suitor with scant sexuality, outspoken and determined and yet feckless and obfuscating at the same time. As Shaw's agent provocateur, however, he is a superb instigator, neatly able to defy and then erode James Morell's self-satisfaction while convincing himself that he loves and is the best possible match for Morell's wife. The mastering irony for Marchbanks, of course, is that his desire for Candida is so strongly qualified by reticence and that hers for him is so mysterious regarding its motivations and goals. Yet such qualifications, significant as they may be, are mitigated in light of Shaw's broader dialectical program. In truth, and as William Irvine points out, if Shaw had wanted a truly potent sexual threat to enter the Morell household, he could easily have made Marchbanks older, more single-minded, and more robust.[1]

Marchbanks's mission in *Candida*, however, is not to be sexually, or even romantically, competent but rather to provide, in his acts of philosophical defiance and both physical and verbal challenge, the optimum co-partnership in a theatricalized Shavian dialectic. In this role he is assuredly successful, and his callowness is no hindrance when it comes to outdoing Morell on the preacher's own turf. If Marchbanks exhibits "genius," however, it is the quality of his abrupt, flashing perceptiveness rather than his poetic gift (of which Shaw provides little to judge) that can justify such an assessment. In fact, Marchbanks isn't very smart at all concerning real-world issues and person-to-person transactions, and it is mostly Shaw's orchestration of this character's behaviors – that is, the dramatic ingeniousness of the carefully pitched assaults and retreats – where a superiority of mind is most tellingly evinced.

Shaw once called *Candida* a "mystery," and the play retains, in spite of a quaintness that perhaps has grown more marked with the passing years, the very enigmatic qualities that have provoked disagreement since its first production. The mystery in *Candida* is usually associated with the play's title character, in particular with the relative decipherability of her motives as regards both her husband and the young poet in the house. Yet the mystery of *Candida*, if it can be called that, pertains to the poet as well as Mrs. Morell, and to the versatile aspect of his alleged "genius." Irvine calls the play "a study of genius in relation to worldly success and happiness." As a genius, says Irvine, Marchbanks "has all the obvious weaknesses and will eventually succeed because the world cannot prevent him." When the play ends and Marchbanks heads out the door, it is Irvine's contention that "the theme of the loneliness and self-sufficiency of genius surges up to dominance" (178). What happens once Marchbanks leaves the Morell household is, though, considerably less pertinent than what occurs while he is inside its oddly parental embrace. Whether or not Marchbanks will succeed with "the world" (a debatable issue, given his social skills) is not nearly so immediate or significant a question as what his in-the-moment sharpness brings to the rondo of Shavian debate on the status quo within the Morell house and its social environs. Perhaps it is for this reason that controversy has attended Marchbanks as a characterization that is truly believable as opposed to dramaturgically successful. On this question, however, the purely theatrical and interpretive factors of acting and directorial choices in a given production can be brought to bear, and the Marchbanks of one performer will assuredly not be that of another. For Irvine, at least,

Marchbanks as a figure of ostensible genius is "psychologically the least satisfactory character" in the play (178).[2]

Dramatic effectiveness, in the case of Eugene Marchbanks, is a profoundly more important quality than "genius," poetic talent, or psychological verisimilitude – perhaps especially so with respect to irony in its dialectical iteration. As the drama's chief catalytic agent, Marchbanks must not only ignite and then sustain the question of which man is best for Candida, but also be a prompt for the critical issues that arise around maternity, marital and extramarital relations, the romantic or idealistic versus pragmatic viewpoint, action versus talk, and the nature of "Prossy's complaint" – in short, many of the dialectical ingredients that Shaw packs into the proceedings. It is a characteristic of this dramatist that not a lot of synthesis emerges from the layered and interwoven play of thesis and antithesis; rather, the dramatic, and even suspenseful, emphasis is placed on the antipathies and complementarities among the terms themselves. Even when Marchbanks makes his enigmatic closing assertion that the "night outside grows impatient" and takes leave of the Morell domain, the audience is still left with questions – indeed, with a mystery – about the degree to which the component parts of the Shavian dialectical argument have come into any discernible or decisive conjunction. Shaw calls for Morell and Candida to "embrace" after Marchbanks's exit, but how so exactly and with what stage image to leave the audience?

With respect to thematics per se, Shaw's employment of irony is markedly different from Ibsen's or Chekhov's, even as all three dramatists gainfully use the gambit of an intrusive outside personality (Hilda Wangel, Natasha, Marchbanks) to heighten the range of ironic implications. The relationship of irony and Shavian dialectic is close, intricate, and revelatory. In a play such as *Candida*, one that is exemplary of Shaw's early dialectical dramas, the ironic is continually emphasized, and indeed is given a place at center stage – but, again, in ways quite different from its manifestations in Ibsen and Chekhov. Shaw is not an ironist along the lines that these other dramatists are, and his characters are not particularly ironic in terms of their worldviews, at least not to the extent that, say, Solness or Lopakhin are. As a dialectician, though, Shaw employs irony implicitly in ways that connect it directly to the dramatic conflicts, tensions, and antitheses themselves – or, in States's phrase, irony as "the very essence of opposition" (*Irony* 6). As in any ironic situation, there is within the dialectic a basis in juxtaposition, as in the relation of one term – character, philosophy, or point of view – to another. That Shaw can conceive a play in which the terms of dramatic character and dialectic are so closely interwoven is, in all actuality, merely symptomatic of the fact that irony and dialectic – and, in fact, drama itself – are concepts that share such affinities among themselves.

Even as Kenneth Burke identifies irony as one of four "master tropes" (metaphor, metonymy, and synecdoche along with irony), he advises that their literal application can be recognized by different but complementary names – and in the case of irony, the alternate term is dialectic. Further, says Burke, the term "dialectic" is equitable with that of "dramatic," particularly in the sense of how ideas and agents of action, as well as agents or characters in ideation, interrelate within a play (*Grammar* 503, 511).[3] In the logic of such a syllogism, then, irony bears an equivalence to drama on intrinsic terms. The Burkean formulation regarding irony is, along these lines at least, directly applicable to Shavian dialectics, particularly in relation to the dramatis personae – that is, to the collective interrelation among antithetical and complementary terms that are represented or embodied by a defined group of characters:

> Irony arises when one tries, by the interaction of terms upon one another, to produce a development which uses all the terms. Hence, from the standpoint of this total form (this "perspective of perspectives"), none of the participating "sub-perspectives" is either right or precisely wrong. They are all voices, or personalities, or positions, integrally affecting one another. When the dialectic is properly formed, they are the number of characters needed to produce the total development.
>
> (*Grammar* 512)

There is a sense here in which the ironic/dialectical commonality can be applied to any play, at least to the degree that the dramatis personae always (or at least ideally) represents the number of voices required for the drama to fully realize itself, as well as all of the latent possibilities for conflict, action, and interrelation. And yet, when the characters are (as in the case of Shaw) so closely connected with their respective "voices" or "positions," this relation becomes particularly acute. In this way, the Shavian characterizations and interrelations between, for example, Undershaft and Major Barbara, Mrs. Warren and Vivie, Ellie Dunn and Captain Shotover, Marchbanks and Morell are appositional in specifically ironic as well as dialectical or dramatic terms.

States calls irony and dialectic the "two most frequent fellow-travelers" for drama (*Irony* 3).[4] Within the terms of this closely connected triad, in fact, certain fundamental behaviors in dramatic action are encountered, including the tendency for action to develop in directions dictated by forces in opposition that propel the characters' interrelations and responses. What States refers to as drama's "entelechial process" is the intrinsic pattern arising, as Burke himself might say, from the fact that "the dramatist is like the dialectician in the sense that he or she is driven on to antithesis, to a continual sharpening of distinctions into ironic oppositions" (*Pleasure* 71–72). This is not, in drama, simply a process of inciting argument; it is rather a matter of insuring opposition with the additional component of directional momentum, or what Susanne Langer would call the "mode of Destiny."[5] The distinctions themselves are what create both conflict and forward motion, or, with reference once more to Burke's theory of progression and alteration, "'what goes forth as A returns as non-A.'" In Burke's framing, again, it is the "essence of drama and dialectic" that is located in "the irony of the 'peripety,' the strategic moment of reversal" (*Grammar* 517).

And yet, it is not simply the reversal or focused instance of peripety that defines the play of irony in drama. Irony can also assist in identifying the component facets of the problems or range of tensions that are being enacted. States finds, indeed, that it is through irony that "the dramatist finds the limits of 'the premise' within which a significant action may be dialectically developed." Irony becomes, along these lines, a principle of selectivity and arrangement of the events. Additionally, it serves as a tool for determining that "all that can be said on the subject has been said" (*Irony* 141). Applied generally to the works of Bernard Shaw, such a concept can take on particular nuances. Shaw famously constructs his dramas from orchestrating the interplay of voices around a given set of ideas and positions, whether the particular issue at hand is, for instance, the manufacture of armaments or the legitimacy of prostitution or the interplay of maternal and romantic love. Shaw's ironies arise, additionally, from his aversion to siding with his characters, a predilection that has practical (or dramaturgical) as well as aesthetic implications. States refers to Shaw as the "archparadoxist" of modern drama, contending that the "characteristic form of irony in the modern dialectical theatre may be paradox, or the irony which shows that things are either the reverse of what we believe them to be, or should be the reverse of what they are" (*Irony* 162).

Eugene Marchbanks must, in these contexts, enact the ironic or paradoxical motive together with the dialectical one. To accomplish this effect, Shaw positions Marchbanks within a triangle, along with James and Candida Morell. Shaw himself called *Candida* a "single situation in three acts," but he might just as well have called it a dialectical situation for three characters (Shaw *On Theatre* 111). It is ostensibly the age-old romantic triangle, albeit with a good deal of ideological freight added in along with matters of matrimony and courtship, poetry and preaching. Shaw extends these three primary sides of embodied argument through the use of other characters (most notably, Proserpine Garnett, or "Prossy"), adding also to the range of contradictory ideas and motives within his primary triumvirate. Marchbanks is the agitator, and in this trait at least he bears resemblance to his creator. As Richard Ohmann notes, all through his life Shaw wrote as "an *opponent,*" a position that arose from his own youthful antagonism toward "Victorian smugness" (28). It is worth noting, too, that in his life Shaw often found himself in – or, just as likely, deliberately created – situations in which he was one side of a triangular, most often romantic, relationship. Michael Holroyd refers to the relation of characters that Shaw created to women that he was interested in as "obsessively replaying the old triangular liaison." In connection to *Candida*, the pattern takes on a more specific manifestation: "The rivalry between Marchbanks and Morell over Morell's wife Candida carries echoes from several of Shaw's three-cornered affairs, in particular that of May Morris and [Henry] Sparling, but was intended as an interpretation of the current drama between himself and the

Charringtons" (315). Charles Charrington was the husband of Janet Achurch, the actress for whom Shaw wrote the part of Candida – an arrangement that, in itself, mirrors the fictional triangle of Mrs. Morell, Marchbanks (perhaps an extension of Shaw the "opponent"), and Reverend Morell. Shaw's preference, in fact, was often for married actresses (as in the case of Achurch) or for women otherwise associated with particular men, as in the case of Ellen Terry (with whom he carried on an epistolary courtship) and Henry Irving. Although such women were not necessarily serving as a theatrical muse in the fashion of, say, Emilie Bardach in the case of Ibsen, they could represent a strong influence, even indirectly, to the creation of Shaw's drama.

The very act of forming the triangle is, dramaturgically, central to both the structural principle and the dialectical (ironic) action of *Candida*, as it is along different lines in *The Master Builder*. Its shape and formation are effectively what set the drama, seen as dialectical process, into motion. Or, put differently, it is with the completion of the triangle that the status quo is significantly upset and challenged. Until Marchbanks arrives at the Morell home, as one of James Morell's "discoveries" (another irony, in light of what Morell himself is made to discover), that home is an epitome of established ways, convictions, and conventions – this in spite of the fact that Morell is supposedly a forward-thinking Fabian socialist minister. Moreover, the home represents a conjugal situation with, as it were, the requisite two sides instead of three. Yet the status quo that is shared by the Morells is an intricate arrangement indeed, and Shaw takes pains, from the outset of his play's action, to lay forth its dimensions.

Shaw, it would seem, could scarcely resist the ornate stage direction. His description of the setting for *Candida* – to wit, the Morell house as it exists near a park in the London suburbs – is described with such thoroughness (and over several pages) that the very weight of detail approaches oppressiveness. Shaw might easily have written something along the lines of, "St. Dominic's Parsonage, Victoria Park, near London, 1884," and left it at that. And yet, his lavish specificity does add, for a reader if not an audience, to the visual portrait of the life that is shared by the Morells. The status quo that is encountered as *Candida* begins is, again, a complex phenomenon, and to simplify it is perhaps to do an injustice. In reductive form, however, the state of affairs in this household has much to do with Morell himself: his perceptions, his ways of conducting himself and directing others, the life he thinks he leads, and of course his marriage. Such circumstances might also include Morell's self-satisfaction, the strength of his convictions, his complacency, his belief-system (religious, social, and conjugal, including their interrelations and hierarchy), his cosmos and place within it. If the mental state of Halvard Solness is key to the initiating circumstances and subsequent trajectory of action in *The Master Builder*, so at least is a set of attitudes indicative in the case of Reverend Morell. In Allan Lewis's description, in *The Contemporary Theatre*, Morell is "handsome and courageous, a Socialist who believes in the decency and equality of all people, who fights against injustice, and who is happy in his well-run home" (85). Morell is, in short, the "Good Man," admired by his parishioners (perhaps especially the women who suffer, like Prossy, from the "complaint" of being attracted to his good looks and hale qualities), appreciated by associates like Alexander Mill ("Lexy"), cherished (or so he believes) by the best wife a cosmos can offer, Candida. As he advises Lexy:

> MORELL (*tenderly*): Ah, my boy, get married: get married to a good woman; and then you'll understand. That's a foretaste of what will be best in the Kingdom of heaven we are trying to establish on earth.

And, continuing: "Get a wife like my Candida; and you'll always be in arrear with your repayment" (7–8).[6] This is Morell, or Morellism, at its most confident, most smug state. And yet, as Burke might say, this is also the point "A" that will gradually, through ironic and dialectical turns, come back as "non-A." A wife "like" Morell's Candida becomes in the course of the play's action a highly indeterminate entity, just as Morell's professed understanding of his wife and marriage turn to perilous uncertainty or, in Shaw's word, to "mystery." For Morell, at the end of the play, "his" Candida will be listening attentively as the upstart Marchbanks bids against him for her devotions.

Life according to Morell is predominantly a prescribed order. From his calendar of appointments and speaking engagements to his sense of social proprieties to his notions concerning the "Kingdom of

Heaven on earth," all factors great and small are integral to Morell's realm, and to his impression of a world and universe that make wonderful sense. So strongly held are Morell's beliefs that other characters (Prossy, Lexy) become extensions of him, whereas others (Marchbanks, Burgess) are decidedly not of his ilk. Within this proto-drama of "Morell" versus "non-Morell," Candida herself stands center stage – appearing to be of the first variety, and then of the other. The dramatic stakes that develop in *Candida* arise here largely from the considerable disparity between what Morell believes in as the play begins and what he is made to see (if not understand) as events transpire. As Eric Bentley puts it, Morell "has been the victim of a life-illusion of Ibsenic proportions: he has thoroughly misunderstood the marriage on which all his boasted confidence and happiness were based" (*Thinker* 133). Regarding the extent of the Morell cosmos, or that of *Candida* more generally, it is important to note that the ironic component does not lead necessarily, as it can with Ibsen and Chekhov, toward inclusive or universalized implications. Here the pattern of irony and dialectic is constrained for the most part to concerns within the Morell home, in spite of Marchbanks's poetic extravagance or the possible associations of Morell's religiosity. This is not to say that attitudes toward marriage or romantic love, for example, cannot be extrapolated to a more wide-ranging significance, but rather to observe that irony here serves a more delimited function pertaining mostly to social relations and conventions.

As a key feature of the play's dialectical workings, Shaw cleverly matches one projection of himself against another, with Candida the wife/mother set between the two male figures. If Shaw the "opponent" resides in Marchbanks, Shaw the Fabian is every bit as alive in Morell. "Morell is the Shavian ideal," says Lewis, "the Fabian Socialist who fights for social reform, dignity for all men. He is well-dressed, well-spoken and a likely member of Shaw's own Fabian group, but he has been so concerned with the ills of society that he has not seen them in his own home" (*Contemporary* 86). Candida herself may ultimately seem, as Bentley offers, to be "an expression of the feminine enigma" (*Thinker* 134); and yet, at the outset of the action she does not seem so mysterious. She returns home, having been away with the children (who are not, significantly, brought along with her), and plans to stay only for two days – as Morell tells Lexy, "to see how we're getting on without her" (7). It is soon apparent that Morell's ability to "get on" worsens considerably now that his wife is back at home. Candida's arrival is not, however, the event that in and of itself disrupts the Morell status quo. It is the other arrival, that of Marchbanks, that not only accomplishes that mission but, in doing so, sets the play's core dialectical mechanics into motion. Marchbanks's catalytic abilities quickly find their succinct expression, and his antagonism of Morell (along with, correspondingly, all that Morell stands for) begins in earnest, with a single line: "I love your wife" (21).

The woman so admired by Eugene is the center and the foundation of Morell's existence: this is *Candida*'s core problem. Candida is thirty-three: seven years younger than Morell and fifteen years older than Marchbanks. She is, one might infer, an arresting presence: attractive and sensuous in a maternal way and, strictly from a performance point of view, a match for the look and acting talents of Janet Achurch. Shaw calls her "well built, well nourished" and with "the double charm of youth and motherhood." "So far," he writes in his stage directions, "she is like any other pretty woman who is just clever enough to make the most of her sexual attractions for trivially selfish ends; but Candida's serene brow, courageous eyes, and well set mouth and chin signify largeness of mind and dignity of character to ennoble her cunning in the affections" (15). Arguably, her "cunning in the affections" is precisely what is not ennobled in the course of things. Rather, it is what finally diminishes not only her two men (nearly destroying the one) but her own projections of integrity and comfort as well. Such cunning is fortunate, however, in the dramaturgical or dialectical sense, and so too are her qualities of sexual attractiveness, maternal care, and indecipherability. The "mystery" of Candida is, to a notable degree, what keeps the dialectical dance of romantic, conjugal, poetic, and maternal love alive over the entire course of the play. Shaw allows one to know Candida – a bit – in the early scenes, but then initiates a steady subtraction in his title character's readability and reliability. Morell and Marchbanks are both, ultimately, confounded by her manner and shifting nature. If she is certain of herself, as it often appears, she is sparing indeed with allowing solid assurances to others. Candida herself may finally be, as Berst has it, "aesthetically dull" (60), but that is mostly in the sense of her limitations regarding such art or poetry as happen, through Marchbanks especially, to come her way.

Like Morell, Candida is ripe for a dialectical rendering. And like both Morell and Marchbanks, she directly reflects aspects of her creator. Bentley sees a specifically maternal side in this relation: "Into Morell Shaw can put that part of himself (a child) which finds Candida irresistible, just as into Candida he can put that part of Woman which he finds irresistible – the mother in her." At the same time, Bentley finds a dramatist who is of two minds on his creation: "Candida is made out of a Shavian ambivalence: he would like to reject this kind of woman, but actually he dotes on her. One quickly senses that he *is* Marchbanks." If Candida is enigmatic, then, part of the mystery may come from the playwright's ambivalent view of her, an ambivalence arising from his own circumstances as well as those of the drama. Bentley argues, in fact, that although "Shaw's intellect is against Candida, his emotions are for her" ("Making" 305–307).

The contradictory aspects within Candida are pronounced, allowing for a dialectical interiority that further complicates her relations with both Morell and Marchbanks. Gail Finney calls her a hybrid, particularly so as a result of the coexisting associations with the Virgin (as visually depicted in Marchbanks's gift of the Titian reproduction, "Assumption of the Virgin") and the New Woman – or, by extension, the play's so-called "Woman" question (193).[7] Finney's characterization – Candida as "that engaging amalgam of the Virgin Mary and the New Woman" – deftly captures her combination of appealing comforts with factors that might in fact be immiscible (204). Candida mothers and coddles both her husband and her young suitor, even as she confounds their respective aims and desires. If *Candida* is, as Shaw told Ellen Terry, "*The* Mother play," a goodly portion of its dialectical complication arises from the interrelation of motherhood with sexual allure and domestic power.[8] And yet, if Candida were only a singular embodiment of motherhood, even with a strongly sensuous aspect, her character would not embody this degree of ambivalence and enigma. Berst's commentary reflects both the charismatic power and the oppositions within the character: "The magnetism of Candida the Mother prevails throughout the play. The power of her self-confidence, the warmth of her maternal affection toward her husband and poet-lover, and the charm of her geniality all project a forceful and humane image. But these elements, strong as they may be, are set in a context which qualifies and at times contradicts them" (44).

Thus the particular, and at times undecipherable, combination of attributes that apply to Candida, when taken together with Morell's established attitudes and present state of affairs, constitute the play's central dramatic situation and potential – or, rather, comprise the latent situation that exists as a tenuous status quo awaiting Marchbanks's catalytic provocations.

> MARCHBANKS (*looking round wildly*): Is it like this for her here always? A woman, with a great soul, craving for reality, truth, freedom, and being fed on metaphors, sermons, stale perorations, mere rhetoric. Do you think a woman's soul can live on your talent for preaching?
>
> MORELL (*stung*): Marchbanks: you make it hard for me to control myself. My talent is like yours insofar as it has any real worth at all. It is the gift of finding words for divine truth.
>
> MARCHBANKS (*impetuously*): It is the gift of gab, nothing more and nothing less.
>
> (23)

Candida's nature does not, of course, always reflect the perceptions of her two admirers, and the play reveals little if any thirst for "reality" and "truth" on her part – save, possibly, for a fixation on her husband's true feelings. "Truth" is the poet's ostensible quest, not Mrs. Morell's – contributing here again to a Shavian irony. "Candida," in this sense at least, is less a real woman than a projection of what Marchbanks – and Morell, for his part – believe and need her to be. But this arrangement suits the play's dialectic, if not Reverend Morell, just fine. By the end of act one, Marchbanks can claim, "I am the happiest of mortals," with Morell ruefully responding, "So was I – an hour ago" (25).

The poet can see into the Morell marriage in ways that the preacher cannot. Or, put differently, he can observe or feel intuitively what is latent – unspoken, unstable, or open to question – in the Morells' relationship. In fact, the acuteness of Marchbanks's

84

sensitivity (possibly his true genius), his primal and instinctive feel for tender spots and vulnerabilities, is what allows for the concurrent verbal assault and chivalric treatment of Morell and Candida respectively. Correspondingly, though, Candida must be available to such attentive wooing from the young outsider, or the catalytic agency has no fertile ground for provocation and development. Just why, it might be asked, would this beloved and admired preacher's wife be open to such courtship – or is she? This is a part of *Candida*'s ongoing "mystery," certainly, and also a critical component in the Shavian dialectic around love, marriage, and "words" – as spoken from the pulpit or through a poet's romantic self-dramatization. Without the arrival of Marchbanks, the status quo continues unperturbed, but with his appearance there can be no continuation by the Morells of business as usual.

The composition of this quasi-romantic triangle provides, as Martin Meisel argues, both a departure from and a commentary upon the more recognizable conventions of Domestic Comedy. In Shavian terms, this implies that the dramaturgical structure exists in dialectical or ironic relationship to an existing dramatic pattern as well as to a widely known existing work – in this case, Ibsen's *A Doll House*, with the man and not the wife as "doll."[9] "A fundamental convention of Domestic Comedy," notes Meisel, "was the triangle composed of a romantic wife, a seemingly prosaic husband, and a seemingly poetic lover." But Candida is "the antithesis of the conventional foolishly romantic wife" in that she is "tempted not by romance, but by the poet's need." Morell, too, is an "inversion," in his case a twist on the expected Domestic role of husband: "Usually the conventional play disclosed progressively the hidden strengths and hidden virtues of the prosaic husband. Morell, on the other hand, is presented initially as a man of magnetic personality and ostensible strength, but in the course of the play Eugene's absurd prediction that he shall shake Morell to his foundations comes true" (230–231).

The "threesome" is, per se, an innately effective and age-old dramatic device. Three, as they say, is a crowd, and the implications of this adage are multifarious for romances, friendships, and rivalries alike. The very act of forming the threesome, or the triangle, can provide the occasion for drama, especially if the component three sides or characters carry with them particular ideological sensibilities or, one might say, dialectical/ironic potentials. In chapter two ("Ideals and Idealists") of *The Quintessence of Ibsenism*, Shaw proposes the triad of realists, idealists, and Philistines (37–45). In *Men and Supermen*, Arthur Nethercot proposes that the "neatest and most concrete specimens of the three types to be found in a single play occur in *Candida*" (7). At the same time, he notes the paucity of critical agreement on how exactly the three types, or any other types, are to be identified: "What *is* the truth about *Candida* the play and Candida the woman?" (9). For Nethercot personally, the solution seems clear, and he doesn't doubt that "Shaw himself intended his three leading characters to represent, primarily, Marchbanks as the developing realist, Morell as the wavering idealist, and Candida – how disillusioning this will be to the romanticists! – as the static Philistine" (10). The assignment of Shavian roles is not so significant, for our purposes here, as is the dialectic among ideologically embodied terms, each with its own range of versatile and suggestive implications. Each one of the three Shavian terms – realist, idealist, Philistine – can be played against the others, singly or in pairs. Additionally, they can be seen in combination with other signature roles within the play – such as mother, father, preacher, romanticist, and so on – with the several combinations serving to augment the resonances around dialectical match-ups and points of opposition and collision. Shades of irony appear naturally and frequently in such pairings, at times as an oxymoron, as when the title character is viewed as a "Philistine" object of poetic desire.

Shaw is infamous for the tendency to embody ideological or behavioral points of dispute in his characters, with the advantage of aiding a dialectical exchange but with the concurrent danger of characters coming across as mouthpieces for his ventriloquism or as partisan vehicles for information.[10] In *Mrs. Warren's Profession*, for example, Vivie has precisely the right convictions to offset her mother's; in *Major Barbara*, Undershaft has exactly the sorts of practical beliefs necessary to question Barbara's idealism. In *Candida*, and as a subset of the primary dialectical motifs and embodiments, Shaw includes the element of shyness, which is vested in Marchbanks but is cleverly paired with its own opposing characteristic. That is, Marchbanks is just as brazen as he is "shy," and this very type of contradiction is part of the glory of the character's charm as well as dialectical/ironic effectiveness.

86

The motif of shyness appears innocently enough when it is first introduced, but turns into one of the more resonant behaviors in Shaw's
larger drama. The implications and consequences of being "shy" first
come to the fore when Marchbanks and Prossy Garnett converse in the
second act:

> MARCHBANKS: Really! Oh, then you are shy, like me.
>
> PROSERPINE: Certainly I am not shy. What do you mean?
>
> MARCHBANKS (*secretly*): You must be: that is the reason there are
> so few love affairs in the world. We all go about longing for love: it
> is the first need of our natures, the first prayer of our hearts; but
> we dare not utter our longing: we are too shy. (*Very earnestly*) Oh,
> Miss Garnett, what would you not give to be without fear,
> without shame –
>
> PROSERPINE (*scandalized*): Well, upon my word!
>
> (27)

Much of the comedy in Marchbanks's character arises from his alternation between cringing away from situations and diving in head-first,
which provides a running dialectical parody on the theme of shyness.
But Shaw's aim is quite serious, and in this instance what Marchbanks
says must be taken, literally, to heart. "We are too shy," says Marchbanks,
and the line might be read as a warning signal against all the weight of
misunderstanding that accrues as the remainder of the play's action
develops. Prossy is naturally too "shy" to admit her "complaint," the
romantic admiration for Morell that she shares with other women; yet
Morell in turn has fallen well shy of recognizing the feelings of those
around him, most notably his admired wife. By deliberately surmounting
his own shyness, even comically, Marchbanks is able not only to stake his
claims but also to sharpen his attack and force the latent issues in the
Morell household into the open.

Within the overall pattern of interaction, Shaw blends such sub-
ordinate motifs into debates on the larger ones, adding both facet and
nuance to the competing terms and characters. It takes Candida herself
to let Morell know that he has female admirers (underscoring what
one already sees as a certain charming obliviousness on the part of the
preacher), but as she does so both Morell's political and religious postures

are brought into the argumentative mix, along with one of the play's primary – and most notorious – dialectical and ironic terms, "Love":

> CANDIDA: Oh, the worse places aren't open: and even if they were, they daren't be seen going to them. Besides, James dear, you preach so splendidly that it's as good as a play for them. Why do you think the women are so enthusiastic?
>
> MORELL (*shocked*): Candida!
>
> CANDIDA: Oh, I know. You silly boy: you think it's your Socialism and your religion: but if it were that, they'd do what you tell them instead of only coming to look at you. They all have Prossy's complaint.
>
> MORELL: Prossy's complaint! What do you mean, Candida?
>
> CANDIDA: Yes, Prossy, and all the other secretaries you've had. Why does Prossy condescend to wash up the things, and to peel potatoes and abase herself in all manner of ways for six shillings a week less than she used to get in a city office? She's in love with you, James: that's the reason. They're all in love with you. And you are in love with preaching because you do it so beautifully. And you think it's all enthusiasm for the kingdom of Heaven on earth; and so do they. You dear silly![11]

Immediately following this exchange, Shaw quickly executes a pivotal move with his dialectical terms, shifting the focus of "love" and attentiveness from Prossy and Morell to Marchbanks. If there is indeed a continual "mystery" in the figure of Candida, this is in part because of what she says to Morell at this juncture. When questioned, she denies jealousy of Prossy, but admits jealousy "for" another: "Not jealous of anybody. Jealous for somebody else, who is not loved as he ought to be."

> MORELL: Me?
>
> CANDIDA: You! Why, you're spoiled with love and worship: you get far more than is good for you. No: I mean Eugene.
>
> MORELL (*startled*): Eugene!
>
> CANDIDA: It seems unfair that all the love should go to you, and none to him; although he needs it so much more than you do.

(*A convulsive movement shakes him in spite of himself.*) What's
the matter? Am I worrying you?

(37–38)

Morell, by this point, is very worried indeed. Yet Shaw needs for him
to worry even more, and needs also for his leading lady to be even more
enigmatic and, at the same time, alluring. Candida asks her husband if
Marchbanks will "forgive" her:

> MORELL: Forgive you for what?
> CANDIDA (*realizing how stupid he is, and a little disappointed,
> though quite tenderly so*): Don't you understand? (*He shakes his
> head. She turns to him again so as to explain with the fondest
> intimacy.*) I mean, will he forgive me for not teaching him
> myself? For abandoning him to the bad women for the sake of my
> goodness, of my purity, as you call it? Ah, James, how little you
> understand me, to talk of your confidence in my goodness and
> purity! I would give them both to poor Eugene as willingly as I
> would give my shawl to a beggar dying of cold, if there were
> nothing else to restrain me. Put your trust in my love for you,
> James: for if that went, I should care very little for your
> sermons: mere phrases that you cheat yourself and others with
> every day.

(39)

This speech, coming near the end of the second act, iterates many of
the key dialectical terms that will motivate the remainder of the action
and animate the attendant discussions. The sentiments expressed in
this sequence by Candida are largely what motivate Morell to leave his
wife and the young poet alone together as he heads off that evening –
with Prossy, Lexy, and Burgess – to the meeting of the Guild of Saint
Matthew.

Yet Morell's "worry," not to say anguish, must be qualified,
even in light of its extremity. Candida would not take a lover, even if
she had the opportunity and if her poet were an older or wiser sort of
romantic. The ostensible opportunity that is presented later that evening by the fireplace is only a sham opportunity, replete with sensual

symbolism but nearly devoid of sexual threat. Candida may be "fasci-
nated" by the poker in her hand, but for Marchbanks at least she wields
more of a weapon than a symbol. Shaw would no more unite the suitor
and his beloved in an overtly sexual way than he would supply resolution for the other issues – that is, the dialectics – among the three
primary figures that comprise his triangle. Their shared dialectic must
also remain mysterious, both here and at the play's end, in the sense
that no solution can take the place of the Shavian paradox. For the
"archparadoxist," there is no other course, no other way to retain the
potency of the dialectical/ironic terms themselves and the questions
which they pose. Moreover, Shaw has not placed his characters in
authentically threatened circumstances, but rather in a situation that
Francis Fergusson likens, in his appraisal of Shavian dramaturgy, to a
"parlor game." Shavian irony, in this context, emerges strongly from a
contradictory tension arising among the playwright's thematic intentions, the conventions of his comic situations, and the absence of an
authentically "real" basis of comparison. As Fergusson puts it, "Shaw
never discovered a publicly acceptable, agreed-upon basis in reality
outside his peculiar comic perspective whereby it might have been
consistently and objectively defined. All comedy is conventional and
hence unreal; but Shaw does not make the distinction between the real
and his own ironic perspective upon it. This is as much as to say that
his perspective, or comic inspiration, is that of romantic irony: the
basis of his theses, of his rationalized characters, and of the movement
of his dialogue is the *unresolved* paradox" (*Idea* 183).[12]

An effective union of comic and dialectical perspectives is, nonetheless, central and essential to Shaw's dramatic development and to the
intended effects of his theatrical debates. Shaw's comedy is not only
mannerly but societal, and is directed quite deliberately toward an audience that the dramatist views as prospective, real-world participants in
decisions about his characters and their circumstances. In his theory
of genre and with specific relation to "ironic comedy," Northrop Frye
speaks directly, in *Anatomy of Criticism*, to the union of irony with the
expression of character and comedic purpose in a social framework: "Just
as tragedy is a vision of the supremacy of *mythos* or the thing done,
and just as irony is a vision of *ethos*, or character individualized against

environment, so comedy is a vision of *dianoia*, a significance which is ultimately social significance, the establishing of a desirable society" (285–286). Here it is quite specifically the union, to use Aristotle's terms, of character and thought – or in Shaw's dramaturgical terms, dialectic – that suggests a correspondence of the ironic and the comedic, with a related social purpose.

"Irony," writes Cleanth Brooks in *The Well-Wrought Urn*, "is the most general term that we have for the kind of qualification which the various elements in a context receive from the context" (209). Shaw might well appreciate Brooks's emphasis on irony, wit, and paradox (209, 257) – and, as noted earlier, although Brooks is looking at the tropes and means of analysis of poetry, the terminologies and functions are strongly similar to their usages in drama. Dramatically, however, the terms of irony and paradox, as well as wit, call necessarily for embodiment and enactment. They must, in other words, find their primary utterance not only in situations of context, juxtaposition, and contrast but also in theatrical characters and their situations. Ironic character may, as Frye might say, be individualized against environment, and irony itself may derive its particular character and flavor from what Brooks calls the context, but these sensibilities in unison provide for particularly opportune dramatic occasions, those that arise when an individual character is thrust into a latent drama – a "context" – with the specific purpose of disrupting a status quo.

The intruder plot

Marchbanks, as intruder into the Morell household, initiating force for change in Morell's status quo, and catalytic agent in Shaw's dialectic, must be situated optimally within a specific, even ideal, relationship to the overall "context" of *Candida*'s events and circumstances as well as to the other members of the dramatis personae. Indeed, it is the perfected quality of the match between the intruder and a play's circumstances or context that can provide the kind of supreme irony that may inform a collective field of characterizations and relationships. Simply put, irony arises when a perfect candidate for disrupting an existing situation and provoking an escalation in dramatic conflict or dialectic arrives upon a scene. From this basic equation, situations with latent potential for a developing dramatic action can achieve complexity, and *Candida* is no exception. Even though the traits and mannerisms given by Shaw to Marchbanks have been subject to varying critical points of view, it is precisely because of these qualities, and not in spite of them, that *Candida* takes the form that it does and yields its particular dialectical and ironic formulations.

The intruder, then, is the newly arrived yet necessary member of the dramatis personae, and, as in the case of Marchbanks (or Hilda Wangel in *The Master Builder* or Natasha in *Three Sisters*), the play cannot achieve its aims without the disruption that results from this figure's appearance. The simplicity of such a formulation belies the fact, however, that the relation of irony to an "intruder" arrangement in drama can produce intricate, and often complicated, results. For plays of this type, the overall arrangement of events, from instigation to end, is dependent upon the intruder and his or her effect upon the prior circumstances. Samar Attar succinctly describes this centrality, with reference to the intruder as "outsider," "stranger," or "newcomer":

> ... he appears suddenly on stage, seemingly from nowhere, unknown to the other participants in the drama; he thrusts himself upon them without permission or welcome and upsets the dramatic *status quo*. The intruder may become the center of the play, the protagonist who drives the dramatic action forward, or he may remain a secondary figure whose function is only to serve as a catalyst to bring out the inherent conflict and differences within the dramatic community upon whom he has intruded. In any case the intruder is responsible for the drama. Without him there would be no conflict or, at least, no open conflict. The importance of the intruder figure then lies not only in his own inherent qualities as a dramatic character, but also in his function in the framework of relations existing among the other characters.
>
> (9)

Such a description can apply to intruders and guest figures ranging across genres historically and geographically from the Dionysus of Euripides to Kaufman and Hart's Sheridan Whiteside to Pinter's notorious outsider figures (Ruth, in *The Homecoming*, is an exemplary case). The intruder need not, however, be a complete stranger. Solness has encountered Hilda in the past (or so she says), the Prozorovs have known Natasha, and Marchbanks is, as Candida tells us, one of James Morell's recent "discoveries." Rather, the intruder must embody the agitating component that enters into an existing situation from the outside; he or she is a member of the dramatis personae yet stands in ironic contrast, again as Brooks might say, to the embracing "context."

The dramatis personae, together with aspects of setting and given circumstances, contain all of a drama's latent possibilities – which is simply to note that a play's overall development can be seen as the result of interchanges among a delimited group of characters that are designed for the purpose. As such, the dramatis personae is not only the listing of a cast but a set of linkages, and the characters included therein bear necessary dramaturgical as well as relational connections with one another. As Burke writes, in *The Philosophy of Literary Form*, "there is obviously a philosophic sense in which agon, protagonist, and antagonist can each be said to exist implicitly in the others" (77), but such coexistence must often express itself dramatically in terms of difference and antipathy. In the context of Burke's famous system of "dramatism," the characters are "agents" who generate action ("acts" and "agency") in given situations and settings ("scenes") for a specific reason ("purpose"). Dramatism is, fundamentally, the system of motives that exists dynamically among these five terms, and one that emerges also from their particular interrelations. In *A Grammar of Motives*, Burke defines this co-participation in terms of equations or ratios between terms – thus, the relation of a given setting and action would be described as a "scene-act ratio." As Burke says: "Using 'scene' in the sense of setting, or background, and 'act' in the sense of action, one could say that 'the scene contains the act.' And using 'agents' in the sense of actors, or acters, one could say that 'the scene contains the agents'" (3). Along these lines, therefore, when the character of Marchbanks steps into the Morell household and incites the dialectical conflict arising from the latent conditions therein, in Burkean terms he is acting out the potentials of a particular "scene-agent" ratio, a juxtaposition that is made ironic not only through juxtaposition but in the ideality of its design.

Such a perfecting of the dramatic agent – in *Candida* the suit-ability of an intruding character's range of traits to the Morells' existing situation – would in Burkean terms be related directly to the "agent-act" ratio as well as to the overall composition of the dramatis personae. In *Perspectives by Incongruity*, Burke indicates that "the *dramatis personae* should be analyzed with reference to what we have elsewhere called the agent-act ratio. That is, the over-all action requires contributions by the characters whose various individual acts (and their corresponding passions) must suit their particular natures. And these acts must mesh with one another, in a dialectic of coopera-tive competition" (167). Burke's oxymoron here is, in fact, neatly and economically suggestive of the Morell-Marchbanks relationship as an antagonism that calls for implicit co-participation. What Burke refers to as the "character recipe" would, for Marchbanks as well as any of the other characters in *Candida*, simply indicate a combination of traits that can nest precisely within the configuration of the play's dialectical situations (*Perspectives* 176).

For the intruder figure, such a recipe calls for particular ingre-dient qualities, and the appropriateness is likely to be marked, in turn, by particular sorts of ironies resulting from juxtaposition. Eugene Marchbanks must be "shy" with Prossy, aggressively challenging with Morell and, concurrently, amorously callow with Candida. Finally he must be sufficiently quixotic to walk away from both of the Morells and leave them with what remains – or has yet to be discovered – regarding their marriage. Indeed, the effectiveness of the intruder – or, more directly, the drama that is provoked by the traits of that figure in combi-nation with others – is determined largely by what develops following the meeting of catalytic agent with the existing set of conditions. Moreover, the perfected aspect of the intruder's characterization derives typically from some vulnerability, or latency, within that status quo – an avail-ability for dramatic development in which the intruder's catalytic traits are especially, if not ideally, provocative.

In the abrupt arrival of Hilda Wangel in the Solness household, Ibsen produces what Barthes would call the acme, that which changes the aleatory ("luck") into a concentrated instance of revelatory signi-fication. By contrast, Natasha's intrusion into the Prozorov home is insidious and attenuated rather than sudden, yet it brings about a result that is also devastating.[13] Hilda must understand the "impossible" in the way that Solness does, Natasha must be insensitive in ways that facilitate her taking over the house, and Marchbanks must be, among other things, an embodied ironic contradiction, the wooer who is not truly a lover. Hilda's dramatic purpose is finally to deliver Solness to the top of the tower, and it is Natasha's purpose to situate her children by Andrei in the bedrooms of his sisters. In each case, there is a definitive result: Solness falls to his death and the Prozorov sisters are vanquished. In the case of Marchbanks, however, the mission of the intruder is to leave a situation suspended, in equipoise – or, to borrow Fergusson's word, as an "unresolved" paradox or dialectic. In *Candida*, the intruder plot concludes just as it should, following a full development among the dialectical terms that Shaw has introduced, intermixed, and brought into various contrapuntal relations. Yet this plot also concludes ironically, with an intruder figure who is ostensibly on a dialectical mission leaving behind a conundrum as opposed to a resolution.

As the play's concluding act begins, it is past ten in the evening. Candida and Marchbanks are together by the fireside, alone in the house, she staring abstractly at the brass poker she holds "upright in her hand," he reciting poetry. Any sexual charge that may be perceived in the scene is, no doubt, suggested more by its symbolism than overt action. Up to this point, though, Marchbanks has seemed ardent and Candida has told her husband that she would gladly be Eugene's teacher, saving him from "bad women" if it weren't for her wifely love. By the fireplace, Eugene says her name over and over: "I never think or feel Mrs. Morell: it is always Candida."

CANDIDA: Of course. And what have you to say to Candida?
MARCHBANKS: Nothing but to repeat your name a thousand times. Don't you feel that every time is a prayer to you?
CANDIDA: Doesn't it make you happy to be able to pray?
MARCHBANKS: Yes, very happy.
CANDIDA: Well, that happiness is the answer to your prayer. Do you want anything more?

MARCHBANKS: No: I have come into heaven, where want is
unknown.

(46)

Morell enters at this moment and "takes in the scene at a glance."
His arrival is opportune, in that it visually recreates the quasi-
romantic threesome as well as the dialectical triangle, but in spite
of appearances to the contrary it doesn't interrupt the "anything
more" that might ensue between Candida and Marchbanks.
Marchbanks has not been a serious wooer, and indeed the scene has
shifted already from subtle sensuality into the religious imagery
that characterizes the remaining interactions between the young
poet and the preacher. Although Michael Holroyd sees Candida offering herself to Marchbanks in this sequence, this seems unlikely given
not only the poet's preoccupations and behaviors but her genuine
surprise when James leaves them alone together.[14] Holroyd points
also to what is essentially a religious taboo that keeps the two apart,
with the ostensibly phallic poker turning rather to a symbol of
"knightly chastity." As he sees it, "the affinity between them is
that of mother and son, and the weapon that guards them from hell
is the taboo of incest. It is because the Virgin Mother outlaws sex that
she is Shaw's ideal. Candida reduces all men to children by emotional
castration" (317).

Castrated or no, both men are made childlike if not ineffectual in
the face of the maternal as well as sexual power that belong to Candida
and with which she rules the Morell environs – which is, importantly,
the domain of a popular and charismatic religious leader. In one sense,
Shaw's sublimation of the teasingly sexual into the religious seems
to pull the punch on the play's implicit eroticism, creating its own sort
of dramaturgical castration. There is another way, however, in which
the very basis for the play's conception – and certainly the manner
in which it plays out in the home of a reverend – is innately a combination of religious and artistic sensibilities. If the inspiration for
Candida arose to a large degree from Shaw's relationship with Janet
Achurch (and from the triangle that included her husband), it also came
about quite specifically, as Holroyd reports, from Shaw's associations

with religious paintings of the Virgin Mother.[15] When Morell questions Marchbanks on what transpired that evening with Candida, Shaw turns the religious imagery to comedic purpose through double entendre:

> MORELL: And you approached the gate of Heaven at last?
>
> MARCHBANKS: Yes.
>
> MORELL: Well? (*Fiercely*) Speak, man: have you no feeling for me?
>
> MARCHBANKS (*softly and musically*): Then she became an angel; and there was a flaming sword that turned every way, so that I couldn't go in; for I saw that that gate was really the gate of Hell.
>
> MORELL (*triumphantly*): She repulsed you!
>
> MARCHBANKS (*rising in wild scorn*): No, you fool: if she had done that I should never have seen that I was in Heaven already. Repulsed me! You think that would have saved us! Virtuous indignation! Oh, you are not worthy to live in the same world with her.
>
> (47)

Marchbanks's image of Candida remains exalted, but the impressions that she herself generates in the play's last act could encourage the opposite opinion. Shaw uses Candida's fluctuations, particularly in relation to how she is perceived by others (including the audience), to shift or redirect the focus of his debates, dialectical arguments, and consequent ironies. The varying interpretations and perceptions of this character thus become increasingly germane to how her position in the dialectical triangle is to be regarded. In Shaw's own words: "Candida is as unscrupulous as Siegfried: Morell himself sees that 'no law will bind her.' She seduces Eugene just exactly as far as it is worth her while to seduce him. She is a woman without 'character' in the conventional sense. Without brains and strength of mind she would be a wretched slattern and voluptuary. She is straight for natural reasons, not for conventional ethical ones."[16] By the third act, Candida is many things at once, leading in one sense to contradiction and "mystery" but in another to an increased complexity concerning what she says and does and how she may be understood by observers. And, as Berst points out, the

97

underscoring of earlier shortcomings takes on a progressively dialectical and ironic effect in the play's later sequences. Berst argues that by the second act, "her deficiencies are manifest – her assertiveness can be brazenly shallow, her humor cruel, and her sensibilities banal." The third act, he says, "reiterates these failings" but also creates a dramatically effective polarization: "Both positive and negative elements coexist in her character to a cumulatively ironic effect, providing her with dramatic vitality and psychological depth, and further contributing to the complexity of the dialectic" (44).

The agon between Marchbanks and Morell comes down, in one view, to who is the "good man" as opposed to the better man. Marchbanks presents a forthright challenge to Morell in this respect, in advance of the one that Candida presents to both of them by asking for a "bid" from each. Marchbanks insists on meeting with the man that Candida married:

> MORELL: The man that – ? Do you mean me?
> MARCHBANKS: I don't mean the Reverend James Mavor Morell, moralist and windbag. I mean the real man that the Reverend James must have hidden somewhere inside his black coat: the man that Candida loves. You can't make a woman like Candida love you by merely buttoning your collar at the back instead of in front.
>
> (47–48)

Among the enigmatic areas in this mysterious play is the reason why Candida married Morell in the first place, especially given the condition to which he is reduced by play's end. Might there really be another man inside Morell, loved by Candida but disguised behind the trappings of his outward show? On the evidence, this seems unlikely, and another of the master ironies of the play is the fact that she does choose Morell's bid, even in light of – or because of – his steady degradation over the course of the action. Irvine argues on the side of "misunderstanding" between the Morells, perhaps a useful idea in terms of dialectic – to the extent that it can keep matters undefined and thus in play – but not as satisfying as an interpretation of motives or results. The action of the play, says Irvine, "is based on a

98

very old dramatic device: a misunderstanding. In the course of the play, husband and wife come for the first time genuinely to understand each other and their actual relationship" (174).[17]

Yet in spite of the acuity of the Shavian debate, there is little to suggest that Morell and Candida can surmount their misunderstandings enough to comprehend one another at all. In fact, a substantial portion of the unresolved aspect of the play's dialectic around marriage pertains exactly to this – that when Marchbanks exits, he leaves behind a union that, apart from "words" and maternal coddling and flirtation, has yet to be defined on more intimate terms.[18] Morell's obliviousness is contributory, but so again are Candida's Philistinism, lack of depth, and offhand cruelty. Berst takes this a step further, and compares her to the wily wife and mother in Strindberg's *The Father*: "Laura taunts her husband with the possibility of the illegitimacy of their child; Candida dangles the possibility of her infidelity before Morell. Laura at last reduces her husband to madness and utter dependence; Candida at last reduces Morell to the child's chair and professions of gratitude for being managed so well." Yet again, this degree of antagonism can serve a dialectical acuteness: "But it is in part a measure of Shaw's art that this current flows subliminally to other dynamic concerns, specifically to the problem and challenge of Marchbanks. The point is made without being intrusive or melodramatic; indeed, it is cloaked in its seeming opposite – the virtue of a good woman – and in this it gains ironic, dramatic, and human force" (54).

The bidding sequence, *Candida*'s most well-known set piece, brings the drama's major dialectical strands into strategic – and, again, triangular – juxtaposition. The scene involves only the three principles and is a dramatic representation of how, in Bentley's phrase, Shaw in his prose tends to "marshal his facts ironically." Bentley remarks that the "chief mark of Shavian prose is its use of ironic antithesis and juxtaposition," but the same can be said of his dramatic technique in scenic constructions such as this one (*Thinker* 125). Hearing of the "choice" that is ostensibly presented, Candida responds: "Oh! I am to choose am I? I suppose it is quite settled that I must belong to one or the other."

MORELL (*firmly*): Quite. You must choose definitely.

MARCHBANKS (*anxiously*): Morell: you don't understand. She means that she belongs to herself.

CANDIDA (*turning on him*): I mean that, and a good deal more, Master Eugene, as you will both find out presently. And pray, my lords and masters, what have you to offer for my choice? I am up for auction it seems. What do you bid, James?

The shape of the triangle is, at this stage at least, sharply outlined. Morell responds with words, Marchbanks with cloying needfulness, and Candida reacts characteristically to the display of male weakness.

MORELL (*with proud humility*): I have nothing to offer you but my strength for your defence, my honesty for your surety, my ability and industry for your livelihood, and my authority and position for your dignity. That is all it becomes a man to offer to a woman.

CANDIDA (*quite quietly*): And you, Eugene? What do you offer?

MARCHBANKS: My weakness. My desolation. My heart's need.

Candida, quite naturally, gives herself to "the weaker of the two," and Marchbanks despairs of his apparent loss. At the play's end, when Candida claims, despite the clear evidence to the contrary, that "I make him master here," she quotes the words of Morell's bid back to him as she strokes his hair and leans her cheek "fondly against his." Shaw's stage direction is that she speaks these words "with sweet irony" (58). There is, indeed, a clear and persistent sense in which the ironies in *Candida* are assuredly "sweet" in their nature, wrapped as they often are in the title character's maternal ministrations, Morell's protestations, or what the preacher would call the poet's "fripperies." Yet sweetness is, more accurately, merely another of Shaw's ingenious guises for a stringent dialectical contest that is waged to a significant degree on emotional terms that are often more treacherous than they appear at first.

Shaw, in this play as in others, is adept at eliciting feelings for his characters as well as responses to their respective viewpoints, engendering attitudes that can, as in the case of *Candida*'s triangle, contribute to – or skew, as the case may be – a dialectical pattern. While *Candida* provides, in one way, a cumulative and dynamic discourse among varying sensibilities or positions (religious, familial, psychological, and so forth), it concurrently embodies these and other notions in specified ways and, in doing so, elicits emotional responses along with appraisals of the characters who stand for them. The characters must embody and enact the dialectical/ironic pattern, representing it through human behaviors even while standing for its more abstract terms. As States puts it, "drama is the extension of oppositional development into the sphere of human action and passion; or, as Burke might say, the dancing of the ironic-dialectical attitude." With reference to Langer's directional conception of the dramatic mode as "Destiny," States says that drama is "irony acted out, or, if you wish, dialectic personified" (*Irony* 23). In a play such as *Candida*, then, the individual characters may stand for particular sensibilities, attitudes, or positions but they are also called upon to be co-participants – in effect, to embody not only individual qualities but also a pattern that, of necessity, calls for more than one person.

Candida may conclude in an unresolved state, yet one can still assume that Shaw has, through his triangulation of primary characters along with the supporting cast, said everything that needs to be said – or, at least, all that he means to say. One function of irony is, in fact, to aid in the thorough statement of a set of ideas in a progressively dramatic way. Again, as States argues, it is irony that aids the dramatist is discovering "the limits of 'the premise'" in which an action is developed through dialectic. Or, in his phrasing, "irony and dialectic are principles of selection and arrangement" (*Irony* 141). Irony, on these terms, is one of the dramatist's "vital modes of discovery," as "he passes through irony, one might say, into dialectic, into arguing *both* sides of the problem fully as opposed to taking one side or another" (*Irony* 34). Here, once again, is the vital co-participation among the related (at times, nearly synonymous) terms of drama, dialectic, and irony. In this relation, Burke identifies the "dialectic substance" as dramatically fundamental: "Whereas there is an implicit irony in the other notions of substance, with the dialectic substance the irony is explicit. For it derives its character from the systematic contemplation of the antinomies attendant upon the fact that we necessarily define a thing in terms of something else" (*Grammar* 33).

To embody and characterize such a notion dramatically would be, from one perspective, to define Candida or Morell or Marchbanks in terms of their "antinomy" to one another; in another sense, as States might say, it would be to describe the overall drama of the three characters as a progressive and fully developed expression of dialectical exploration, with a basis in irony. The fact that Shaw does not push his antithetical characters or terms toward a final synthesis, even while presumably saying all that there is to say, suggests that irresolution is in fact the dialectical goal.[19] In Søren Kierkegaard's conception anyway, the idea of a "hovering" dialectic can be one attribute of inquiry and solution: "There is a dialectic which, in constant movement, is always watching to see that the problem does not become ensnared in an accidental conception; a dialectic which, never fatigued, is always ready to set the problem afloat should it ever go aground; in short a dialectic which always knows how to keep the problem hovering, and precisely in and through this seeks to solve it" (151).

There is, perhaps, no way for Shaw to keep *Candida*'s "problem" from hovering, if only because he has included so many different "antinomies" along with the additional and unresolved questions of where Marchbanks will go and, more significantly, what will become of the Morell marriage. Morell's penultimate line – "You are my wife, my mother, my sisters: you are the sum of all loving care to me" – is spoken with conviction, but it is not received on the same terms.

> CANDIDA (*in his arms, smiling, to Eugene*): Am I your mother and sisters to you, Eugene?
> MARCHBANKS (*rising with a fierce gesture of disgust*): Ah, never. Out, then, into the night with me!
>
> (59)

Morell has, by this point, been reduced to a fool, a confessor not only to his utter dependence upon Candida but concerning his sexual confusion and familial conflations as well. Allan Lewis, having referred to Shaw's title character as "a bit of a vixen" but with the "unassailable masquerade of the 'good woman'" and "delicately dishonorable," sums up Morell's situation: "Morell falls flat on his lifelong illusions, leaving his wife queen of the household. He who would run the world cannot run his own house, as his wife most subtly reminds him" (*Contemporary* 87). If Berst is correct, that within Shaw's "threefold perspective" Morell is the "most significant dramatic and dialectic epicenter," then Morell's condition and circumstances certainly call for reassessment at play's end.[20] The same figure who at the beginning of the action counseled, "Ah, my boy, get married: get married to a good woman; and then you'll understand," now arrives at the Burkean "non-A," a point of ironically reversed circumstances. Marchbanks is, at the end, misled and compromised but not defeated; he can run off into the poetic night with a final frippery, a line that is at once marvelously evocative and indecipherable: "In a hundred years, we shall be the same age. But I have a better secret than that in my heart. Let me go now. The night outside grows impatient" (59). Morell, though, is stuck, frozen in what can be nothing but dialectical stasis. In Bentley's assessment, "Morell finally loses his image of his wife and of himself. The curtain has to be rung down to save us from the Strindberg play that would have to follow" (*Making* 308). The Morells may not have quite so grim or embattled a future as that before them, yet Candida's "sweet" ironies prove to be crueler than her maternal fussing might have suggested. Again, however, this very contradiction nurtures both the irony and the dialectic, and as Bentley so aptly points out in *The Playwright as Thinker*, "*Candida* is the sweeter for not being all sugar" (136).

4 Pirandello's "Father" – and Brecht's "Mother"

The Father in Luigi Pirandello's *Six Characters in Search of an Author* is among the most renowned yet most anonymous figures in all of modern drama. He has no name other than the generic one, and his identity is dependent largely upon his status as an uncompleted, and therefore stranded, fictional character, the invention of an author who had an idea for a play, and a scene or two, but who left a story unfinished. The Father has a background but is without a readable future, and his present existence is only tangible to the extent that theatrical artistry can enable and reflect it on stage. He suffers terribly, primarily through remorse (the signature figure, or mask, that Pirandello associates with him) but also through comparison of his ontological status and perceptions with those of others, particularly the Director who attempts vainly to understand and to enact the Characters' shared story. The Father knowingly and perpetually embodies a set of contradictions, and his mastering irony is that of a figure whose condition – fictive and yet truthful, partial yet consistent – is eternally at odds with the less "real" personages upon whom he and his family are modeled. Severed from his dramatist creator, the Father can live only on stage, searching for wholeness and the sort of vindication that his unfinished story cannot bring.

The Father's anguish, together with his fierce pursuit of ontological authenticity, can be heard and seen only in the aesthetic pale between artistic conception and creation, between writer and character, actor and performed action. The Father is unique, an *homme de théâtre* who is not an actor, director, or writer but a figure who belongs nonetheless only to the drama. He is iconic, an impresario of the modernist theatre, and both his stature and his identity arise directly from the layered ironies of his condition and the necessarily prismatic manner of their delivery on a stage. The Father is also worldly: he is familiar with a spectrum of life experiences and exhibits qualities that reflect the fullness of his endeavors. Yet his own depiction is, at the same time, always delimited by a single fateful scene, the meeting with his Stepdaughter in a back room at Madame Pace's dress shop and place of assignation. The Father is an ironist, as revealed in his personal responses to circumstances as well as in his exchanges with the stage director, and the ironic standpoint is both self-reflexive and painful. A versatile figure, the Father is constrained and branded nonetheless by definitions imposed after that one encounter, the single Scene. As Susan Bassnett-McGuire remarks, the Father's "protest is against the irony that has condemned him to such fixity, with no additional scenes that might alter the balance in any way" (43).

Throughout *Six Characters*, the offsetting motifs of fixity and fluidity are contrasted and brought into collision, particularly in relation to the Characters as they exist in the opposing realms of their unfinished background story and their current transactions in the theatre with the Actors and Director. Present time is portrayed as transitory and ephemeral – seemingly more so because of the impromptu nature of a disrupted and redirected rehearsal process – while the past, or written, scenes that define the Characters' experiences are fixed and apparently unalterable. No matter how strenuously the Father protests against being categorized only by the unintended and abhorred meeting at Madame Pace's, he cannot escape the fixity, the definition, or the shame:

> Ah, the wretchedness, the wretchedness, truly, of a man alone who despises squalid liaisons, not yet old enough to do without women, and not young enough to be able, normally and without embarrassment, to look for one. Did I say "wretchedness"? It's worse than that. A horror! A horror! Because no woman will give him love. And when you've understood that ... I suppose you ought to do without.

For the Father, the result of the accidental meeting with the Stepdaughter is a grievous loss of "dignity," the face that one shows to the world voluntarily, the one that reflects an exterior composure as against an inward turmoil, a personal or shameful intimacy: "Each of us, for the eyes of others, dresses himself in a certain dignity, while at the same time we all know perfectly well what's going on in our intimate selves. Unspeakable" (225).[1]

That the Father is wedded to a single scene and its inherent shame is especially ironic given the different qualities that are his according to the Characters' shared back story. In this regard, his given title, "Father," becomes in itself a redoubled irony. The word in place of a name binds him strictly to his guilt: were it not for the familial connection, the encounter at Madame Pace's would simply represent a paid-for tryst with a much younger woman (the Stepdaughter is eighteen, the Father in his fifties) rather than an occasion of self-definition and loss of dignity. Additionally, the back room scene is interrupted and witnessed by the parental counterpart, the Mother, whose horror at what she discovers becomes for the Father a permanent reminder of regret. And, even though she comes unsuspectingly upon the scene, the arrival is so opportune as to connote its own fatefulness. In a further irony, the unlucky encounter among the three characters takes place by happenstance yet precisely in a space designed for clandestine meetings. The Mother, once sent away by the Father to be with her lover, and the Stepdaughter, watched from a distance by him when she was a schoolgirl, are now reunited with him under the most ill-timed yet ironically appropriate circumstances. Here it is a chance meeting that "signifies," that becomes an acme in Barthes's sense, as an apparent accident is turned into irony by what is "no longer chance."

Still, the Father has a complex past, a background story that suggests a different personality than the one that is witnessed under the immediate theatrical circumstances or in the encounter at Madame Pace's. The Father is preeminently philosophical, with a nature that he claims is not only thoughtful but also generous (an image vigorously disputed by the Stepdaughter). In the past, he has acted according to what he thought best for the Mother, even after her relationship with his clerk, and following their separation he developed a concern and regard for his wife's new family. Such qualities, though, are incidental, even meaningless, by comparison to his shame and to his "fixity." As Roger Oliver puts it, the Father's "intellectuality, his kindness, and all his other good sentiments and deeds are ignored. His life is summed up in the one action dramatized, an action representative of his carnal weakness as a man. Not only must he be known by just this one action, but he must repeat it in the eternity of art, and be tormented for it by his Stepdaughter, who also knows him only at this one moment" (56–57). The Stepdaughter, whose claim it is that the Father used to watch and follow and wave at her after school, is the personified agency of this fixed definition and his consequent despair.

Pirandello presents the differing viewpoints on the Scene at Madame Pace's – from the colliding perspectives of the Father, Stepdaughter, and Mother as well as the Actors and Director – scenically as well as in the Characters' recollection. The most vivid instance of misunderstanding, not to say ontological dissociation, occurs on stage when the Actors attempt to enact the reality and torment of the Characters in an improvised setting meant to stand for Madame Pace's dress shop. Yet the back story, including the Father's reasons for sending his wife away with his employee and his professed feelings for family members, can be conveyed only through disputed recollections as opposed to being staged and given a degree of authentic life under current conditions. Pirandello's resulting dialectic, which includes the finished scenes in the Characters' lives, their existentially incomplete status, and their present desires and motives, is thus played out in a theatrical milieu that, by its very nature and aesthetic processes, further complicates any effort toward locating truthfulness in the situation. More pointedly, the intricate layering of refraction and paradox in *Six Characters* is such that the Pirandellian dialectic itself (with its corresponding ironic behaviors) acquires a dimensional aspect in which the participating terms are not simply left in provocative equipoise, as in *Candida*, but must finally cancel one another out. In Pirandello's hands, irony turns here into a powerfully negative proposition, in dramaturgical, philosophical, and finally ontological terms. That the theatre can deliver the total import of this combination through stage discourse and imagery is at the core of this play's transcendent and ongoing impact.

Paradox may be, as Anne Paolucci suggests, the "heartbeat of the Pirandellian world" ("Comedy" 337), yet paradox in *Six Characters* is not the phenomenon that is encountered in *Candida* or other works by Shaw, whom States calls the "archparadoxist." Shaw's paradoxes tend to be constructed so as to keep a play of ideas in perpetual spin, feed the comic potentials at the same time, and leave resolutions in the lap of the audience. Pirandello frames his play of ideas in a realm of theatrical illusion, casts conflicting points of view through a prism, and, having constructed an aesthetic house of mirrors, denies the possibility of an agreed-upon reality or reliable context for judgment. Irony here, in its close relation to paradox of the Pirandellian variety, is of a radical sort, moving from the satirical toward the tragic if not the nihilistic.[2] Francis Fergusson writes that, in a certain sense, points of contention among Characters and Actors in *Six Characters* are "based on paradoxes in the Shavian manner: romantically unresolved ambiguities" (187) – that is, the sort of conundrum the audience is left with following Marchbanks's departure into the night. However, Fergusson goes on to argue that Pirandello's drama "transcends the Shavian irony, and at the same time realizes the farce of rationalizing with a depth and a consistency beyond that of Shaw" (190). The two dramatists may be alike in the "brilliance" of their paradoxical conceptions, with the "unresolvable paradox" resembling the "basis of 'free' Shavian irony." Yet Pirandello, says Fergusson, is finally unlike Shaw in that he "transcends his paradoxes by accepting them as final – or rather (since he does not, like Shaw, see human action as rationalizing only, and the world as merely conceptualized) he accepts his paradoxes as various versions of a final split in human nature and destiny itself" (*Idea* 191). Shaw himself called *Six Characters* the "most original play ever written" (Gilman *Making* 172), and its uniqueness owes in large measure to the radical nature of its dialectical components as well as theatrical process. The Father asserts:

> For me the drama is precisely in that, in my consciousness that I, that each of us, in fact, believes himself to be one person, when that's not true. Each of us is many persons, many, depending on all the possibilities for being within us. For this man we're one person, for that one another. We're multiple. Yet we live with the

illusion that we're the same for everyone – always the same person in everything we do. It's not true!

The Father protests against the "treachery" of the Stepdaughter who would define him according to one act, the one meeting, in a single situation where "we ought never to have existed for each other" (227). Concurrently, he insists upon his kinship with "each of us," and upon the existential situation of being "multiple." This fundamental association, between the Father's definition as a character in a theatrical situation and the situation of "us" as represented by Actors as well as audience, provides Pirandello with the fundamental terms of his dialectic. In Gilman's view, the basis of Pirandello's originality resides in precisely this relation, in the playwright's vision of theatre and life in dialectical partnership. Pirandello saw that "we move between life and theatre or art (imaginary life) in an unceasing tension, because we are existentially trapped between the claims of truth and reality, the desire for permanence, such as only forms possess, and for physical actuality, with its instability and ineluctable mortality" (*Making* 188). Such unceasing tension, however, also means irresolvable conflict, precisely because of a dialectical process in which both aesthetic and ontological terms are in play in the same time and place. The dialectician, again as States has phrased it, is "driven on to antithesis" (*Pleasure* 72); in the case of Pirandello, the result is a multidimensional discourse in which the participating terms ironize one another in a pattern of mutual and perpetual negation. The dialectical form of *Six Characters* is, to borrow Wylie Sypher's term, cubist, with the contrasting realms and viewpoints of Characters and Actors presented as coexistent and delivered concurrently: "All these levels of representation are held together in a simultaneous perspective of transparent dramatic planes to be read in many directions at the same time" (69).[3]

The dialectic among these interconnected planes depends centrally upon the Father, particularly in terms of his relationships to the other Characters, to the Actors and the Director, and in regard to his questions and convictions having to do with identity and definition. If, as in *Candida*, a play's dramatis personae stands implicitly for a set of dialectical patterns and ironic interrelations, such representation takes on multiple dimensions in a case where the persons of the drama include fictional Characters as well as Actors and where the setting is a theatrical space meant for rehearsal and performance. Here the question of "who" the Father is takes on greater significance and a more complicated range of implications; correspondingly, his particular traits, relationships, and interactions, in the back story and present stage action, expand the play's dialectics in philosophical as well as in dramaturgical ways. The Father is a character, a member of the dramatis personae of *Six Characters*, and at the same time he is a "Character," a fiction, an embodiment of an author's idea for a play. This exact relation, of character to "Character," encapsulates the central ironies upon which the play is based. The Father is the drama's instigating agent, its point of origin personified.[4] As such, he implicitly calls up the fundamental Burkean theorem of ironic relations: the question of "what new characters, born of a given prior character, will be the 'inevitable' vessels of the prior character's disposition" (*Grammar* 517). Given the complexity of the Father's particular "disposition," the "new" characters – that is, the remaining members of the dramatis personae – ironize his situation through a full spectrum of means and viewpoints.

The character of Dr. Fileno, the earlier incarnation of the Father who appears in Pirandello's story "The Tragedy of Character," speaks these lines:

> One is born into life in so many ways, my dear sir, and you know very well that nature avails herself of the instrument of human fantasy in order to pursue her work of creation. And the man who's born as a result of this creative activity, which has its seat in the spirit of man, is destined by nature to a life greatly superior to that of anyone born of the mortal womb of woman.
>
> (99)

In his "Preface" to *Six Characters*, Pirandello remembers the Father's birth, when the character came to his mind as "a man about fifty years old, in a dark jacket and light trousers, with a frowning air and ill-natured, mortified eyes" (363–364). Pirandello recalls entertaining the premise of a group of such figures who, having come alive in his mind, "do not resign themselves to remaining excluded from the world of art." They are "dramatic characters, characters that can move and talk on their own initiative; already see themselves as such; have learned to defend themselves against me; will even know how to defend themselves against others" (366). The Father must, as a dramatic character, have his drama in order to be, to exist – "that is, a drama in which he may be a character and for which he *is* a character. This drama is the character's *raison d'être*, his vital function, necessary for his existence" (368). In *Six Characters*, however, the Father's necessary "drama" is redoubled and mirrored back upon itself: it exists in the background story, including the encounter in the back room at Madame Pace's; it is played out on stage in the recreated, "acted" version of that Scene with the Stepdaughter and Mother; it informs the play throughout as a core agon among planes of refracted truth and illusion.

"Who" is the Father? Is there a discernible point, wonders Joseph Wood Krutch, when he is "being himself" or not being such, given his behaviors in all the various instances? Does he truly have a "character" apart from what Krutch would call his inconsistencies? (82–83). The Father is given motivations and feelings and reasons for doing things in the back story; in this respect he is even given psychological depth and dimension, particularly regarding familial relations. Perhaps, as Domenico Vittorini suggests, the Father's ill fate has been "superinduced" by his own "tortuous mental processes" (294). And yet, in the present interactions on stage, the Father is a man of precise thought, forceful debate, and philosophical acumen. Walter Starkie argues that the Father "cannot, like real human beings change from one personality to another, for he has been crystallized as one personality" (218). And yet, even given the Father's remorse over the fixity that results from the back room meeting with the Stepdaughter, Pirandello presents him in total as a multidimensional figure. "*Who is the Father?*" inquires Eric Bentley in "Father's Day." What does he do? – and where does he live? (58). Bentley calls the Father the "propeller" of the play's action, its "prime mover," noting that along with his demand that "his drama be staged" what he does primarily is talk – or, more precisely, the Father is "talking to live," talking to "avoid getting killed" (63, 66).[5] On the contrary, however, the Father's over-arching purpose for Pirandello is not to talk or even to propel the action; it is to insure, through ironic and embodied contrasts between himself and the dramatis personae, a fully articulated dialectical scheme.

The Father stands for, enacts, and embodies the Pirandellian dialectic; in *Six Characters* he is its focal nexus and primary conduit. In the Burkean pattern, the Father assumes the "role of *primus inter pares.*" In the context of dialectical (ironic) co-participation, Burke writes in *A Grammar of Motives*: "For whereas any of the characters may be viewed in terms of any other, this one character may be taken as the summarizing vessel, or synecdochic representative, of the develop-ment as a whole" (516). This is not the position of Marchbanks, Morell, or even of Candida – although she comes the closest, in *Candida*, to such emblematic status. To be the "synechdochic representative" of a dramatic development with the intricacy of *Six Characters* calls for a different conception altogether, and indeed for an altered perspective on ironic interrelations. The Father, who is a character performed by an actor and observed by an audience, and is also a Character in scenes with Actors and, further yet, is a Character who is fully aware of his own status as a character, complete with the ontological and aesthetic implications, represents a radical variance from the standard ratio of individual character to dramatis personae.

The very fact that the cast of *Six Characters* includes Characters and Actors, when taken together with the role of the Director and, implicitly, the presence of an audience at the performance, insures the intricacy of this variation. The spectrum of stage figures, or what Burke would refer to as the "sub-perspectives" in dialectic, comprise the necessary components of Pirandello's elaborate deconstruction of iden-tity and artistic representation. And, when the number of voices called for includes not only the roles to be played but also the agents of performance, the dialectic is refracted away from the social into aesthetic and existential planes. Here again the Father provides a key point of interconnection, as in act two when he, like the Stepdaughter, is at first so flummoxed by the idea of an actor playing *him*, not to mention being able to understand the feelings brought on by the regretted encounter in Madame Pace's back room. The Father asks of the Director: "what do you mean a rehearsal?"

> DIRECTOR: A rehearsal. A rehearsal for them (*he indicates the Actors.*)
> FATHER: But if we are the characters ...
> DIRECTOR: All right, you're the characters, if you say so. But here, my dear sir, characters don't perform. Here actors perform. The characters are there, in the text (*He points to the prompter's well*) – when there is a text.
> FATHER: Exactly. And since there isn't one and you have the good luck to have the characters here in front of you, alive ...
> DIRECTOR: Oh, splendid! You want to do it all yourselves? To act, to appear before the public?
> FATHER: Yes, just as we are.
>
> (232)

In situations such as this (and *Six Characters* reiterates this basic aesthetic problem), the role of irony is to define, through a successive opposition of terms, the contour of the argument – or "premise," in States's term – that is at hand. Here, though, it is not only Pirandello's premise that is multidimensional, but the factor of irony as well.

The Characters are consistently made ironic by the presence of the Actors – and vice versa. The attempt by the Actors to enact the Scene at Madame Pace's ironizes the experience of the Father and the Stepdaughter, and in doing so takes away the affective authenticity. By contrast, the very truthfulness of that scene – its definitiveness – marginalizes the Actors and Director by consigning them to a realm of falsity – that is, of imitation. The dimensional aspect of the Father's character, along with his resistance to being encapsulated within a set definition, stands in ironic contrast to the individual Actors whose business it is to be versatile and "multiple" – many beings rather than one. When such a complexity in the dramatis personae is examined in the context of Burke's system of dramatism, the layers of irony and dialectic are expanded exponentially. The "scene–act" ratio, in a situation where the scene is a stage and the act involves rehearsal and replication of event, is an arbitration not only of setting and action

113

but of theatrical art and process. When the "scene" is Madame Pace's back room, and the "act" is the meeting among the Father, the Stepdaughter, and the Mother, then such a ratio is implicitly offset and made ironic by the scene and act on stage when the back story is imitated and thus made false – turned to "pretense" by the Actors. Theatrical spectacle enforces the ironic impression through a perpetual contradiction between what is seen and what can, under the circumstances of this play, be believed by an observer.

Burkean theory suggests, again, that the dramatis personae should be investigated in line with the "agent-act" ratio (*Perspectives* 167), which is simply to observe that the characters as a group may be understood by the totality as well as the individuality of traits and actions, and that plays are built in accord with this correspondence. Yet such a total participation becomes, in the case of *Six Characters*, a formula for dialectic that is all but confounding in its multidimensionality and inclusiveness. Pirandello's configuration is, quite literally, a house of mirrors. The business of the Actors is to mirror the human models upon whom character is based; the Characters, in turn, are the mirrors of the action that was invented, but left incomplete, by their original author. The Pirandellian mask, in this situation, is more than an alterable face of character or personage before the observant world; it is the representation of an extreme, indeed ultimate, variation and indeterminacy, Dionysian in both its spirit and versatility. Here the Burkean idea of "character recipe" is both fragmented and extended, at once. If the ostensible purpose of such a recipe is, for an author, to guarantee the traits necessary to both individual characters and, by extension, the dramatis personae, such qualities are multiplied and also abstracted in Pirandello's vision. In Burke's directive, the dramatist should achieve the illusion of completed character "by *so building a character-recipe in accord with the demands of the action that every trait the character does have is saliently expressed in action or through action*. Here is the way to get 'actualization'" (*Perspectives* 176).

Actualization, a term that certainly earns its quotation marks in the case of *Six Characters*, results in Pirandello's play from a character recipe built of necessity for Actors, Characters, Director, and a "Madame Pace" who is summoned and appears as if from thin air.

The concept of "traits," in such a context, is fluid indeed. The primary trait that is needed for the Actors is, ostensibly, a performing ability, and perhaps a degree of mocking skepticism when confronted by the Characters. The Characters, by contrast, have such traits as were given to them by their creator but are, of necessity, incomplete and, in this sense anyway, undefined. Yet the Actors, in order to perform the roles suggested by the Characters, must base their activity upon observable traits and behaviors – and so the conundrum builds. If drama is, as States suggests, "conflict informed by ironic necessity" (*Irony* 24), the opposition among these terms of agent, act, and scene could scarcely, in *Six Characters*, be more radically conceived.

Indeed, the fundamental relation of actors and characters upon which Pirandello's play is built contains an implicit aesthetic dependency (actors need characters to perform; characters require actors to give them life), but with the particular variety of oppositions added in, this connection turns dialectical and profoundly ironic. The Characters insist on performing the roles of themselves in order to claim and embody the authenticity of their story; the Actors scorn the Characters for not being human, for not being real. And yet, the "real" and the "illusory" are also consubstantial; they belong to one another, even as they are set in opposition. Gilman calls it a "deep irony" that "illusion has always to be seen through, known in its status as an arm or instrumentality of the real" (*Making* 188–189). Or, in J. L. Styan's words, Pirandellian drama shows that "illusion is not only inseparable from the reality, but often *is* the reality" ("Games" 149).

Within Pirandello's house of mirrors, the Father is reflected in a multitude of ways and from a number of angles, including the variations of his own self-projection and image. If, as Brustein suggests in *The Theatre of Revolt*, the mirror is the "central prop" of the Pirandellian theatre (302), its metaphorical associations are particularly acute in the case of this one figure, Pirandello's philosophical spokesman and, again, among his dramatis personae the *primus inter pares*. Throughout *Six Characters*, the Father is positioned before one symbolic mirror or another: he is castigated and defined by the Stepdaughter; his behavior at Madame Pace's is recreated on the stage by an Actor; his background story constantly underlies and comments upon his present circumstances. And, as perhaps the most painful aspect of the Father's ontological suffering, he is faced perpetually with his own image – that is, with his self-awareness as a Character, with his fixity, with his defining trait or mask of guilty regret. Indeed, what Marvin Rosenberg refers to as the "essential fact" pertaining to the Father is "his eternal reliving of an ugly experience that commands endless remorse" (140). In spite of his energetic, not to say desperate, defense of his case and point of view, and despite the doggedness of his debate with the Director over "who" he (or anybody) is, the Father is finally stuck among the mirrors – with his philosophy, his traits, and the ironies of all his past behaviors.

> STEPDAUGHTER: For anyone who has gone wrong, isn't the person who caused the first lapse responsible for everything? For me he's that person, and it all goes back to even before I was born. Look at him, see if it's not true.
> DIRECTOR: All right. And does this burden of remorse seem nothing to you? Give him a chance to show it!
> STEPDAUGHTER: But how, if you don't mind my asking? How can he show all his "noble" remorse, all his "moral" torment, if you're going to spare him the horror of one fine day finding in his arms, after having invited her to take off her mourning clothes, the little girl he used to watch coming out of school, that same little girl who's now a whore?
>
> (244)

Here then is the fix, as well as the fixity, from which the Father cannot free himself. On the stage, within the present action, his desire to see his own version of the Scene vindicated is countermanded by the Stepdaughter who insists to the Director that her version of actuality – "The truth, sir, the truth!" – be the one that is staged and thus actualized. And yet it is the back story, mirrored in that present moment, that contains the more basic ironies of the Father's situations, and the ones that most provoke his remorse. Pirandello juxtaposes an image of a man who claims such regard for the extended family – his wife's children including the young Stepdaughter – with the same man who ends up in the back room at Madame Pace's, with the Mother arriving there opportunely as witness to his horror. Moreover, it is he, the Father, who has brought all this upon himself by sending his wife away with his employee – generously, in his view – in the first place. Thus the Father becomes, precisely to the degree that he both instigates and perpetuates his story as well as his own unceasing remorse, his own author.

> FATHER: The eternal moment. As I tried to tell you, sir. She (he indicates the Stepdaughter) she's here to hold me, to fix me, to keep me hooked and suspended, forever in pillory, in that one fugitive, shameful moment of my life. She can't let go and you, sir, you can't save me from it.
>
> (245)

The Pirandellian situation, exemplified most tellingly in *Six Characters* by the Father, is built upon such polarized situations, often ironically counterpoised so as to reflect and comment upon one another. Pirandello, observes Anne Paolucci, "has perceived the opposite in life, and perceived the opposite of the opposite myriadfold. And it is out of the depths of mirrored opposites that he brings up his dramatis personae as creatures of his *sentimento del contraria*, the feeling of the opposite" ("Comedy" 324–325). Here also there is a relation of opposition and polarity to what Burke calls the "dialectic substance," a dependence upon irony, and "the fact that we necessarily define a thing in terms of something else" (*Grammar* 33). Actors are defined by characters and, to an even larger degree, characters by actors. Any authenticity lent to the Scene at Madame Pace's must account for both the enacted recreation and the points of view that belong to the back story. Pirandello's *sentimento del contraria* extends, however, from the play's immediate situations and arguments to a more embracing, universalized vision of paradox and irresolvable polarity. While the cosmic reach of irony can, for Ibsen, include a vision of metaphysical, if mysterious, appropriateness, or for Chekhov the revelation of character within a vast and impenetrable web of time and meaningful happenstance, the ironic for Pirandello is finally an existential conundrum rooted in the mask and the mirror: variable, intractable, contradictory, yet part of the world's make-up and, as such,

intrinsic to both the theatre and the ontological situations and perspectives it would replicate.

> FATHER: But of course, ladies and gentlemen. What other reality
> exists for us? What for you is an illusion, something to be
> fabricated, is for us, instead, our only reality. (*Brief pause. He
> comes forward a few steps toward the Director and then goes on.*)
> And that's true not only for us, you know. Think about it
> carefully. (*He looks in the Director's eyes.*) Can you tell me who
> you are? (*He keeps his finger pointed at the Director.*)
> DIRECTOR: (*Upset, but with half a smile*). What do you mean,
> who am I? – I'm me!
> FATHER: And what if I said that isn't true, because you're me?
>
> (247)

Here the ironical play of "you" and "I" is cast against a background in
which "Characters," as a subset of dramatis personae, are in performance with other characters; when taken together with the particular
opposition of Characters and Actors and the multiplicity of the
Father's roles, the *sentimento del contraria* is manifest on all levels,
extending in all directions. Compounding this situation, the exterior-
ized stage figure – vividly represented by the Characters as well as the
Actors – is continually placed in juxtaposition, not with a tangible or
defined interiority but with antithetical possibilities which make mul-
tiples of what Bentley calls the playwright's "antithesis of mask and
face" (*Thinker* 150).[6]

In this milieu, the relation of Pirandellian irony to embodiment
and enactment achieves a range of application not previously encountered in the theatre. If Pirandello is, as Brustein would say, the "most
seminal dramatist of our time" (*Revolt* 316), part of his originality owes
to the ways he vivifies abstract ideas through stage characters and
reifies the existential quandaries they represent through versatile
employments of the theatrical environment itself. For Pirandello, the
concurrently truthful and illusory nature of the stage characters and
their situations reflect the ontological impossibility of a determinate
self and mutually understood surroundings or circumstances – that is,
the basic configuration given voice and body by the Father and the

Stepdaughter. Here again the contrast with Shaw is implicit, but Pirandello extends the Shavian principle of embodied dialectic – as a play of contrapuntal voices around specified thematics – to a prismatic expansion of how the relation of the self to circumstances and to other selves might be enacted on the stage. States notes the comparison to Shaw and Shakespeare in this context, observing that the latter's works, like Pirandello's, "are valuable as examples of how a play can personify the content which philosophy takes up discursively" (*Irony* 169).

The Father is, first and foremost, a dramatic character; as such, he "must have his drama." In *Six Characters*, though, it is not simply that the characters fit naturally into a story told in dramatic terms; it is, rather, a matter of urgency that the Characters find their expression, their completed drama, and so the "must" is accentuated. As Walter Starkie describes this situation, the Characters "owe their existence to dramatic creation, they cannot prevent themselves from rushing to express themselves: they must get the opportunity of reaching their completion as parts of the drama" (209). The Characters' shared and overarching intention, beside which other traits and motives are subsumed, is toward completion, toward fully represented selfhood, and this can only be achieved through enactment and embodiment, not only of their story but of this motive. They are "dramatic embodiments of will," as Anne Paolucci puts it, "and in their single-minded purpose, the dramatist has recognized the multiplicity of intentions and actions which make up personality." These characters exist, in Paolucci's phrase, in a "state of passionate awareness of self" (*Theater* 48, 54). The Father, in particular, must bear the awareness of his status as a Character:

> FATHER (*with dignity but no trace of annoyance*): A character, dear sir, can always ask a man who he is. Because a character truly has a life of his own, one stamped by his own specific traits, traits which always declare he's "somebody." While a man – I'm not speaking of you now – a man, so-to-speak in general, can be "nobody."
>
> (247–248)

Even as he performs as Pirandello's spokesman and *"raisonneur"* –
increasingly so, as the action advances – the Father is most notably a
philosopher of his own condition.[7] He is a Character, complete with a
background story in which many of his qualities are apparent; he is also
the driving agent and conscience of the immediate stage action, which
must include scenic detail from that background even as it advances,
within the current environs, a dialectic of existential authenticity and
theatricality. In this multidimensional setting, the Father both performs and personifies the play of irony that coalesces around him as
Pirandello's focal figure and most singular representative.

The Father stands for a drama that is projected on two primary
levels, each one marked by ironic juxtaposition. In the background scene
at Madame Pace's, irony arises when the Father arrives at the point of
assignation only to be met by his Stepdaughter and then, with ideally
adverse timing, her Mother. When the Scene is placed in the hands of the
Actors, in present time, the factor of reenactment estranges the action and
turns it ironic by comparison with the original motives and deeds, especially so because the Characters are so ill-served by the agents who
ostensibly should be the ones able to deliver their story. As Bentley
notes in "Father's Day": "The crowning, and Pirandellian, irony comes
when the Director's contribution to the proposed 'drama,' instead of
enriching it, actually impoverishes it further" (68). The stagy delivery of
the Scene, with Actors standing in for the Father and Stepdaughter, is a
travesty of the original encounter, especially in its dissociation from the
motives and passions that, for the Characters, created it. Such enactment,
as a fiction, can only be an abstract and ironic version of what "happened"
in the Characters' vision of actuality.

By contrast, the Father embodies authenticity – at least to the
extent that he is "somebody." Yet he is also a supreme embodiment of
ironic interconnectiveness. The Father *is* the situation and the quandary: he stands, at once, as a representative of the truthfulness of
character and of the impossibility of defined selfhood. As a further
irony, he is self-aware – stricken with such awareness, in Pirandello's
rendering – in an environment in which others, particularly the "real"
characters such as the Director, are so lacking in perception of their
own ontological situations. And, of course, irony is compounded as

those who would seek ontological truth and permanence exist in a pale of fluctuating identity, revealed in the transience of the enactment itself. From the Pirandellian perspective, in fact, humankind is doomed to enactment. As Bentley characterizes the situation in *The Life of the Drama,* "we men can only play roles, we cannot just be. We can conceive of creatures who just are, but we cannot be them, we can only enact them. Hence the paradox of these characters who just are, yet whose 'being' cannot be communicated to us except through enactment. For us then, the enactment, not the thing acted, remains the ultimate term. Simulation is the only thing not simulated. Pretense is the ultimate reality" (191).

> FATHER (*very softly, with something like honeyed humility*):
> I ask you, sir, only to learn if you see yourself now, really, to be the same as you were once, if, given the perspective of time, with all you know now about the illusions of that time, all the things within you and around you, as they seemed then – and as they were, yes, real for you? Well, thinking back on those illusions, long since discarded, all those things which no longer seem what in fact they *were* then, don't you think that tomorrow, not merely the floorboards of this stage, but what you are feeling now as well, your reality for today, in fact the very earth beneath your feet, might also seem an illusion?
>
> (248)

Pirandello's theatre centers, finally, on the variations implicit in role playing, in the case of *Six Characters* a multidimensional projection of masks and mirrors, "illusions" and embodied perspectives. In the Father's speech above, were it not for the metatheatrical references, one might almost hear Vershinin's voice, and the Chekhovian perspective on time and "tomorrow." Yet the Father allows for a much different embodiment of irony than Vershinin or Lopakhin – or Hilda Wangel or Eugene Marchbanks – can stand for. His particular embodiments and enactments refract the ironic standpoint, not only into a complexity of variations but also toward a negativity that belongs to Pirandello's vision in particular.

Maurice Valency writes, in *The End of the World*, that "the essence of irony" for Pirandello "was an awareness that being is insubstantial, an illusion peopled by shadows. Thus, what is experienced as tragic is actually comic, and our entire life-experience is a pitiful absurdity" (101). Here, the playwright's *sentimento del contraria* extends from dramatic polarity and opposition to self-nullifying contradiction. Existence is questionable, and projections of selfhood so unreliable and lacking in authenticity that only negation can result. What Pirandello dramatizes, in Rosenberg's phrasing, is "the absurdity of identity" (127). On such terms, the Father's quest – for vindication, completeness, validation, and escape from the confines of "Character" – can only end in negation. For Starkie, Pirandello is a "metaphysician" as well as a "master of irony," but the metaphysics of irony are such, for this dramatist, that self-awareness is cut off and removed forever from any universalized sense of meaningfulness. Hence the necessary plight of Pirandello's characters is often, as Bentley points out in *The Life of the Drama*, "metaphysical anguish" (134). The Father may carry "remorse" as the dominant trait as regards his background story with the Stepdaughter, but the ontological suffering that he embodies extends beyond the parameters of a single experience to an all-embracing alienation. Giovanni Sinicropi speaks to the extremity of this condition: "The impossibility of contact with the transcendental source of existence separates unequivocally the metaphysical dimension from the immanent one. The only content that catharsis can assume in this theatre is that of an existential checkmate" (370).

Irony has, as States would say, a "negativity," a directional quality that arises from its own antithetical properties and gravitates toward progressive stages of cancellation.[8] "Ironic thinking," as Eric Gans points out, is "potentially tragic," with a central tragic figure becoming available to "sparagmatic violence" (66). The Father, who is not a tragic character per se, is nonetheless made to experience precisely this ironic impression; that is, the identity that he would claim – and which becomes, by extension, the embodiment of an existential questioning of identity – is torn apart by his drama's own processes, with a sparagmos that is wrought by the contradictory planes of interaction through which he is presented. Sparagmos, with its historic associations with tragedy, is in this situation allied intimately with irony. In Northrop Frye's conception: "Sparagmos, or the sense that heroism and effective action are absent, disorganized or foredoomed to defeat, and that confusion and anarchy reign over the world, is the archetypal theme of irony and satire" (*Anatomy* 192). In the Pirandellian world, such "anarchy" pertains quite literally to an absence, if not of law then of objectivity, definition, and identity. In this sense, the Father can stand for dismemberment, even as he defends his own cohesiveness, reality, and truthfulness, with sparagmos becoming emblematic not only of his case but of the fault lines that characterize identity more generally.

The fragmentation that the Father represents is epitomized and galvanized by his status as both Character and character, a figure with a past history but only a present life on stage, self-aware but without adequate means of communicating his plight – with all of this existing simultaneously but with each variation on a different plane of the dramatic construction. Thus Pirandello's characters, most notably the Father, pursue an impossible course of self-completion. They construct identity with conviction and determination – what Pirandello refers to as *costruirsi*, the building up of the self – but that task is innately futile. As Brustein writes: "No matter how well these roles are played, however, none of them reveals the face of the actor. They are disguises, designed to give purpose and form to a meaningless existence – masks in an infinite comedy of illusion" (*Revolt* 289). Moreover, as David McDonald emphasizes, the Father and the other Characters are "written beings" (423), and this status also informs the fragmentation along with the Father's quandaries, aesthetic and ontological:

> The Characters are to exist in-between the real and the unreal, the natural and the supernatural. The Characters are presented as *mimemes*, mimetic units, *indices* to a story without a decided plot. More so than the Ghost in Hamlet, they are "floating signifiers," or traces of their own effaced presence. Their mode of being – if not poetic – is, at least, semiotic. They are signs of their

own absence. They are written, or more precisely, being written and rewritten, as they are seen and heard or read. Their story, their identity, begins and ends in a writing (*l'écriture*) or a protowriting, a first writing, the mark and trace of their *dasein*, their being-there.

(425)

Written yet searching for an Author, stage figures who claim truth but stand for their own incompleteness, the Characters are suspended in half-light, in irresolution. The existential irony that attends them is also, inevitably, an aesthetic one: in McDonald's phrase, they "are not, never have been, and never will be fully present" (426). The Father is eternally parenthetical; no matter the single aspect of his persona that happens to be reflected in given moments, there is always the other one, and the next one after that, in successive brackets of dimension, opposition, and abstraction.

Irony that is a product of dramatic character linked to "character," and irony that arises through parenthetical representation of character in given contexts, mark Bertolt Brecht's plays as well as Pirandello's, but on notably different terms and with varying implications. Brecht's parent figure, "Mother Courage," is also, like Pirandello's "Father," an icon of modernism in the theatre. Indeed, there are singular images, such as Mother Courage hitched as if eternally to her wagon, or the actress Helene Weigel's silent scream, that transcend the gestus of a particular work and stand more extensively for the theatrical consciousness of an era. In this respect, both Mother Courage and Pirandello's Father are figures who represent, in his or her own way, a modernist theatrical method and philosophy as well as an ironic standpoint. Whereas Pirandello's Father is an embodied dialectic of authenticity, selfhood, and theatrical illusion, Brecht's Mother is a personified gest, an epitomized dialectic of contradictions that are localized in character yet ironized through Brecht's scenic design and presentational techniques.

The parental status of each figure adds a noteworthy dimension to the ironic commentary that ensues. The Father's portrayal must be matched directly with that of the Stepdaughter, and by extension the

Mother, in order for his quandaries and guiltiness to be fully dramatized. His remorse, the poignancy of his situation generally, and the
philosophic cogency of his expression derive in large part from familial
linkages in both his background story and in present action in the
theatre. As instigator of the drama within several interrelated frames,
the Father "fathers" the play's origin and also its later course. In
Mother Courage and Her Children, the title character's fate, as part
of Brecht's dialectic around war, family alliances, and profiteering,
depends as much upon her maternal relation to Eilif, Kattrin, and
Swiss Cheese as on the conditions of the war itself and her methods
of buying and selling. Even Anna Fierling's nickname has, in Gilman's
phrase, a "grossly ironic origin" (*Making* 225):

> MOTHER COURAGE: They call me Mother Courage 'cause I was
> afraid I'd be ruined, so I drove through the bombardment of Riga
> like a madwoman, with fifty loaves of bread in my car. They were
> going moldy, what else could I do?
>
> (25)[9]

Here, Courage turns to "courage," a woman's nickname that becomes
not only ironic but ludicrous when blind tenacity is juxtaposed with
the stakes at hand and also the results – that is, when such a combination affords a succinct snapshot of the play's larger thematic demonstrations. Courage is Brecht's focal embodiment and title character,
but only fully so as a mother in combination with her children, with
all four of them needed to completely embody the brutal consequence
of maternal investment coupled with battle and her haggling to
survive.[10]

From this perspective, Courage's status as mother belongs necessarily to the play's master ironies. The relationship to her children,
individually and as a family, is offset continually with her buying and
selling as well as the effort to survive in an atmosphere of brutal
motives and consequences. Courage knows irony when she sees it,
but doesn't always see it in herself or her own experience, a blindness
that comes across most poignantly on the occasions of her children's
deaths, the ones she knows about and the one she doesn't. Or, in

Ronald Speirs's phrasing, she would seem at first "to be a master of irony rather than its object" (96). Courage has many faces to show, to the children as well as to others, as the action advances and she meets steadfastly with the rigorous circumstances. Indeed, her ready adaptability is part of a talent for survival – but also, and consequently, of the price she must pay to survive. Courage is, as Karl Schoeps sees it, one of Brecht's "split characters" (258), and perhaps the most profound of her divisions is that between motherhood and the instinct for trade; it is in this regard that Franz Mennemeier cites Brecht's own characterization of Courage as an embodied contradiction, as the "merchant-mother" (140). Indeed, Mother Courage is a role based not only in opposition but in contradiction, and Speirs points to the "most obvious contradiction in her life" as that "between her trade and her role as mother" (93). Arguably the sharpest single expression of this mastering irony – "I believe – I've haggled too long" (64) – comes in scene three when Swiss Cheese is shot for not giving up the regimental cash box and then Courage, too busy to notice what was occurring, is made to view the body without betraying that it belongs to her.

Irony and dialectic, in *Mother Courage and Her Children*, are wedded necessarily to a principle of contradiction, one that is dramatized largely through gestus and, in the case of the title figure, embodied in the character herself. Even as Courage stands obliquely for the "courage" of will and tenacity, at the same time she demonstrates the catastrophic effects of her exertions, in telling vignettes as well as the overall pattern of action. Contradiction, in this view, is apparent in both the character and the circumstances of Brecht's epic story, with the relationship between these accentuated continually by analogy. The directness of this linkage between irony and contradiction in Brechtian dramaturgy is underscored by Speirs, who notes that the playwright's aim was "to enable the spectator to gain the kind of historical conspectus of her situation that Courage, caught up in the thick of things, cannot sustain. One of his principal means of doing this was to expose the contradictions in Mother Courage's experience, another was to incorporate these contradictions in patterns of irony" (93). Within such patterns, says Speirs, Courage is a "dialectically conceived figure" (93). She embodies so alterable a range of attitudes, in other words, that only internal contradiction can result. The playwright's ideological ends are achieved, however, primarily through ironic apposition of these perspectives, and the standpoint of irony becomes key, not only from the title character's point of view but – especially – from that of the audience. "The audience is encouraged," writes Speirs, "to criticize the war with Mother Courage, but also to develop a critical view of her attitudes and behaviour. In fact, Mother Courage's very perceptiveness contributes importantly to the ironic presentation of her fate" (95).

The mastering irony in *Mother Courage and Her Children* is delivered not only through contradiction or apposition but also repetition. The audience witnesses the deaths of the children – Swiss Cheese, then Eilif, then Kattrin – one by one, and sees Courage's level of participation, as well as her reactions, all the while. What has value in the face of these deaths? Over what does Courage haggle that is worth the loss of a child? What does "courage" amount to in such reiterated circumstances? Gilman points to the "ironic perspective" that issues from Courage's "survival at the cost of everything that has seemed to matter." And, it is not only the fact that children die as Courage haggles or looks the other way. Rather, the ironic perspective is such that the dialectical terms of motherhood and profiteering are presented on intimate as well as persistent terms, with the one aspect quick to assume the altered face of the other. "The deaths of her children," says Gilman, "all take place as more or less direct results of her making the living that is designed to sustain them." Here the most profound contradiction of all, that between a mother's creation and a war's destruction, is set repeatedly before the observer as intolerable yet ongoing – and also intrinsic to the circumstances. Courage, as Gilman puts it, is "held in the bitter contradiction by which the attempt to maintain her children in life – to 'love' them in the only way she can, materially, by providing sustenance – becomes the very principle of their being lost to her" (*Making* 225, 227).

> MOTHER COURAGE: Sometimes I see myself driving through hell with this wagon and selling brimstone. And sometimes I'm driving through heaven handing out provisions to wandering

souls! If only we could find a place where there's no shooting, me
and my children – what's left of 'em – we might rest a while.

(96)

There will be no "rest" for Courage, and no place where there is no
shooting. Even when the illusion of peace "breaks out," it only lasts
long enough for Eilif to be killed for what would, in war, be heroism. By
the time that Courage imagines herself "driving through hell" (scene
nine), only Kattrin remains alive, and this will not be the case for long.
Courage remains unaware of Eilif's death, even at the play's end, but
the "we" to which she refers above – the "we" that has been the
impetus for so much of her bargaining – has become impossible, even
as she hitches herself once more to the wagon.[11]

Mother Courage is, then, a stage figure who continually enacts
and personifies irony, in her actions as well as her adaptable inclinations. For Bentley, her intentions are connected not only to immediate circumstance but also to a total Brechtian pattern: she "had gone
to all lengths to trim her sails to the wind but even then the ship
wouldn't move. So there is irony within irony (as, in Brecht's work,
there usually is)" (*Commentaries* 160). Courage stands for motherhood and the business instinct simultaneously, not to say symbioti-
cally, with the concurrent impulses making for particularly ironic
arrangements against the backdrop of unceasing warfare. And yet,
by comparison to such embodiment, the way in which Courage's
character delivers the performative enactment of Brechtian irony is,
though closely related to the embodying tendency, a more intricate
matter.

In this context, in fact, the comparisons to Pirandellian enactment, as exemplified by the Father, are the richest in yield. In each
instance, with Pirandello's "Father" and Brecht's "Mother," it is not
only the character but also the aesthetic mode of theatrical communication that informs the profoundly ironic quality of what is presented.
Enactment for the Father is a mode of being; he is fully manifest only on
the stage, the place of performance. Moreover, he is trapped within a
stasis of incomplete, or unwritten, enactment (the play that has yet to
be finished), yet is tormented by *re*-enactment, that is, the futile

repetition of the Scene which can only be inadequate in its reiteration by the Actors. The prismatic effects of the cumulative action in *Six Characters* – as it involves the Characters' background story, the select scenes of their prospective play, and the current action on the theatre stage – arise in large measure from the refractions among these varied yet interrelated planes of enactment.

The ironic content of the Brechtian gest in *Mother Courage* arises from the theatrical milieu itself as well as the presented story, and it emerges likewise from a situation in which the depicted stage figure exists in parenthetical relation to himself or herself, the character side by side with "character." The Father, in the context of present action in *Six Characters*, is always in parenthetical, and thus ironic, relation to himself as perceived and defined by the Stepdaughter, or as he exists in the back story, or as misunderstood by the Actors and Director. And, of course, he is first and foremost a "Character." In the theatre, and especially in relation to Brecht's epic presentational style, Mother Courage is also a parenthetical figure, made so not only by her traits, ironic viewpoints, or even her contradictions, but also because of the Brechtian performance method that requires an actress to ironize the demonstration of character so that an audience apprehends her as something recreated – "quoted" – rather than as a persona that might engender empathy or identification. Both Pirandello and Brecht offer an artistic frame through which their respective leading character is to be viewed, each in its own way creating an ironic perspective that arises fundamentally from the theatrical setting itself, insuring in the case of Brecht a detachment that can serve to compound the resonances of irony for the viewer.

Brechtian alienation is, as States puts it, "the extreme form of ironic distancing" (*Irony* 176). Put differently, one could say that creating a Brechtian estrangement between audience and action is a radical means of insuring irony, or of enforcing the ironic perspective. To the extent that Brecht's design in *Mother Courage* is to estrange in the sense of insuring aesthetic distance, and to do so by historicizing events and delivering a demonstration of the characters as if in the third person, the epic approach itself will have a multiplying effect, particularly so in the performance of an ironist such as

Mother Courage. At the same time, Courage's contradictory nature is utterly appropriate to Brechtian performance technique. As the playwright himself writes, in "New Technique of Acting": "When reading his part the actor's attitude should be one of a man who is astounded and contradicts." And, from the "Short Organum" (#53): "The coherence of the character is in fact shown by the way in which its individual qualities contradict one another" (Brecht *On Theatre* 137, 196).

To perform the role of Courage, then, is to combine a contrary character with a performance method dependent in itself upon what is contradictory. The ironic facility benefits greatly in such circumstances, and so does the dramatist's ability to either underscore a multiplicity of perspectives or highlight an altered viewpoint through deliberate, ironic contrasts among a character, the play's given circumstances, and the performance style. Brecht, like Shaw, is a dialectician, and while their respective ways and means are different, each dramatist endeavors to argue toward irresolution, leaving the debate in equipoise and with the audience deciding on outcomes for themselves. In Robert Leach's words, Brechtian dramaturgy consists of "components which interact dialectically but never synthesize" (130). A familiar yet core principle of Brecht's epic theatre involves interruption of the action, intervention of a sort that, in essence, counteracts the tendency toward synthesis. Moreover, the interruption encourages the parenthetical standpoint; through intrusion – through song, recitation, dance, choral intervention, or other means – into an otherwise fluid action, that action becomes a quotation, becomes bracketed. That is, it assumes a frame, and one with an essentially ironic purpose and effect. Irony, along these lines, is militant as well as theatrical. In Leach's phrase, the "technique of interrupting is active and interventionist," the purpose being to encourage a stimulation of the spectator toward "an awareness of the possibility for change." *Mother Courage and Her Children*, Leach argues, is "an almost programmatic illustration of this alternative kind of dialectical theatre, because its power derives precisely from the relationship between the material, the technique and the function, the 'gesture,' the 'interruption' and the 'stimulation'" (131).[12]

The Brechtian stage effect is not prismatic in the manner of Pirandello, but each playwright uses irony and its effects to create a multitude of perspectives, albeit to different ends. Pirandello breaks up and then refracts the planes of action and perception to a point where anyone's proposed "reality" is alterable, abstract, and contestable. Brecht, on the other hand, intrudes upon and alienates the action until the range of perspectives on his characters' situations become multiple – and, indeed, changeable by design. By interrupting the stage action, says Leach, "by fragmenting the totality and using montage, interruptions, non-psychological characters and gesture, Brecht confronts the spectator not with reality itself, but with attitudes toward reality" (138). Again, such technique is employed fundamentally to encourage the parenthetical standpoint, and in both cases the result is a variegated perspective achieved through purposefully theatrical and performative means. Both figures, the Father and Mother Courage, are characters integrated within the bounds of his or her respective story; yet each one also exists, and simultaneously so, as a "character," a figure who is always at a remove from that integrity, displaced in order that Pirandello and Brecht can accomplish their distinctive phenomenological inquiries, in the setting of a theatre's stage or on a battlefield, by notably ironic means.

5   Absurdist irony: Ionesco's "anti-play"

The glorious illogic of Eugene Ionesco's *The Bald Soprano*, and the causal disruptions that characterize the playwright's vision more generally, have a basis in extreme contradiction, and that contradictory principle is, in turn, situated fundamentally in irony. Indeed, the play's subtitle, "Anti-play," can be understood as referring to an intrinsic pattern of opposition that affects character qualities and behaviors (Mr. and Mrs. Smith and Mr. and Mrs. Martin, most notably), whimsical matchings of cause and effect in relation to time, location, and event, and the fundamentals of dramaturgical structure. For Ionesco, in fact, such opposition is not so much an effect of the dramatic proceedings as it is an underlying precept for the sensibility as well as the disharmonious action of *The Bald Soprano*.[1] In this sense primarily, a pervasive antagonism in Ionesco's theatre can be distinguished from more typical understandings of conflict and also from the ironic aspect of dialectic as examined here in association with Bernard Shaw and Luigi Pirandello in particular. Just as the Pirandellian theatre is marked by a *sentimento del contraria* (the "feeling of the opposite" that becomes progressively more inclusive in accord with its own tendencies toward the negative), Ionesco's vision is characterized typically by perpetually negating correlations, as words and ideas elicit, and tend often to cancel out, their referential partners. In the context of this inclination, Rosette Lamont identifies a pervasive "anti-attitude" in Ionesco's drama and associates this with the playwright's "all-embracing irony" (*Imperatives* 5).[2]

If Shaw is the "arch-paradoxist," and the "heartbeat of the Pirandellian world" is paradox, then in this vein Ionesco most resembles

132

the latter dramatist, particularly in connection with the negativity, as against the dialectical potentials, of paradoxical language and situations. Paradox for Ionesco connotes, therefore, not so much a provocative ideological quandary as it does an insinuation of non-meaning that extends to preposterousness and then to chaotic breakdown – brought about in large part by a pervasive "anti" with a built-in, intensely parodistic component of derisiveness. Expectations are not only inverted or negated but also mocked. When the doorbell rings in *The Bald Soprano*, for example, it is unclear whether someone will be at the door or not, despite the apparently reasonable expectation on the part of the Smiths and Martins that such ringing requires human agency. The stage picture here, suggesting both presence and absence and a resultant stasis, is signaled clearly in the dialogue:

> MR. SMITH: Goodness, someone is ringing.
>
> MRS. SMITH: I'm not going to open the door.
>
> MR. SMITH: Yes, but there must be someone there.
>
> MRS. SMITH: The first time there was no one. The second time, no one. Why do you think that there is someone there now?
>
> MR. SMITH: Because someone has rung!
>
> MRS. MARTIN: That's no reason.
>
> (22–23)[3]

Here, a more commonplace assumption of "reason," in this case an expectation that when a doorbell announces an arrival a person must be "there," is turned inside out, first by the absence of a bell-ringer, then by the equally paradoxical (and improbable) arrival of the Fire Chief, and finally by the fact that there is no tangible correlation between the ringing of the bell and whether or not a person is doing the ringing. Furthermore, and in the particularly "English" environs of the play, there is no particular reason for assuming that any "there" exists outside of the "middle class English interior" in the first place. In Ionesco's cosmos, the behavior of a doorbell is not only whimsical but existential, contributing as it does to a basic questioning of identity and presence as well as who a prospective guest or intruder might be.

MRS. SMITH (*in a fit of anger*): Don't send me to that door again! You've seen that it was useless. Experience teaches us that when one hears the doorbell ring it is because there is never anyone there.

(23)

In this instance, the language of paradox (apart from Mrs. Smith's fit of anger, her line perfectly echoes Oscar Wilde) refers essentially to a negation that is made apparent in ironic terms: an assumption, paired directly with negation, of logic and reasonableness. Ionesco, as Valency notes in *The End of the World*, is "a specialist in paradox. Underlying his plays and his critical and polemical writings is the useful assumption that every statement implies its contrary" (348). Defined thus, paradox becomes once again the natural partner of irony, but in purposefully negating terms.

Contrariness, when manifested at such extremes, carries with it a directional component, a self-sustaining pattern of cancellation, ending in zero (or, as the final movement of the play makes vivid, in chaotic babel). Sense, in spite of the several characters' efforts to locate it, erodes steadily in proportion to the diminishing capabilities of language as well as to the erratic progress of events. "Contradiction follows contradiction," writes Allan Lewis in *Ionesco*, "for in the absence of objective criteria the opposite of a statement is equally true" (35). Objectivity, of course, is inconceivable, indeed impossible, in Ionesco's universe, again in spite of the characters' strenuous efforts to secure it. The concept of a "fact" is, in itself, a ludicrous proposal:

MR. MARTIN: Excuse me, madam, but it seems to me, unless I'm mistaken, that I've met you somewhere before.
MRS. MARTIN: I, too, sir. It seems to me that I've met you somewhere before.
MR. MARTIN: Was it, by any chance, at Manchester that I caught a glimpse of you, madam?
MRS. MARTIN: That is very possible. I am originally from the city of Manchester. But I do not have a good memory, sir. I cannot say whether it was there that I caught a glimpse of you or not!

(15)

Immediately following this exchange, Mr. and Mrs. Martin conduct an elaborate inquiry into the possibility of their being acquainted with one another, carefully evaluating the accumulating evidence of not only shared train rides but a mutual place of residence (flat number 8 at 19 Bromfield Street), deducing finally that they are Donald and Elizabeth, man and wife. However, ensuing quickly upon this apparently success-ful process of deduction, the Martins' intricate construction crumbles in the version of the truth provided by the maid, Mary. Prior to identifying herself as "Sherlock Holmes," Mary proclaims: "In spite of the extra-ordinary coincidences which seem to be definitive proofs, Donald and Elizabeth, not being the parents of the same child, are not Donald and Elizabeth. It is in vain that he thinks he is Donald, it is in vain that she thinks she is Elizabeth." Who is one to believe, Mary or the Martins? One cannot know, and the very premise of certainty is made ridiculous in the circumstances. Even Mary opts ultimately for indeterminacy: "Who has any interest in prolonging this confusion? I don't know. Let's not try to know. Let's leave things as they are" (19). Again, as in the case of the nonsensical doorbell sequence, the logical course of determination spirals steadily into nullity. Lewis refers to *The Bald Soprano* as "a play in which the theme of nothingness runs through every scene," and Ionesco's reali-zation of this motif is achieved primarily through ironic and oppositional arguments that propel themselves along by self-cancellation. In this regard, and in consideration of such innate extremity, Lewis names Ionesco, in *The Contemporary Theatre*, as "the recognized leader of the theatre of negation" (272).

And yet *The Bald Soprano*'s negativity has, in a further irony, a predominantly comic nature, as if nothingness can only be confronted by inanity, or at least by parody of the attempts by well-intentioned individuals such as the Smiths and Martins to cover it over with chatter and hypothesis. And in this context too, Ionesco's paradoxical assumptions can be distinguished from Pirandello's. In particular, the aspect of finality that Fergusson locates in the Pirandellian paradox does not derive, in *Six Characters in Search of an Author*, from a vision that is principally comedic – in spite of the Father's wryness, the Director's discomfort, or the sustained motif of mistaken identity. Indeed, it is precisely with respect to a concept of identity, and the fallibility therein, that Pirandello's sensibility is, at bottom, least comedic. Nor does the

Pirandellian *sentimento del contraria* issue primarily from a satiric or parodistic (not to say absurdist) standpoint. For him, rather, the feeling of opposition is an existential given, especially in relation to matters of selfhood, and the consequent antagonisms are, in their extremes, intractable, irresolvable, and ultimately tragic.

Valency's comment in regard to Pirandello's drama, that "what is experienced as tragic is actually comic, and our entire life-experience is a pitiful absurdity" (*End* 101), can be turned upside down in the case of Ionesco, for whom the comic experience, in extremis, finally turns ruinous, with "absurdity" being an a priori, an ontological circumstance that precedes any affective or intellectual standpoint. While Pirandello may dramatize, in Rosenberg's phrase, the "absurdity of identity" (127), in the environment of *The Bald Soprano* the absurdity is what turns "identity" into something meaningless, beside the point, a concept to be strenuously parodied rather than mourned. Ionesco carries this mission forward through determinedly ironic means as the characters focus attention on sundry matters related to personal identification – which, in their conceptions, have mostly to do with allegedly ancestral lineages and kinships.

> MRS. SMITH: That would be proper. And Bobby Watson's aunt, old Bobby Watson, might very well, in her turn, pay for the education of Bobby Watson, Bobby Watson's daughter. That way Bobby, Bobby Watson's mother, could remarry. Has she anyone in mind?
> MR. SMITH: Yes, a cousin of Bobby Watson's.
> MRS. SMITH: Who? Bobby Watson?
> MR. SMITH: Which Bobby Watson do you mean?
> MRS. SMITH: Why, Bobby Watson, the son of old Bobby Watson, the late Bobby Watson's other uncle.
>
> (12–13)

Sometime later, the Fire Chief offers to tell stories for the Smiths and Martins, including "The Dog and the Cow" and, more notably in this context of absurd "identity," "The Head Cold," an exaggeratedly detailed riff on heritage, family relations, occupational and marital status, amounting finally to an ornate elaboration of nonsense. "A curious story," remarks Mrs. Smith. "Almost unbelievable" (35).

136

In Ionesco's works among others, it is "metaphysical anguish" (Esslin's phrasing) that goes hand in hand with the laughable and the ridiculous.[4] Irony's intrinsic negativity is allied naturally with tragic patterns and associations; and yet, concurrently, irony's partnerships with satire and parody make for comic intrusions and disruptions. Absurdist irony, with reference to *The Bald Soprano* as a deservedly exemplary case, pertains quite specifically to matters of genre. And yet, and as a complication of this relationship, absurdism is in itself a disruption of genre, and the "anti-play" a parody of theatrical categories. The paradox here is productive, in the case of *The Bald Soprano*, of an ironic inquiry into the very processes of theatre and employment of language as well as the more ostensible, if ludicrous, concerns and habits of discourse among the Smiths and Martins. As the playwright remarks, in "The World of Ionesco": "In *The Bald Soprano*, which is a completely unserious play where I was most concerned with solving purely theatrical problems, some people have seen a satire on bourgeois society, a criticism of life in England, and heaven knows what. In actual fact, if it is a criticism of anything, it must be of all societies, of language, of clichés – a parody of human behavior, and therefore a parody of the theatre, too" (480).

Ionesco accomplishes his "parody of the theatre" in large measure by framing the action of *The Bald Soprano* in a context of ironic juxtapositions, with iterations of boulevard melodrama and comedy of manners serving especially as reflections of genre that, along with the tragical and comical per se, are played consistently against the "anti" genre of unruly absurdism. In one of his diary entries (1951, following soon after the initial production of *The Bald Soprano*), Ionesco underscores the full scope of the "anti" through reiteration: "Abstract theatre. Pure drama. Anti-thematic, anti-ideological, anti-social-realist, anti-philosophical, anti-boulevard psychology, anti-bourgeois, the rediscovery of a new free theatre" (*Notes* 181). Here, a broadly inclusive motif of antagonism reaches beyond a principle of opposition to an "anti" definition of theatre, a discovery of new theatrical possibilities at the expense of long-established behaviors. Ionesco parodies melodramatic encounters, opportune meetings, and theatrical coincidence generally when the Martins rediscover one another as Donald and Elizabeth, and then when the maid, Mary, is reunited with the Fire Chief as his self-proclaimed "little fire hose."

> MRS. SMITH: You two know each other?
> FIRE CHIEF: And how!

(35)

But the parody goes further than a joke at the expense of theatrical conventions. In fact, and within the play's ironic format and parody of logic, the Fire Chief and Mary *must* know one another from before, must be reunited, just as the Martins must rediscover their marriage and cohabitation, in order for the oxymoron of full vacuity to be realized on Ionesco's terms.

"Anti" comedy of manners becomes, in this vein, a particularly successful gambit, providing as it does the occasion for redoubled irony. That is, if comedy of manners is itself a parody (albeit a potentially appreciative one) of social custom, staging a mockery of such comedy becomes, in its turn, a means of re-enforcing the satiric point. Ionesco initiates the satire straight away, with the many references to "English"-ness in the opening stage directions, and with immediate attention to the manners of how and what people eat and drink. The clock strikes seventeen English strokes as, in the theatre, the play opens with an aural as well as visually satiric commentary:

> MRS. SMITH: There, it's nine o'clock. We've drunk the soup, and eaten the fish and chips, and the English salad. The children have drunk English water. We've eaten well this evening. That's because we live in the suburbs of London and because our name is Smith.

(9)

Later, yet still in the context of "manners," the character of Mary is turned into a comic type, a standard figuration of genre, a role that includes her Holmesian perspicacity when it comes to the non-marriage and non-identities of Donald and Elizabeth. Her job as a stock character of genre is to make announcements and admit guests but also to be the smart servant who knows more than the lords and ladies of the manor – but in the case of *The Bald Soprano*, ridiculously so.[5]

> MARY: Mr. and Mrs. Martin, your guests, are at the door. They were waiting for me. They didn't dare come in by themselves. They were supposed to have dinner with you this evening.

MRS. SMITH: Oh, yes. We were expecting them. And we were hungry. Since they didn't put in an appearance, we were going to start dinner without them. We've had nothing to eat all day. You should not have gone out!

MARY: But it was you who gave me permission.

MR. SMITH: We didn't do it on purpose.

(14)

The play's "Englishness" can be seen also, in the metatheatrical context, as related directly to the parody of "manners." In fact, it can be understood as a hint that ancestral ties relating to genre as well as to unseen characters such as Bobby Watson may be incorporated freely in this play, ties that relate it, if eccentrically, to the theatrical worlds of Wilde, Shaw, or Coward. Once again, though, Ionesco employs what is in fact one of the play's key terms – "English" – to compound an irony, in that *The Bald Soprano* is not only a critique of genre and of theatrical convention, but is even more notoriously a critique of language and (anti) communication. Built into this critique, however, is a deliberate use of language to accentuate the satire of manners and, by extension, of theatrical genre. As Nancy Lane points out, much of the play's comedy arises from "devices as old as theatre itself: parody, punning, and wordplay" – devices typically associated with the primacy of wittiness in comedy of manners (35).

If an effect of absurdist irony is to ridicule, and even defy, the concept of genre, it is also to oppose, unite, or cross-pollinate the traditional categories, with the component parts reacting against or commenting upon one another on typically ironic terms. In this scenario, the behaviors of the Smiths and Martins are played out against a background of familiarity – that is, against the archetypal "Smiths" and the "Martins" that we already know, in our lives or in other plays.[6] A parody of manners, when combined with a satire on melodramatic convention, heightens the ridiculous aspects in the case of both targets, especially when portrayed in a frenzied realm of intensifying anarchy. Indeed, as the action of *The Bald Soprano* advances, it becomes more and more farcical: as the pace accelerates, mistakes multiply, and the characters lose their propriety, "manners" are subsumed in the chaos of, among other factors, disparate comedic genres.

How bizarre, as a Smith or Martin might declare, and what a strange coincidence that one sub-genre of comedy (farce, satire, manners) can upstage or displace another in such a way. The effect of genres upon one another in *The Bald Soprano* provides for an intricate dialectic, and one that contributes pointedly to the dramatist's critique of theatrical machinery. To borrow a term used in connection with Brecht and Pirandello, Ionesco's dramaturgy becomes "parenthetical" with respect to this type of referentiality. As one play among many, *The Bald Soprano* exists in implicit and ironic relationship to other plays that it references and in fact borrows from: comedies of manners, melodramas, and boulevard farces, but with each of these queried or fragmented by the presence, implicit or explicit, of the others.

For Ionesco, the differentiation of comic and tragic may be artificial (or non-existent, or laughable), yet in *The Bald Soprano* the playwright uses exactly that division to intensify certain effects of each generic term. This is particularly true when the issue is one of affect, tone, and ontological import rather than dramaturgical convention per se. The stark vacuity of both character and situation might be extremely funny, but the emptiness itself is frightening, especially in its all-inclusiveness. As Pronko notes, Ionesco finds the tragic and the comic to be "inextricable": "In fact, he is not certain what differentiates them, for the comic is the intuition of the absurdity of a universe in which man has neither dignity nor absolutes, and therefore a more starkly depressing universe than that of tragedy, which confers upon man a certain nobility and meaning in the midst of his defeat" (11). Once again, the reference is not only to a vision of experience but to a dramatic genre; in this instance, to specific attributes commonly associated with tragedy. Notable in this context is Ionesco's subtitle for *The Chairs* as a "tragic farce," the apparent oxymoron serving to conflate, or make indistinguishable, what would otherwise seem to be opposing sensibilities with respect to genre.

There is an element of absurdity in relating the typically tragic qualities that Pronko mentions ("dignity," "nobility," "meaning") to characters such as the Smiths and Martins, and that aspect can be variously humorous or pitiable, or both. In *The End of the World*, Valency concludes that, finally, *The Bald Soprano* "is not funny. It evokes laughter, of course, but even more certainly it arouses pity and terror. In the course of time, Ionesco has characterized his play in ways to suit every taste, but he has never lost sight of its tragic undertone" (342). From this point of view, the reference is not, again, to the more philosophical aspects of tragedy or tragic vision, or even to specific tragedies, but to one of the most prominent (and contestable) aspects of Aristotle's tragic definition and criteria. To combine *eleos* and *phobos* – or a coexistence of the two – with laughter is a recipe that would be inconceivable for Aristotle, but for Ionesco such mismatches add notably to the ironic effect of one genre upon another – again, the effect these varying theatrical typologies have on each other when placed in preposterous interrelation. *The Bald Soprano* is, indeed, deliberately satirical in its treatment of genres; in Ionesco's words, it is a "parody of a play, a comedy of comedies" (*Notes* 179). While it may be doubtful that audiences would pity the Smiths or the Martins (or Mary or the Fire Chief) or be terrified at their preposterous circumstances, it may still be the case that, as the familiar motifs of theatrical representation cancel one another out over the course of *The Bald Soprano*, the void that is left might evoke, if not catharsis, then a palpable unease at the resulting lifelikeness.

Together with the ironies of cross-breeding among generic types, *The Bald Soprano* achieves its ends and effects, as plays tend to do, through the behaviors of its characters. The quality and impact of dramatic characterization is, however, substantially altered by the unique circumstances of this play, a result that pertains to Ionesco's individuation of roles and his use of language as well as to prescriptions of genre. The dramatis personae of *The Bald Soprano* is comprised of figures who, in effect, stand for a set of self-reflexive ironies: in one sense, they signify recognizable human beings, as dramatic characters generally do; in another, they represent "characters," the stock figures of genre, beings not of life but of theatre. Finally, and even as they go about their respective actions and exchanges, they defy individuation and end up, as Ionesco himself says, "interchangeable: Martin can change places with Smith and vice versa, no one would notice the difference" (*Notes* 180). The Smiths and the Martins are, finally and deliberately on the part of the dramatist, "anti" characters, caricatures of character.

The extremity of such caricature is obvious in the contrast between the characters in *The Bald Soprano* and theatrical figures who are fashioned naturalistically, especially those constituted in accord with the recommendations of, say, Emile Zola or August Strindberg.[7] In fact, the successful characterization of a Martin or a Smith depends in large measure on their ironic position with respect to an ancestry of dramatic characters, ones with past histories and qualities of personality that emerge from discernible causes, incidents, and relationships. By contrast, and for the purposes of Ionesco's drama, Mr. Smith needs no background, no place or time of birth, no parents, no traumas or telling dreams, no physiological complaints, no upbringing or influential environment, and no economic worries. The characters may, as noted, place considerable importance on matters of heritage and kinship, but only in the most nonsensical ways, as in the case of the ubiquitous "Bobby Watson." In truth, Mr. Smith gets along quite nicely with neither a past nor a memory, and with no particular concerns about money, personal motives, or, certainly, mortality.[8] Mr. Smith must, however, be married, be "English," have a maid, and be "anti" witty enough to utter a balanced but unintelligible aphorism such as: "Take a circle, caress it, and it will turn vicious" (38). But then, so do the other characters in the play. From this angle, the Martins and Smiths are better understood as theatrical functionaries rather than characters. Or, as Richard Schechner puts it, they are "'parts' – that is, sets of verbal notations, just as a musical part is a set of musical notations. These parts in themselves have no feelings" ("Inquiry" 28).

Just as the Smiths and Martins have no tangible pasts (or futures, given the bedlam and role reversals of the play's final sequence), they exist in a present moment that is abstracted from quotidian measures of time. The English clock (another "part," as Schechner might say) may have an assigned place of origin but is continually mistaken concerning its ostensible function, to keep track of the exact hour of the day. And yet, in the context of "anti" time, the dramatic function of a clock is to *not* keep the time, but rather to argue with time, to make a jest of time:

MR. SMITH: Here's a thing I don't understand. In the newspaper they always give the age of deceased persons but never the age of the newly born. That doesn't make sense.

MRS. SMITH: I never thought of that!
[*Another moment of silence. The clock strikes seven times. Silence. The clock strikes three times. Silence. The clock doesn't strike.*]

(11)

Later on, when the Fire Chief wonders if he will have sufficient time to tell his stories, Mr. Smith apologizes that the clock "runs badly. It is contradictory, and always indicates the opposite of what the hour really is" (34). Measured time, in this universe, is a mockery; the exactitude of, say, Lopakhin's watch or his timetable is something foreign, incomprehensible. Here instead the clock is, as Valency notes with appropriate anthropomorphism, "a free spirit" (*End* 341).[9] Time itself is "contradictory" in *The Bald Soprano*, and the characters are bereft, not only of the exact hours and minutes of their "day" (whatever that is) but of an embracing context, a life continuum. In Richard Coe's assessment, it is the absence of such a continuum that can be related directly to the problem of character traits or personality: "A 'personality,' in the classical concept of the term, implies at least a minimum of continuity from one moment to the next, and not merely an unrelated sequence of 'states of existence' accidentally confined within the same material body. But this minimum of continuity is precisely what is lacking. Each 'state of existence' owes nothing but an arbitrary debt of coincidence to the one before it" (30–31). Character, in *The Bald Soprano*, is a quality that the Smiths and the Martins themselves cannot hold onto, at least not with any consistency. Time is abstracted, and the interactions among the couples become more and more disjointed as the play moves forward. The characters may begin as embodied parodies of stock theatrical figures, but, as Lane discerns, they "lose even that degree of coherence as the play progresses. They lack any discernible motivations, rationality, or internal life; rather, they are like puppets from guignol, automata as mechanical as the clock that chimes in at will on the dialogue throughout the play" (38).

Dramatic characters may communicate and reveal themselves through linguistic expressiveness, but Ionesco's people suffer a progressive diminishment, and finally a disintegration, of language's ability to convey thought or feeling or make sense of phenomena. *The*

143

Bald Soprano is, in Ionesco's own conception, a "tragedy of language," and the mutual breakdown that is experienced by the Smiths and Martins is finally brought about by frustration followed by violent rage at the loss of words and, consequently, meaning (*Notes* 175). The characters attempt to locate or express wisdom – and for much of the play they persist gamely, as if in pursuit of reliable truth or knowledge – but the quest is doomed in spite of their cheery, "English" earnestness.

> MR. SMITH: One walks on his feet, but one heats with electricity or coal.
>
> MR. MARTIN: He who sells an ox today, will have an egg tomorrow.
>
> MRS. SMITH: In real life, one must look out of the window.
>
> MRS. MARTIN: One can sit down on a chair, when the chair doesn't have any.
>
> MR. SMITH: One must always think of everything.
>
> MR. MARTIN: The ceiling is above, the floor is below.
>
> (38)

The lines are thoughtfully phrased, evenly balanced, epigrammatic. Moreover, there is an implicit sense of return, reciprocity, or of one phenomenon set in relation to another – "I'll give you my mother-in-law's slippers if you give me your husband's coffin," says Mrs. Martin (39). And yet, such balances, which in the speaking can neatly reflect the witty symmetries of comedy of manners, are not proportional at all. Instead, they are declarations of mismatch, of disjuncture, and finally of a consciousness unable to reliably assign names to a world outside of being. Immediately following this sequence in the play, the language moves from simple illogic to total disintegration, and from clauses, queries, and sentences to sounds thrown together in desperation, to "cascades of cacas" (40).

The story is familiar concerning Ionesco's fortuitous experience with learning a foreign language, and so is his account, in "The Tragedy of Language," of how his own study of English, and the use of a conversation manual in particular, prepared for the circumstances as well as the characterizations in *The Bald Soprano*. Here, too, there is an indication of how the dramatist came upon the antithetical motif (ceiling above, floor below) as well as the mannerly phraseology of his characters:

> I bought an English-French Conversation Manual for Beginners.
> I set to work. I conscientiously copied out phrases from my
> manual in order to learn them by heart. Then I found, reading
> them over attentively, that I was learning not English but some
> very surprising truths: that there are seven days in the week, for
> example, which I happened to know before; or that the floor is
> below us, the ceiling above us, another thing that I may well have
> known before but had never thought seriously about or had
> forgotten, and suddenly it seemed to me as stupefying as it was
> indisputably true.
>
> *(Notes* 175)

Ionesco recounts how two couples, the Smiths and Martins, were invented by the author of the instructional manual to create dialogue (including Mrs. Smith's assertions, "perfectly irrefutable truisms"), to provide an "English" setting, and to identify phenomena of the world through conversation. He recalls the realization that such dialogue was essentially dramatic – "So what I had to produce was a play" – and then remembers the transformation from the book characters' exacting phraseology into the "anti" expressiveness of the play to come: "After a time, those inspired yet simple sentences which I had so painstakingly copied into my schoolboy's exercise book, detached themselves from the pages on which they had been written, changed places all by themselves, became garbled and corrupted." At first, Ionesco thought of calling his play *English Made Easy* *(Notes* 177–178).

"English" is the substance of this play in translation, in the sense that for Ionesco a newly discovered language and pattern of dialogue is brought to theatrical life in *The Bald Soprano*'s primary, and ironic, mode of expressiveness, or "anti" communication. The linguistic behavior of the play, the "English" spoken by the "English" characters, is placed in ironic relation to standardized English and its anticipated usage – that is, to a manner of discourse that is expected in accord with the norms of dramatic genre or with conventional idioms of conversation. "English," from this perspective, is both the root and the stylistic means of Ionesco's comedy, especially in regard to the play's epigram-as-nonsense style of "anti" mannerly wit. "English," too, provides both a predisposition and a vehicle for *The Bald Soprano*'s tragic progression. In this instance, the tragedy of the play is felt most poignantly not as individualized calamity or loss but as a failure of naming and, by extension, of thinking, knowing, and ultimately, of "being" for all the characters. In "The Tragedy of Language," Ionesco refers to such deficiency: "The Smiths and the Martins no longer know how to talk because they no longer know how to think, they no longer know how to think because they are no longer capable of being moved, they have no passions, they no longer know how to be, they can become anyone or anything, for as they are no longer themselves, in an impersonal world, they can only be someone else, they are interchangeable" (*Notes* 180).

The Bald Soprano's language is, in Pronko's view, substantive in the sense of a texture; words are tactile, and are used "as a kind of property rather than in the usual literary way. The words and sentences become brittle and take on an almost solidified existence of their own." In terms of the dramaturgy, the situation of the play is "disarticulated, exploded, exaggerated until something monstrous and violent is achieved" (7–9). Disarticulation, as a linguistic strategy or as pattern of action, is in itself an occasion for irony that bears a resemblance, once more, to Eric Gans's reference to "sparagmatic violence," associated in this instance with characters defined by use of language as against thinking per se. The words themselves (in other words) are the occasion for sparagmos, the tragic rending of a represented character in drama. "English," consequently, is an active and vital force in this absurdist drama, despite its failure to provide sense or context, and the effects of this are felt most strongly as an unlocalized and disassociative energy, an unpredictable wild card of "anti" signification that operates as a power turned loose among the characters. Schechner sees language in *The Bald Soprano* as parasitic, something that cannot accomplish its work without the hosting agency supplied by the characters: "The language needs people because it is not able to live on its own, purely; people are its means of being, its host." Understood thus, it is "English" that impels the action and provides its substance, rather than the Smiths and the Martins alone. "Mrs. Smith is not using language," says Schechner. "It is using her." Language is alienated from thought (what, after all, can the characters be thinking?) but not from action; rather, the language – "English" – *is* the action, and words are "the initiators of dramatic events" ("Inquiry" 23–25).[10]

The effect of "anti" language in *The Bald Soprano* is, first, to exacerbate and then to demolish the tension that already exists, that is built-in, between signification and what is signified.

> MRS. MARTIN: Don't ruche my brooch!
> MR. MARTIN: Don't smooch the brooch!
>
> (40)

By the later movements of the play, and especially the end sequence, words are divested of all meaning. "Brooch" means nothing; it only rhymes with "smooch," which is also meaningless. "English," which in the play's opening beats was fully capable of differentiating fish and chips from an English salad, is by this point utterly bereft of signifying power. Language itself turns tragic, more so perhaps than the characters who struggle to use it with specificity. And yet, language is fallible to begin with, and in this sense the "disarticulation," the linguistic sparagmos that occurs in *The Bald Soprano*, represents a difference from other discourses in terms of the degree of the disjuncture rather than in the nature of the problem per se. "By creating ways of thinking and being," notes Steven Kern, "language also 'lies' by narrowing and distorting what we take for experience. We name things with words according to metaphors that express only partial and accidental relations between things and ourselves" (118).

This fallibility, the innate imperfection of language, is what *The Bald Soprano* employs to such theatrical effect, as "anti" language enlarges ironically and exponentially upon deficiencies that "English" has to begin with. If, in Kern's phrasing, "language does not so much represent the world as it creates our experience of it," then the Smiths and the Martins (on Schechner's terms, the host vehicles for words) can fashion a preposterous cosmos through verbiage alone:

> MRS. MARTIN: Silly gobblegobblers, silly gobblegobblers.
> MR. MARTIN: Marietta, spot the pot!
> MRS. SMITH: Krishnamurti, Krishnamurti, Krishnamurti!

MR. SMITH: The pope elopes! The pope's got no horoscope. The
horoscope's bespoke.

MRS. MARTIN: Bazaar, Balzac, bazooka!

MRS. MARTIN: Bizarre, beaux-arts, brassieres!

(41)

The relation of the signifier to the signified, says Saussure, is "arbitrary,"
with no empirical connection between the two (69).[11] "English," as the
"anti" language of *The Bald Soprano*, magnifies such arbitrariness into
gibberish, though not, here, at the expense of alliteration. The characters
can still imitate, still compete with one another, still hear one another –
"Bazaar"/"Bizarre" – but they cannot produce or understand a thought or
create a readable environment through logic or a causal system supplied
by words. In ironic terms, the very weakness of language has, in *The Bald
Soprano*, a reverse effect. That is, language may be the primary energy at
work in the action of the play, acting through the characters to constitute
a world of uncertainty and non sequitur. At the very same time, however,
language itself is compromised and made frail in essential ways by its
own imprecision: "Language is radically powerless," notes Saussure, "to
defend itself against the forces which from one moment to the next are
shifting the relationship between the signified and the signifier. This
is one of the consequences of the arbitrary nature of the sign" (75).[12]

MR. SMITH: It's!

MRS. MARTIN: Not!

MR. MARTIN: That!

MRS. MARTIN: Way!

MR. SMITH: It's!

MRS. MARTIN: O!

MR. MARTIN: Ver!

MRS. SMITH: Here!

(41)

Ironically, the final lines of *The Bald Soprano*, as a fugue of voices and
then as a chorus of Smiths and Martins, do make notable sense, if only
as a statement of denial and displacement, of "signifiers" and their
referents that are forever at odds, and always somewhere else.

148

Catachresis, the employment of a wrong word for the context, assumes multiple implications in *The Bald Soprano*. On the one hand, the notion of a "wrong" word is made problematic by the indeterminacy, not to say impossibility, of a "right" word. Moreover, the idea of a "context," while not arbitrary (it is "English"), is innately questionable. And finally, if the concept of a context is in itself questionable, the rights and wrongs of word choices must also be subjectively determined. Still, the phenomenon of the "wrong" choice, in direct relation to use of "English," is highly germane in terms of its ironic implications in particular. As Hayden White notes: "The basic figurative tactic of Irony is catachresis (literally 'misuse'), the manifestly absurd thing characterized or the inadequacy of the characterization itself." In Ionesco's drama, of course, both situations are apparent, as absurdity is characterized and the means of characterization ("English") is shown to be manifestly inadequate. Along such lines, irony is related directly to the fallibility of language with regard, not only to catachresis per se, but to the very tendency of language to insure opportunities for slippage and for gaps among signifiers and signifieds. As White argues:

> It can be seen immediately that Irony is in one sense
> metatropological, for it is deployed in the self-conscious
> awareness of the possible misuse of figurative language. Irony
> presupposes the occupation of a "realistic" perspective on reality,
> from which a nonfigurative representation of the world of
> experience might be provided. Irony thus represents a stage of
> consciousness in which the problematical nature of language
> itself has become recognized. It points to the potential
> foolishness of all linguistic characterizations of reality as much as
> to the absurdity of the beliefs it parodies. It is therefore
> "dialectical," as Kenneth Burke has noted, though not so much in
> its apprehension of the process of the world as in its apprehension
> of the capacity of language to obscure more than it clarifies in
> any act of verbal figuration. In Irony, figurative language folds
> back on itself and brings its own potentialities for distorting
> perception under question.
>
> (37)

Here the presence of the ironic is wedded closely to the concept of misuse, and to the capabilities of language for producing faulty connotations, a pattern that underlies much of the action and, indeed, the originating premise of *The Bald Soprano*. And yet, the disparity between a wrong and right word choice cannot be wholly arbitrary. On the contrary, it must be potentially meaningful in itself if an ironic effect is to be successfully achieved. In this regard, the impression of the "anti" in Ionesco's drama can be understood, not only in relation to, but as inclusive of the concept of irony itself.

"Anti" irony is, in this view, not so much a double negative as it is a redoubling of ironic potentials, a magnification of the trope's range of import through extreme exaggeration of its own innate properties and tendencies, especially the basic trait of signifying opposition. Coupled with such expansion, however, is a concurrent, and precipitous, diminishment in the trope's natural ability to connote context or, more embracingly, sense. Here the concept of a sensible, universalized, or cosmic irony, as identified in relation to Ibsen or Chekhov especially, becomes impossible, transformed into something that is potentially inclusive but is chaotic and without meaning at the same time. With respect to *The Bald Soprano* in particular, the exaggeration of the ironic is achieved predominantly through irony's intrinsic relation to language, and from an "anti" kinship between words and what they are meant to denote. Irony is, of course, based fundamentally in wording, and the greater the degree of play in language, of potential indeterminacy among signifying terms, the greater the opportunity for ironic insinuation and commentary.

Irony's ancestry is in wording; or, as Gans puts it, irony "is a characteristic of the historical human sign-system of language." With reference to what he identifies as the "vertical" difference ("the basis of the opposition within the sign-system between signifier and signified"), Gans argues that irony arises naturally in the situation in which "the primary characteristic of the sign is that it occupies a different level of being from the reality it designates." Absurdist irony, or, as Ionesco might have it, "anti" irony, becomes in this alignment a hyperextension of what is already an innate condition of opposition and possible contradiction situated in the capabilities of language and sign-making generally. Gans explains: "Irony is the expression, necessarily indirect, of the fragility of the absolute or 'vertical' formal difference inaugurated by the sign with respect to its source, the relative or 'horizontal' difference in the real world between the subject and the object of desire ... Irony is the necessarily indirect and allusive expression of the deconstructability of the formal structure of language that is the model for all formal structure, all of which are in the last analysis structures of representation" (65–66). It is exactly this "deconstructability" – or, to recall Pronko's term, "disarticulation" – which insures the vulnerability necessary for what Ionesco refers to as a "tragedy of language" and what Gans calls "sparagmatic violence": not the tearing apart of a tragic hero but of a tragic thinker and speaker who cannot think or speak in any language but one of ironic non-referentiality. In the dark at the play's end, the characters chant:

> ALL TOGETHER: It's not that way, it's over here, it's not that way, it's over here, it's not that way, it's over here, it's not that way, it's over here.
>
> (42)

And so *The Bald Soprano* ends, ironically, as it began, folding back upon itself with the Martins turning into the Smiths and, one supposes, vice versa. The lights come back up, and now it is the Martins who "say exactly the same lines as the Smiths in the first scene, as the curtain softly falls" (42). Even as the "English" language regains, for a moment, the sense it had early on ("There, it's nine o'clock."), the play concludes with an ironic punctuation that is more visual than linguistic, with its reversal stated more pungently in a stage image than in words.

As an "anti-play," *The Bald Soprano* disrupts logic, causality, time, and location. Ionesco ironizes theatrical genres as well as familiar modes of characterization and speech, primarily through derisively robbing language of its alleged capabilities regarding precise articulation and signification. In terms of genre per se, the zone between comedy and tragedy in the play may be indistinct or non-existent – as Valency remarks, *La Cantatrice Chauve* is "as funny as the tragic can be" (*End* 350). Both generic terms bespeak, in such a situation, not only an ironic context but also a parenthetical relation to one another. Still, implicit in the concept of genre is an assumption of order, and in the context of irony there is often a general presumption of sense, or at least of aptness, however fathomable or mysterious the case may be. Were it not for the typically wry, satiric, fateful, or whimsical element of import or even sense, the "vertical" aspect of ironic referentiality would lose considerably in degrees of suggestiveness. Even amid the accelerating chaos, the order of events in *The Bald Soprano* has logic and is precisely wrought in accord with the play's unique operating principles. All the while, however, it is the strengthening of an "anti" ironic impression, in tandem with a relentless "disarticulation," that finally takes a necessary, even tragical, element of sense away from a theatrical cosmos and, at the same time, from irony's more frequently recognized powers of connotation.

6   "Ironist First Class": Stoppard's *Arcadia*

If there is a rival, or perhaps an heir, to Bernard Shaw as "archparadoxist" it is most assuredly Tom Stoppard, especially in the realms of verbal and situational irony. In Stoppard's *Arcadia*, the figure of Septimus Hodge, the tutor-turned-hermit, provides one of the most intricate and layered embodiments of Stoppard's renowned tendency toward irony in the form of paradox, witticism, literary allusion, and historical juxtaposition. Stoppard has been called an "Ironist First Class"; his fondness for paradox and tautology is familiar, well-documented, and repeatedly in evidence in his plays; his habitual fondness for literary references (writers and their works alike) and situational quirks in history is amply demonstrated.[1] Remarking on the dramatist's style of dialogue, Stephen Schiff points to Stoppard's "paradox-happy logorrhea," and the playwright himself confesses that paradox and tautology "don't have to mean anything, lead anywhere, be part of anything else. I just like them. I've got an unhealthy love affair for them" (155, 215).[2]

In the play that first brought Stoppard notoriety, *Rosencrantz and Guildenstern are Dead* (1966), the master irony is based on an inversion of focus with regard to *Hamlet,* one that brings Shakespeare's two doomed courtiers, insignificant in the tragedy's action, to the forefront in both philosophic and dramatic terms. The two are assigned promi- nence, in Stoppard's telling, by the very fact that they are so unaware of their purpose or place in the cosmic scheme of events, or in the plot that has allowed them to exist in the first place. In *Travesties,* the literary allusions are not to Shakespeare but rather to James Joyce and Oscar Wilde. The former is seen as a character in the play (Joyce, in the telling,

happens to be in Zurich, c. 1917, along with Tristan Tzara and Lenin),
whereas the latter is unseen but is instead a continual point of reference, particularly with respect to *The Importance of Being Earnest* and
its characters. Ironies arise repeatedly in the co-mingling of the three
historical figures, their interactions with characters such as "Cecily"
and "Gwendolen," and from the fact that events are presented through
the skewed and patently unreliable filter of storyteller Henry Carr's
memory. Stoppard has long been compared to Wilde, as wit and farceur,
and in this context *Travesties* provides a highly representative case
for how successfully the dramatist can tune and calibrate the clausal
balances necessary for Wildean wittiness, or, in John Fleming's phrase,
"Wildean epigrams of inversion" (108).[3] In *Arcadia*, this tradition continues, with Septimus Hodge as the exemplar of performative and
self-reflexive verbal irony as well as an erotic sensibility that, purposefully or not, pays homage to the truewits that preceeded him, in the
Restoration and after, in the theatre of comic manners. Mr. Horner
and Mr. Dorimant, could they transcend the intricate boundaries of
their own intrigues in *The Country Wife* or *The Man of Mode*, respectively, might recognize the situation:

> SEPTIMUS: Mrs. Chater demanded satisfaction and now you are
> demanding satisfaction. I cannot spend my time day and night
> satisfying the demands of the Chater family. As for your wife's
> reputation, it stands where it ever stood.
> CHATER: You blackguard!
> SEPTIMUS: I assure you. Mrs. Chater is charming and spirited,
> with a pleasing voice and a dainty step, she is the epitome of all
> the qualities society applauds in her sex – and yet her chief
> renown is for a readiness that keeps her in a state of tropical
> humidity as would grow orchids in her drawers in January.
> CHATER: Damn you, Hodge, I will not listen to this! Will you fight
> or not?
> SEPTIMUS: Not!

(7)[4]

Quite apart from the trysts and offhand assignations that liven
Septimus's existence at Sidley Park (Lady Croom is another, more

serious, romantic conquest), he is also a young scholar (aged twenty-two in 1809, then twenty-five) with a sharply scientific and mathematical turn of mind. Indeed, his primary role at the estate is to be tutor for the relentlessly curious young genius, Thomasina Coverly, who is aged thirteen as the play begins and nearly seventeen as it ends. Septimus's own brilliance and erudition, together with Thomasina's verve and demand for knowledge, infuse *Arcadia*'s scenes in the early nineteenth century, just as the effort to discover his identity and personal history, largely a project of the garden historian Hannah Jarvis, defines a major portion of the play's contemporary action. Septimus is, to be sure, a vintage Stoppardian character, made so especially by his witty perspicacity but also by his metatheatrical qualities and predispositions. Septimus is a master of spectatorship: not only is he an alert and astute observer of those around him and of goings-on at the estate, he serves also as an ideally informed audience for his own utterance and performance. The tone of bemused irony that he brings to the encounter with Ezra Chater is lost on his conversation partner, but Septimus himself seems to enjoy the interaction immensely – as, in theory, does the actual theatre audience attending *Arcadia*. As a performative ironist, indeed, Septimus is observed simultaneously by himself, by others with whom he engages in scenic interplay, by the theatre audience, and by characters in the contemporary scenes that endeavor without success to understand him and his protégé in their shared historical frame. As an elaborately wrought Stoppardian creation, Septimus shows off a classical education of notable breadth, a rampant intellectual as well as sensual curiosity, and an opportune, not to say requisite, connection with a famous figure of literature – in the case of *Arcadia*, the Romantic poet, Lord Byron. It is not surprising, surely, that Septimus's ironic disposition is revealed primarily by verbal means, but the ironies he embodies and enacts are also situational, and on several interactive levels at once.

Stoppard, a veteran devotee of signifying contradiction, is masterful with the sort of mannered and contrapuntal dialogue that is designed to insure, along the lines of Shavian dialectics, a complex and likely irreconcilable spectrum of facets to a problem. John Lahr quotes the playwright on this dynamic: "I put a position, rebut it, refute the rebuttal and rebut the refutation. Forever" (*Coast* 95). In *Arcadia*, Septimus stands for the Stoppardian principle of contradiction, and he does so largely on ironic terms. Hodge may be a recognizable figure of genre (and of comedy of manners in particular), yet his fate, as discerned by Hannah Jarvis and the others who observe him from the present day, transcends the predictable bounds of genre and, while not authentically tragic, is certainly dismal – and dismally fateful. The theatre audience for *Arcadia* can never observe Septimus directly as the hermit of Sidley Park, yet by the play's end it can sadly imagine the deranged and isolated figure that the erudite and debonair tutor has become. As the play nears its close and the couples from both eras are waltzing, the specter of Septimus and Thomasina "crushes us" – to borrow Joseph Hynes's phrasing (653) – in that the audience knows by then of the young woman's imminent death by fire. Thomasina precociously intuits the second law of thermodynamics, but then dies as if to illustrate and embody it. It is, of course, her death as well as her science that creates the Sidley Park hermit, the mathematical "scribbler" so inscrutable to researchers in the play's present day. Irony, as I. A. Richards describes it in general terms, is a "bringing in of the opposite, the complementary impulses" (250). *Arcadia* exemplifies, in this respect, not only ironic contradiction per se but also a dialectic among interrelated, or complementary, terms. And yet, the fundamental principle of contradiction, elaborated by Stoppard and embodied especially by Septimus (as tutor and as hermit), extends well beyond the situational motif of *Arcadia*'s split time frame. The conventions of verbal irony mark the play's action throughout; the juxtapositions of present and past create continual opportunities for sardonic connotation; yet the total spectrum of ironies in the play includes Romantic, cosmic, and postmodern perspectives.

A single line of Lady Croom's will suffice as evidence, not only of Stoppard's debt to Oscar Wilde, but of *Arcadia*'s style of conscious verbal irony: "It is a defect of God's humour," she proclaims, "that he directs our hearts everywhere but to those who have a right to them" (71). Taken together, Lady Croom's words and tone perfectly reflect the sophistication and the world-weariness brought on by a repeated witnessing of the disparity between what *is* and what ought to be – to wit, the age-old ontological gap that makes for continual sources of ironic commentary. Played against the background of *Arcadia*'s debates, spoken and implicit, concerning determinism and free will, Lady Croom's line bears a lightly cosmic touch, aligning as it does the will of an Almighty to a whimsical sensibility with regard to human affairs. Verbal irony can, of course, be epitomized in conversational discourse as well as individual observations:

> THOMASINA: Septimus, what is carnal embrace?
> SEPTIMUS: Carnal embrace is the practice of throwing one's arms around a side of beef.
> THOMASINA: Is that all?
>
> (1)

Here once again, in the sequence that initiates *Arcadia*'s action, Septimus is observed in the reflexive state of being his own best audience. He is not, of course, aware of being a dramatic character, yet he is theatrical nonetheless, and a consciously performative ironist in the bargain. Ostensibly, there is no one in the room to appreciate his joke, yet he enjoys it anyway, simply on the merits. "Verbal irony implies an ironist," as D. C. Muecke notes succinctly in *The Compass of Irony*, "someone consciously and intentionally employing a technique" (42). With regard to Stoppard and Septimus, indeed, there are two ironists at work, each with his own motive. The playwright initiates the play's dialogue with a Wildean spin on phraseology, while his ironist character casts himself in the roles of dutiful tutor to the young and, at the same time, one with ample, if unconfessed, knowledge of carnal embrace. Septimus is seen here, as elsewhere, in possession of the "generous skepticism" that William Empson assigns to irony (44). The exchange with Thomasina also provides a neatly fashioned microcosm of the play's larger purview, in that the discrepancy between what is known and not known, by whom and at what given times, comprises a goodly portion of *Arcadia*'s philosophic inquiry as well as dramaturgical style and structure. Moreover, there is immediate if tacit reference to the lusts and attractions which, as the play makes clear, are forces in nature that are forever outside of mathematics: "The attraction that Newton left out," as Valentine Coverly calls it (74).

With regard to knowledge and the quest for it per se, Septimus and Thomasina together provide especially opportune occasions for what Muecke describes as an all-embracing, or "general," irony: "In the field of human knowledge there is wide scope for general irony since there is an opposition, not always recognized, between the obstacles to knowledge and the impulse, desire, and self-imposed obligation to know ... It becomes ironic, however, when we recognize in what various ways our knowledge and understanding is necessarily limited and at the same time feel that it ought not to be limited, that we ought to know everything" (*Compass* 151). Muecke's inclusive characterization of this variety of irony is enacted on specific terms by Thomasina and Septimus, especially so in the context of knowledge and of knowing:

> THOMASINA: ... God's truth, Septimus, if there is an equation for a curve like a bell, there must be an equation for one like a bluebell, and if a bluebell, why not a rose? Do we believe nature is written in numbers?
> SEPTIMUS: We do.
> THOMASINA: Then why do your equations only describe the shapes of manufacture?
> SEPTIMUS: I do not know.
> THOMASINA: Armed thus, God could only make a cabinet.
> SEPTIMUS: He has mastery of equations which lead into infinities where we cannot follow.
> THOMASINA: What a faint heart!
>
> (37)

This vignette, one among several that reveal Thomasina's adamant refusal to stop short of thorough and exacting knowledge, is precisely revelatory of the nature of "general" irony in relation to the possibility versus impossibility of knowing. Here again, the motif of attainable understanding is played against the larger canvas of *Arcadia*'s action, especially in relation to the largely futile efforts of Hannah Jarvis and Bernard Nightingale to know the past from the vantage point of the present day.

The powerful effects of situational or dramatic irony in *Arcadia* arise from much more than conventionally discrepant degrees of awareness among the characters in the play or between the audience and the characters. Observers of Stoppard's play are, to be sure, privileged in being able to witness the scenes in both time frames, nineteenth and twentieth centuries, whereas the characters themselves cannot do so; the audience, therefore, can behold the consistent ironies that issue from the two eras in combination.[5] The schism between past and present is, however, drawn so severely that at times there seems to be little connection at all, apart from the inanimate props ("The Couch of Eros," Thomasina's notebooks, etc.) that survive from one epoch to the next in the benevolent embrace of the Sidley Park manor house itself. Even as *Arcadia* examines the mechanisms of history – in nature, deeds, and through scholarship – it steadfastly questions the ability of historical inquiry to determine the personalities and passions, if not the events, of ages past. Prapassaree and Jeffrey Kramer refer to a past history that, in Stoppard's play, is "tantalizingly close but ultimately untouchable" (7), itself a situation that is continually productive of an ironized perspective on the action.

In the context of *Arcadia*'s broader entertainment of chaos theory (or nonlinear dynamics), particularly in relation to the spectacle of intertwined human deeds and actions over time, the past becomes increasingly questionable, not to say indecipherable, from the contemporary standpoint. Daniel Jernigan argues in this connection that, "At its very core, the play is about the practical impossibility of doing historical research, since all the hidden variables make such research infinitely difficult" (20). Or, put differently, the play is very much concerned with the irony of being determined to know (exemplified by characters in both eras) in an atmosphere where knowledge in any total sense will be impossible – or worse, as in Bernard's hapless search for Byron, be misguided and finally ludicrous. Hannah Jarvis probes the available evidence for the hermit of Sidley Park, even as Valentine uncovers the truth concerning Thomasina's discoveries – which, in turn, are part of what has driven Septimus to madness and to a solitary existence in the estate's hermitage in the first place. Hannah draws her conclusions about the hermit, which are accurate to a degree, but *Arcadia*'s audience is able to see just how much she (and Bernard and Valentine) have missed. And yet, it is not only the ironic slippage between eras that marks the difficulty of these quests, but also the gaps of understanding between persons in each of the respective time frames. Stoppard expertly underscores the kinship as well as the alienation between the time periods, providing both Septimus and Valentine with a tortoise (Plautus and Lightning, respectively) and the setting with a transhistoric apple and wine glass. "As Hannah drinks from Septimus's glass," write Sternlieb and Selleck, "so irony builds up in all the overlaps and near misses of what she and Septimus are learning and what Val and Thomasina are teaching." Hannah's personal irony, which owes primarily to her profession as historian, also pertains to this situation of a past that remains obdurate against recovery: "For Hannah the biographer will never be able to capture her subject. She will never find the real Caroline Lamb, the real Septimus Hodge, the real Thomasina Coverly" (492, 497).[6]

Arcadia's theatre audience is allowed the direct observation of only one Septimus Hodge, not the hermit of Sidley Park but rather the engaging young scholar who tutors Thomasina, denies Ezra Chater his duel, romances Lady Croom, and exhibits a quick and extravagant gift for tersely ironic witticism:

> THOMASINA: Septimus, do you think God is a Newtonian?
> SEPTIMUS: An Etonian? Almost certainly, I'm afraid. We must ask your brother to make it his first inquiry.
>
> (5)

At such moments, as in the sequence when Thomasina's question on "carnal embrace" is provisionally answered, Septimus neatly embodies Muecke's characterization of the ironist with "awareness of himself as the unobserved observer" (Compass 218), one able to sustain an ironic attitude without betraying any intent behind one's observations. Septimus, from this perspective, is so fundamentally and concurrently the private as well as public ironist that certain of his qualities and attitudes can be assessed in relation to "alazony," including its originating implications. That is, if irony's theatrical as well as etymological origins exist to some degree in the apposition of eiron and alazon figures, there are ways in which Septimus Hodge can suggest, in each of his incarnations and from the perspective of two time periods, qualities of

160

both of these archetypal figures. Irony is fundamentally hierarchical: the *eiron*, traditionally, is clever beyond his or her humble status and is victorious in relation to the vanity or the bragging of the *alazon*.[7] In this respect, Septimus's position as a hireling at Sidley Park – "not quite a guest but rather more than a steward" (24), as Hannah puts it – is offset by his brilliance and panache. Yet still, he can be vain enough to be vulnerable to the implications and outcomes of his own pride of intellect.

"In Theophrastus," notes Muecke in *Irony and the Ironic*, "both the Eiron and the Alazon were dissemblers, the one concealing himself behind evasive, non-committal, self-deprecative masks, the other behind a façade of boasts. But the modern ironist, whether he plays an eironic or alazonic part, dissembles or rather, pretends, not in order to be believed but ... in order to be understood" (35). Septimus Hodge, born in 1787, is neither an ancient nor a "modern ironist" in terms of his epoch; he is, however, the creation of a modern sensibility and he is scrutinized in *Arcadia* by contemporary characters; in particular, he comes to represent several longstanding and generic attributes and behaviors of comedy, especially in the contexts of "manners" and of farce. Septimus is certainly a "dissembler" (how could he conduct his myriad affairs at Sidley Park and not be?) even as he is avidly forthright in his teaching and studies. And, to the extent that irony informs his world-view, Septimus is certainly not above the employment of an arch persona or point of view "in order to be understood," even if such understanding is more to the benefit of *Arcadia*'s audience as opposed to fellow characters on stage. As a Stoppardian emissary, in fact, Septimus is possessed of far and away the wittiest sensibility among *Arcadia*'s characters, one that often foils rather than abets the understanding of those of lesser wit. Sternlieb and Selleck suggest, in this context, that the voluble Septimus tends at times to actually halt discourse: "Septimus is, of course, a marvelous speaker, but his wit is actually more apt to *stop* conversation. Through his wit, he distorts others' meanings so as to leave them speechless, or anticipates their words while willfully disregarding their direction, or recklessly provides misinformation that makes nonsense of their participation. Only with Lady Croom can he engage in a fair battle of wits; otherwise, he is the only one with a loaded weapon" (490).

Though an employee at Sidley Park, Septimus glories in his position within the hierarchical society of the estate; up until the point of his undoing after the fire, he is abundantly successful in his manipulations of that social order. Muecke stipulates, in *Irony and the Ironic*, that "irony needs 'alazony,' which is Greek for self-assurance or naivety" (4). And, as a further personification of the term: "Alazony varies widely in several respects. The alazon may be totally unreflective, or boldly confident; or he may be infinitely circumspect, seeing every trap but the one he falls into" (37). Here once again, Septimus can be understood as resembling the *alazon* as much as the *eiron*, especially to the extent that degrees of superiority and cleverness – the "only one with a loaded weapon" – blind him to the possibility of what will indeed befall him. Septimus is both the clever underdog who delights in playful dissembling and the self-congratulatory victim who cannot see what is coming. The Septimus who enchants Thomasina with his diverse charms and stores of knowledge comes to suffer, because of that association, a pitiful rather than a comedic fate, becoming in the process what no one, least of all himself, could possibly have imagined. In his relationship with Thomasina, Septimus moves from ironic (and protective) detachment toward intimacy; yet his feelings for her, and the manner of her death, are precisely what prompt his self-exile and the more radical detachment into utter solitude. Septimus's fate is in no way comical, even in light of the character's generic associations and within the larger comedic frame of *Arcadia*. His destiny is only bearable, in the comic frame, insofar as we don't witness it first hand and because the audience's final image of him is a joyous one. Still, in his embodiment of these basic characterizations of the dramatically and comedically ironic, both the *eiron* and the *alazon*, Septimus is inherently representative of personified irony in theatrical terms.

Concurrently, however, there is an important sense in which Septimus's persona and perspective are not ironic at all. He may be an arch and evasive dissembler with characters such as Ezra Chater; he may be wry and entertaining in his tutorial sessions with

Thomasina; and he may endeavor to protect her with verbal elaboration against knowing too much too soon; but when it comes to his scientific or mathematical observations he is far from oblique. Instead, he is direct with his questions and forthright concerning his own interests and what he intends for his avid pupil to learn. Contrasting Septimus with Byron, the Romantic poet of the same age (and with similarities in terms of "acuteness, social poise, bravado, and . . . sexual arrogance"), Jim Hunter underscores the way in which Stoppard's character departs from irony when it comes to matters of teaching: "Where Septimus seems also unlike Byron is his concern, strengthened by Thomasina, for knowledge and the quite unironic pursuit of scientific and mathematical truth" (186–187). Not only is Septimus a committed scientist and scholar, he believes optimistically and without equivocation, ironic or otherwise, in a principle of what is retained rather than lost to history or, as Thomasina will theorize (without using the word), to entropy.

> THOMASINA: . . . Oh, Septimus! How can we bear it? All the lost
> plays of the Athenians! Two hundred at least by Aeschylus,
> Sophocles, Euripides – thousands of poems – Aristotle's own
> library brought to Egypt by the noodle's ancestors! How can we
> sleep for grief?
> SEPTIMUS: By counting our stock. Seven plays from Aeschylus,
> seven from Sophocles, *nineteen* from Euripides, my lady! You
> should no more grieve for the rest than for a buckle lost from your
> first shoe, or for your lesson book which will be lost when you are
> old. We shed as we pick up, like travellers who must carry
> everything in their arms, and what we let fall will be picked up by
> those left behind. The procession is very long and life is very
> short. We die on the march. But there is nothing outside the
> march so nothing can be lost to it. The missing plays of Sophocles
> will turn up piece by piece, or be written again in another
> language.
>
> (38)

As noted, Muecke argues on behalf of the modern ironist's intention to be understood; yet Kierkegaard, says Jonathan Culler, "maintains that the true ironist does not wish to be understood, and though true ironists may be rare we can at least say that irony always offers the possibility of misunderstanding" (154). For Septimus, perhaps, either alternative is possible, but in his teaching, if not always in his wordplay with Thomasina, he is possessed of an unwavering and steadfastly unironic attitude of conviction.

Yet still again, this very situation is the basis for the profoundest irony of all with respect to Septimus and his relationship with Thomasina: that is, the terrible contradiction between what he believes is retained in nature and history and what, in actuality, is forever lost to him. In this context, Hunter identifies the encounter referred to above, in scene three, as having a "grim dramatic irony because Thomasina will die in a fire and Septimus will go mad trying to deal with her mathematics" (162). The contrast extends from the individual character, a "grim casualty," to the era he might stand for: "Septimus, the youthful, elegant and gifted product of the Enlightenment is transformed into a lunatic hermit ... a figure of Gothic gloom and extremity" (187). The circumstances that bring about Septimus's madness and demise are, in themselves, provocative with respect to one of *Arcadia*'s key motifs and points of argument regarding what is freely willed, what is determined, and what arises unpredictably from a complexity of co-dependent energies and systems. In her computations as well as from her insights, Thomasina intuits a version of modern chaos theory along with the second law of thermodynamics. The circumstances of her final hours, her death, and Septimus's reactions to her loss are, in differing ways, illustrations of these varied readings of nature.

In *Arcadia*'s final scene (seven), when Stoppard conjoins the two eras and characters from both historical settings share the stage, there is a brief, four-part fugue among Septimus and Thomasina, Valentine and Hannah, a succinct and poignant riff on time and thermodynamics. The sequence is a visual and choreographic coup de théâtre, with the sets of characters apart in time yet together and complementary in the room at Sidley Park. Valentine tells Hannah what Thomasina has seen: that with respect to heat, the progression will not run backwards:

> VALENTINE: She saw why. You can put back the bits of glass but you can't collect up the heat of the smash. It's gone.

SEPTIMUS: So the Improved Newtonian Universe must cease and grow cold. Dear me.

VALENTINE: The heat goes into the mix.

(*He gestures to indicate the air in the room, in the universe.*)

THOMASINA: Yes, we must hurry if we are going to dance.

VALENTINE: And everything is mixing the same way, all the time, irreversibly . . .

SEPTIMUS: Oh, we have time, I think.

VALENTINE: . . . till there's no time left. That's what time means.

SEPTIMUS: When we have found all the mysteries and lost all the meaning, we will be alone, on an empty shore.

THOMASINA: Then we will dance. Is this a waltz?

SEPTIMUS: It will serve.

(94)

The audience can see that Septimus is urbane and Valentine sunny in the face of ultimate ruin – he declares the world "still doomed" with equanimity. Still, the scene holds in it not only Thomasina's imminent death and Septimus's self-inflicted madness, but also the specter of universal death and emptiness. As Valentine has stated it earlier: "What's happening to your tea is happening to everything everywhere. The sun and the stars. It'll take a while but we're all going to end up at room temperature" (78). Later, in the four-part sequence, Valentine's cosmic "a while" is neatly juxtaposed with Septimus's wryly stated expectation that "we have time" – another sentiment that the audience must realize is sadly inaccurate. As Lucy Melbourne observes, "Septimus's phrase 'we have time' assumes doubly poignant dramatic irony with reference to Thomasina and to his own quest for knowledge" (571).

Septimus, by *Arcadia*'s end, is in love with Thomasina, just as she is with him. Together with the fierceness of the hermit's project to disprove her theory of entropy, this is the passion that so abundantly underlies his mania.[8] His adoration of Thomasina is so strongly felt, in fact, that one can imagine Septimus spending his years in solitude refuting her theory, on the grounds that he cannot imagine or abide such terminality, *or* his attempting to prove her theory's validity by way of honoring the significance of the loss that he himself contributed directly to bringing about. *Arcadia* concludes with a waltz, with Thomasina very much alive in Septimus's arms – but he has already lit the candle that she will take to her room. The conjoining of these two gestures, lighting the candle and leading Thomasina in a waltz, provides an arresting correlative for Septimus's later suffering. In John Fleming's phrasing, Thomasina's "intuition about the heat death of the universe becomes painfully and poignantly personal" (206). Thomasina will die by fire, and ironies redouble in the knowledge that she once drew a picture of Septimus in Richard Noakes's empty hermitage, by way of supplying life and habitation for the structure.[9] As the action of the play advances, and as the setting in the past moves from 1809 to 1812, the question of who tutors whom, between Septimus and Thomasina, becomes increasingly subjective. What is certain, however, is that the mechanisms of their varied inquiries and beliefs bring about a profoundly ironic reversal: Septimus becomes the victim of exactly what he has professed, and is placed in such a position, unwittingly, at the hands of his well-meaning student.

Both of Thomasina's major insights, regarding the second law of thermodynamics and nonlinear dynamics, come to defeat what Septimus would defend. As Prapassaree and Jeffrey Kramer suggest, "it is the discoveries pioneered by Septimus's pupil which destroy the foundations of Septimus's faith. The laws of thermodynamics tell us that the world and the human race are no more immortal than we are as individuals, and the discoveries of chaos theory tell us that the existence of Sophocles was dependent on so many circumstances of such minute precision that there is essentially no possibility of ever reproducing him or his works, even in an everlasting world" (8). And further: "A darker irony follows: when Thomasina deprives Septimus of a foundation for his faith that all loss is ultimately an illusion, she also apparently deprives him of the resources needed to mentally survive his greatest loss, that of Thomasina herself" (8). It is an especial irony, of course, that Septimus is presented with the opportunity to save himself from madness if not from disenchantment. Just before their last waltz, Thomasina asks Septimus to her room, providing yet another occasion in this play for Stoppard to underscore and test out the parameters of free will:

THOMASINA: I will wait for you to come.
SEPTIMUS: I cannot.
THOMASINA: You may.
SEPTIMUS: I may not.
THOMASINA: You must.
SEPTIMUS: I will not.

$$(96)^{10}$$

Had Septimus acquiesced, and accompanied his cherished student to her quarters, she would likely have escaped her fate and thereby precluded the destiny that Hannah Jarvis struggles to decipher nearly 200 years later. As it stands, however, Septimus is left vulnerable to what Hunter calls a "bitter ironic remorse for having acted so honourably on that final night" (181).

Septimus embodies, along with the contradictory aspects of his two incarnations, a clash of intellect and insanity, genius and derangement. As such, he uniquely personifies Stoppard's exploration, in *Arcadia*, of contrasting modes of formality versus disorder, of rational thought versus emotion, of classicism and Romanticism. Of course, the way in which the landscape at Sidley Park has been altered in accord with the tastes of different eras also represents these contrasts, with particular attention to what constitutes order as opposed to what is natural or "picturesque." The fact that Septimus, the loquacious and classically trained scholar, ends up demented in the garden, is exactly illustrative of these shifting and opposing strains in the play. It is early in the action when Hannah Jarvis brings attention to precisely what Septimus might stand for, calling him the "perfect symbol."

BERNARD: Oh, yes. Of what?
HANNAH: The whole Romantic sham, Bernard! It's what happened to the Enlightenment, isn't it? A century of intellectual rigour turned in on itself. A mind in chaos suspected of genius.

$$(27)$$

In fact, what Hannah refers to as a "decline from thinking to feeling" is, with regard to Septimus, a multifaceted proposition, pertaining not least of all to his "Romantic" qualities as well as his more classical associations. Here again, Septimus is not only contradictory as an individual figure but stands also for oppositions that, cumulatively, *Arcadia* explores and emphasizes through reiteration. In relation to Thomasina, Septimus begins the play at a respectable intellectual remove, appropriate to his status as tutor and necessary for his survival at Sidley Park. By the play's end, he is on much more intimate terms with her, emotionally and physically, and she dances in his arms even as she unknowingly insures his destiny. "It was Septimus Hodge," writes Paul Edwards, "who begins the play as a 'classical' optimist, blithe, witty, and apparently completely imperturbable." In utter contrast stands the "scribbling" Septimus we can picture only through the same evidence that Hannah discovers. As Edwards puts it, "His 'madness' consists in spending twenty-two years reiterating Thomasina's equations after her death, desperate to overturn this pessimistic conviction through restoring pattern and the promise of life in the ocean of ashes. This is 'mad' because it can only be done through a computer; the classical Septimus has become his opposite, a full-blooded Romantic" (182).[11]

In fact, the "Romantic" associations of Septimus Hodge are critical in both the historical and philosophical dialectics of *Arcadia*, not only because of their relation to the period of Byron, or their contrasts with classical or postmodern orders or disorders, but in their specific relations to irony. "Romantic" irony is, first of all, a singular category among ironic modes; and second, there is a natural association between Romantic irony and the drama, particularly so in relation to plays with a metatheatrical aspect. Muecke points to Stoppard (and, in particular, *Rosencrantz and Guildenstern are Dead*) and Pirandello along with Shakespeare and also Sheridan in this context. Whereas self-reflexive plays such as *Rosencrantz and Guildenstern*, *Six Characters in Search of an Author*, or Sheridan's *The Critic* call deliberate attention to their theatrical identities through reference to other dramatic works (such as *Hamlet*) or to the theatre itself (as in showing a play in rehearsal, as occurs in both Pirandello and Sheridan), *Arcadia* does so through performative behaviors, tacit references to established comedic genres, and the device of the split time frame that implicitly involves the contemporary

audience as observers that are made conscious of a theatrical convention. "The irony involved in these plays that draw attention, explicitly
or implicitly, to their status as a play, to their illusory nature, is
Romantic irony," writes Muecke in *Irony and the Ironic*. "In
Romantic irony the inherent limitation of art, the inability of a work
of art, as something created, fully to capture and represent the complex
and dynamic creativity of life is itself imaginatively raised to consciousness by being given thematic recognition" (73). Here especially,
it is the doubling of historical settings in *Arcadia* that provides, among
other perspectives, the Romantic aspect (including, of course, the fact
that one of the two eras is the age of Romanticism). Further, the play's
metatheatrical quality serves not so much as a critique of the art's
limitations but, analogously, an accentuation of the thematic motif
of the characters' struggles – through their lessons, theories, and
research projects – to fully or accurately "capture and represent the
complex and dynamic creativity of life." Stoppard's focus is sustained,
in *Arcadia*, on questions that the play treats multidimensionally,
including as it does so a steady contemplation of human interactions
set in relation to processes in nature, to theories of nonlinear dynamics
and determinism, and to varied mathematical representations of the
workings of the cosmos.

What Hannah Jarvis refers to as "the whole Romantic sham," or
the "decline from thinking to feeling," comes across in the larger
dialectic of *Arcadia* as simply a characterization of one mode – existing
in company and comparison with others – of being and of conceiving
the modes and manifestations of nature. In this relation, the play is
concerned profoundly with the dynamics of natural flux, the extent to
which such can be determined, and the situations of the depicted
persons within a cosmic system. In this way primarily, the specifically
ontological connotations of Romantic irony can be related directly to
the action and to the philosophical dialectics of this play. Claire
Colebrook notes that, "Romantic irony, broadly defined, regards
irony as something like a human condition or predicament." For her,
such irony is characterized by "anti-humanism," to the extent that
human nature lacks fixity: "It is precisely because we are human and
capable of speaking, creating and engaging with others that human life

has no fixed nature; any definition it gives of itself will only be one more creation, which can never exhaust the infinite possibilities for future creation" (48). So too, in the doubled historical frames of *Arcadia*, do events and character behaviors alike arise from flux rather than fixity. If the play's science predicts – and cheerfully so, through Valentine and Thomasina – that cosmic change ultimately spells universal coldness and doom, the attitudes of Septimus are much more closely aligned with a cosmos of perpetual rejuvenation. Romantic irony is transcendental and yet immediate; its stipulations are not only literary but also pragmatic and existential. As Colebrook points out, this variety of irony is not understood solely as a literary device, but rather with an understanding that "all life is ironic or subject to the conditions of trope and metaphor" (51). Along these lines, irony of the Romantic sort can be seen as having a particular alliance with drama and theatrical representation, particularly so as "a style of existence rather than a rhetorical figure" and, as for the German Romantics, "the only true mode of life" (Colebrook 52).

The "cosmos" of *Arcadia* is, in one sense, suggested by the omniscient view that is afforded the contemporary audience of the two time periods, one recent and the other removed by some 200 years. At the same time, there are linkages between the eras that provide a unifying effect – the Coverly ancestry itself, the manor house at Sidley Park, the tortoises and the various props – and in doing so suggest an order or a pattern to events. In this connection, Susanne Vees-Gulani borrows a term from chaos theory and identifies certain of the play's analogous and connective motifs and clusters of reference as "strange attractors," here also with a unifying aspect. "Apart from the similarities around strange attractors, Stoppard adds many more connections between the past and the present. Together they result in a close-knit set of relations brought on the stage in *Arcadia* which then, despite covering three different time spheres, still appears as a unit" (419). The play's cosmic aspect applies, in this way, to what is sensical as well as what is universalized. The characters in the present day struggle to make sense of the past, even as persons in both eras endeavor to make sense of nature. In a play that centers so directly on matters of determinism, nonlinear dynamics, time, and, as Thomasina would say, a mathematical "formula for all the future," a cosmic element becomes intrinsic. In *Arcadia*, less attention may be paid to the falling sparrow than to the configuration of an apple leaf, yet from so fine a microcosm as that, the play can draw universal analogies.

A cosmic dimension of irony, as considered here in relation to Ibsen and Chekhov in particular, relates also to an element of apparent meaningfulness, sense, appropriateness, or fateful quality in addition to an implied universality. The cosmic irony of *Arcadia*, however, is quite pointedly concerned with the way in which lives are lived by comparison with the systems that govern, however understandably, that living process. In this instance, yet again, Septimus can be seen as the exemplar of cruel yet cosmic ironic twists: the universe turns out, after all, not to behave as he thought, and the death of the young woman he esteems, representing as it does the very kind of loss he suspected of not being permanent, drives him to self-exile. As Colebrook indicates with respect to this type of situation, "the word irony refers to the limits of human meaning; we do not see the effects of what we do, the outcomes of our actions, or the forces that exceed our choices. Such irony is cosmic irony, or the irony of fate" (14) – a definition that, even with its inclusive generality, can relate more specifically to the unforeseen destiny of Septimus Hodge. Chaos, determinism, and thermodynamics are cosmic propositions, to be sure, yet cosmic irony is what, in *Arcadia*, lends the sciences that connote a universality their immediate dramatic impression, particularly through the linked fates of Septimus and Thomasina Coverly.[12] To the extent that *Arcadia* enacts and uses chaos theory as an image for, in Michael Vanden Heuvel's phrase, a "strange dance of order and disorder" (225), Septimus as tutor and as hermit becomes the analog and personification of both.

Science and mathematics in *Arcadia* are broadly concerned with the nature of pattern formation. On the one hand, there is puzzling on the part of the characters, especially those in the present circumstances, about what constitutes a readable pattern. And here again, Stoppard's audience is allowed a special perspective, placed in the omniscient position of seeing where and how certain patterns form or have application over time, a view that is mostly denied to the characters – that is, to those who inhabit the play's individual eras only. At the same time, the play organizes its inquiries concerning pattern formation around a set of discernible polarities – and once again Septimus Hodge is the figure who most centrally embodies and enacts the drama's principles of opposition. In this respect, *Arcadia* is concerned with more than its past/present or classical/Romantic relations, the contrast of benevolent tutor and solitary hermit, or the contradiction of Septimus as passionate intellectual and as madman.

> HANNAH: The hermit was placed in the landscape exactly as one might place a pottery gnome. And there he lived out his life as a garden ornament.
>
> BERNARD: Did he do anything?
>
> HANNAH: Oh, he was very busy. When he died, the cottage was stacked solid with paper. Hundreds of pages. Thousands. Peacock says he was suspected of genius. It turned out, of course, he was off his head.
>
> (27)

Indeed, within the overall frame of action, Stoppard juxtaposes the genius of Thomasina or of Septimus, not only with the latter's mental breakdown but with the foolishness or inanity of other characters. The resulting pattern in the action is thus characterized by inspired insight in direct relation to its dialectical partners, foolishness or obliviousness. The contrast between Septimus and Chater that initiates the action is mirrored and reiterated several times over, primarily through the contemporary and hapless figure of Bernard Nightingale, who is determined yet utterly wrongheaded in believing that he has discovered literary secrets concerning Lord Byron. And, as a ready analog for its genius/foolishness appositions, *Arcadia* also emphasizes a fast versus slow alternation, exemplified in large measure by the same characters (Septimus and Chater / Valentine and Bernard), but also represented by the key comparison between Thomasina's pencil and Valentine's computer – and succinctly, of course, by Valentine's inert tortoise whose name is "Lightning." The larger patterns that take shape in *Arcadia* are rarely readable by the characters on stage (that is, in the immediate historical moment) and what is ostensibly simple

in the play's interactions can actually be complex or even inscrutable –
and vice versa. As Vees-Gulani notes, *Arcadia* depicts "a world where
the utmost simplicity can nevertheless become too complex for us
fully to comprehend or control" (422), an observation that can apply
equally to characters, events, and natural phenomena.

The interplay of past and present accentuates these other, corresponding oppositions, and the resulting totality of contrasts contributes strongly, along with Thomasina's apple leaf and "Geometry of
Irregular Forms," to the drama's more extensive formation or intima-
tion of patterns, whether decipherable or not. The Romantic ideal of
"genius," as localized in the inspired artist or more generally as an
inspiration in nature (celebrated, say, in the garden at Sidley Park), is
both exalted and questioned in *Arcadia*. The genius of insight or curiosity on the part of one character, most notably Thomasina, is continually undercut by equally misguided ideas and actions – as, pointedly,
when Thomasina brings about her own death by fire. In this regard,
perhaps, Thomasina's fate is engendered more by pattern formation on
the part of the dramatist than by natural circumstances or traits of
character. Thomasina must perish, in Stoppard's equation and within
the cosmos of *Arcadia*, in order that she can enact her own theory
and at the same time send her tutor to the hermitage that she herself
has unwittingly made his destiny, through her art as well as in action.
To this extent at least, Thomasina's death is no more logical or organic
an outcome than that of Marguerite Gautier, in *La Dame aux Camélias*,
another heroine who, along with the analogous figure of Olympe Taverny
(*Olympe's Marriage*), dies for thematics. Even while focusing on natural
processes, in fact, *Arcadia* can seem at times to be confected around its
own aesthetic behaviors and points of historical or scientific reference.
Septimus, too, as Hannah's "idiot in the landscape" (66), is consigned to
insanity as much by an aesthetic demand for a correlative pattern in the
action as by his own traits or ostensible future.

Arcadia's patterns of scientific or aesthetic referentiality, taken
together with those arising from historical alternation or opposition,
relate the play most directly to a postmodern sensibility and, by association, to postmodern irony. Whereas Stoppard has, in other works
(including *Travesties*), been given more to what Linda Hutcheon calls

"ironic intertextuality" (40), *Arcadia* also exhibits a notable range of postmodernist tendencies.[13] In particular, the double time frame accentuates particular manners and means by which the past is accessed and regarded. The master irony associated with the play's two time frames exists primarily, as noted, in the discrepant understandings, on the part of characters in the present, with regard to those in the early nineteenth century. In addition to the characters' behaviors and points of view, however, *Arcadia* also proposes, tacitly and explicitly, particular ways of viewing and understanding the earlier setting and events. The history of Sidley Park is not romanticized, despite its Romantic associations; on the contrary, the estate is seen from several perspectives in relation to natural processes as well as changes in fashion. In this connection, Hutcheon emphasizes a contrast between "nostalgic return" and "critical revisiting" as well as the postmodern tendency toward "an ironic dialogue with the past" (4). Indeed, the past is ironized in *Arcadia* through a "critical reworking" – as Hutcheon might say (4) – that proceeds largely from the play's sustained dissonance between what Hannah, Bernard, and Valentine seek and what the audience can see for themselves with respect to Septimus, Thomasina, and Chater among others. The historical debate between classical and Romantic thought and aesthetics, coupled with scientific and mathematical theories of order and randomness, are brought into direct relation with contemporary equipment, methods, and sensibilities, but never nostalgically (even given the pathos of Thomasina's death and Septimus's future). Rather, the past is presented as a source of referentiality, or quotation, even as it is enacted in one time frame on its own immediate terms. The historical warp between eras is attributed directly by Stoppard to the subjectivity of human perception per se as well as the capricious quality of how objects (such as the "Couch of Eros" or Thomasina's notebooks and drawings) traverse one age into another. Hutcheon calls attention to "postmodernism's orientation toward the 'presence of the past,'" and characterizes its aims in this regard:

> ... to make us look at the past from the acknowledged distance of the present, a distance which inevitably conditions our ability to

know that past. The ironies produced by that distancing are what
prevent the postmodern from being nostalgic: there is no desire to
return to the past as a time of simpler or more worthy values.
These ironies also prevent antiquarianism: there is no value to
the past in and of itself. It is the conjunction of the present and the
past that is intended to make us question – analyze, try to
understand – both how we make and make sense of our culture.

(230)

By contrast, Colebrook identifies irony with the "huge problems of
postmodernity," arguing, with respect to the contemporary historical
context, that "all we can do now is quote and dissimulate. But even in a
world of postmodern irony, the very sense that everything is somehow
quoted or simulated relies on a lost sense of the truly valuable or
original" (1–3). At the same time, though, and while Stoppard certainly
quotes and dissimulates with respect to the relation of present to past,
Arcadia is more typically dispassionate with regard to the particular
and comparative values in one epoch as against another. In spite of the
charm and ingratiating wittiness that Septimus and Thomasina share,
not to mention the convivial atmosphere and buoyant behaviors
among the earlier Coverlys, Stoppard is not out to portray his past as
innately more appealing than his present. Neither era is entirely privileged over the other, in spite of Valentine's ironic observation concerning his own day: "It's the best possible time to be alive, when
almost everything you thought you knew is wrong" (48).

Regarding irony's connection with, and reflection of, postmodernity, Colebrook presents contrasting opinions. Pointing out that
"many have argued that our entire epoch, as postmodern, is ironic"
(18), she offers also that "one way to understand postmodernity is to see
it as a radical rejection or redefinition of irony."

> If irony demands some idea or point of view above language,
> contexts or received voices, postmodernity acknowledges that all
> we have are competing contexts and that any implied "other"
> position would itself be a context. Postmodernity would be a
> society of simulation and immanence with no privileged point
> from which competing voices could be judged. One would have to

accept one's own position as one among others, and as thoroughly unoriginal. One could be ironic, not by breaking with contexts but in recognizing any voice as an effect of context, and then allowing contexts to generate as much conflict, collision and contradiction as possible, thereby precluding any fixity or meta-position.

And yet: "Alternatively, one could see postmodernity as the impossibility of overcoming irony. Any attempt to reduce the world to discourses, contexts, language-games, or relative points of view would itself generate a point of view of recognition" (164–165).[14]

Irony in its postmodern iteration is, on terms such as these, predictably antithetical, yet its presences in *Arcadia* can be understood as aiding Stoppard's project nonetheless. The historical frames of his play offer, in large measure, a skewed vision of events and personalities; the Septimus Hodge that is described by Hannah seems utterly unlike the Septimus that the audience comes to know in alternating sequences. Septimus becomes, in the garden historian's view, more "quotation" – of Romanticism, "Gothic gloom," hermetic gnome – than the energetic figure with both a flair for witty alliteration ("perpendicular poke") and deeply held values concerning the pursuit and constancy of knowledge. The contrast, for *Arcadia*'s audience, is illuminating, especially with ironic reference to how lacking in accuracy "quotation" can be. The Septimus known to the audience is, in his own present-day context, more likely to be found in the estate's gazebo, and in good company, than in an unimaginable hermitage buried in paper and equations. The contexts and discourses of *Arcadia*, varied and wide-ranging as they are, center nevertheless around an eddy of order and disorder, as patterns form and disappear, only to emerge and become apparent again. The play concludes (in a forward projection of time) in madness and death; yet on stage and in the audience's (and characters') present moment it concludes, as comedies traditionally do, in a dance, with Septimus and Thomasina embracing in a waltz. In this regard anyway, the play's point of view, like Thomasina's, is "Oh, phooey to Death" (13). *Arcadia*'s intentions are, along these lines at least, as much concerned with unification as with postmodern disassociation. Vanden Heuvel arbitrates effectively for Stoppard's "compromise formation" with postmodernism, with *Arcadia* as a prime exemplar of that negotiation: "While maintaining faith in the postmodern slippages and flux of language, signs, history, identities, and interpretations, Stoppard nevertheless insists that when structure and stability emerge, attention must be paid" (227).[15]

Above all, perhaps, *Arcadia* stands for a particular sort of intimacy among irony, dramaturgy, and theatrical performance, and to this extent Stoppard's play is indeed a "first class" celebration of ironic modes and their myriad means of interplay. The author is predisposed not only to paradox, tautology, and Wildean wryness but also to the dramatic juxtapositions and appositions that often go hand in glove with irony. In his own words: "I write plays because dialogue is the most respectable way of contradicting myself" (Tynan 44). In addition, it is always theatrical dialogue itself that provides the latent field for ironic speech and interaction. "All speech is haunted by irony," says Colebrook, an observation that also points to factors of ironic opposition. For her, "insofar as speaking creates some event of decision, force and difference, or makes a claim about what is other than itself, it must refer to what is not itself. One can only make a statement about the world, or really say something, if one recognizes the force of contradiction" (165). In this regard, even Stoppard's titular reference, with its double entendre, contains the ironic tension of what is and is not. "Et in Arcadia ego" is a dichotomy, and one that applies immediately and personally to the figure of Septimus Hodge. It is Septimus who counters Lady Croom's assertion ("Here I am in Arcadia") with his own reading, which turns out to be a prophecy concerning death's presence: "Even in Arcadia, there am I" (13).

Arcadia contains multiple instances of conventional dramatic irony, if only because of its many levels of discrepancy regarding what is known and not known to the characters at given times and in the different eras.[16] Yet also, and in its abundance of ironic expressiveness – dramatic and situational, cosmic, Romantic, and postmodern – the play is illustrative of just how closely related the modes of irony are to fundamentals of dramaturgy and theatre aesthetics in addition to dramatic speech per se. The first scene of *Arcadia* concludes with a sequence that, as a microcosm of ironic drama, contains portents for a goodly part of the play's later development:

THOMASINA: Oh, phooey to Death!
(She dips a pen and takes it to the reading stand.)
I will put in a hermit, for what is a hermitage without a hermit?
Are you in love with my mother, Septimus?
SEPTIMUS: You must not be cleverer than your elders. It is not polite.
THOMASINA: Am I cleverer?
SEPTIMUS: Yes. Much.
THOMASINA: Well, I am sorry, Septimus. *(She pauses in her drawing and produces a small envelope from her pocket.)* Mrs. Chater came to the music room with a note for you. She said it was of scant importance, and that therefore I should carry it to you with the utmost safety, urgency, and discretion. Does carnal embrace addle the brain?
SEPTIMUS: *(Taking the letter)* Invariably. Thank you. That is enough education for today.
THOMASINA: There. I have made him like the Baptist in the wilderness.
SEPTIMUS: How picturesque.

(13–14)

"Even a brief ironical remark," notes Muecke, "in being both a challenge and a response, is drama in miniature with both peripeteia and anagnorisis, both reversal in the addressee's understanding and recognition of the ironist's real intent. Moreover, in being ironical, the ironist can be seen as putting on a one-man show: he assumes his role of naif and speaks, writes, or behaves as if he really were the sort of person who might hold the views the irony is intent on destroying or subverting" (*Ironic* 68). In the sequence above, as elsewhere in *Arcadia*, Septimus is, in one sense, a dissembler in the process of staging a "one man show"; at the same time, though, he is in discourse with, and tutoring, a student who is absorbing lessons in irony as well as literature and mathematics – as evidenced by her sly reference to "scant importance" as well as to the effects of "carnal embrace." The vignette's "drama in miniature" points not only to the present and future relationship between the two, but to Septimus's ironic fate in its full perspective. Over the total course of *Arcadia*'s action, Septimus comes to embody a profound ironic peripety; the corresponding anagnorisis, however, is felt not as an abrupt recognition but as a progression on the part of Septimus the "picturesque" hermit in the direction of a cosmic (and dooming) mathematical truth. The sheer scope of Septimus's reversal and implicit discoveries or quandaries, with the many strands of determinism and accident that are contributory, underscore the ways in which *Arcadia* is built upon a foundation and a latticework of ironies, a characteristic that ties the play fundamentally to theatrical process itself. Drama is at least "typically ironic," says Muecke in *Irony and the Ironic*, "and perhaps essentially ironigenic, that is, productive of irony" (71). The ironist, for his or her part, can be resigned, albeit learnedly so, even while keeping the one (or two) person show steadfastly in progress: "Irony," Muecke concludes, "may be not merely the natural or merely the best way but perhaps the only way to deal with life" (*Ironic* 235). The Septimus who is observed by *Arcadia*'s audience embodies this very attitude; it is the unseen Septimus who, ironically, loses that perspective.

7 American ironies: Wasserstein and Kushner

In Eugene O'Neill's *Beyond the Horizon* (1920), an ostensibly simple ironic turn of events provokes a chain of circumstances that becomes tragic in magnitude and inclusiveness. Two brothers, Robert and Andrew Mayo, are all set to pursue what appear to be their respective natural directions in life, Rob to go to sea in search of the play's titular promise, Andrew to stay home and work the farm, following his father James's lead and fond desire. Yet the love of each brother for one young woman, Ruth Atkins, causes an abrupt reversal in these destinies, and Rob, who is utterly unsuited to working the land, stays behind to marry Ruth and be a farmer while Andy takes his brother's place on the sea voyage. Ruth, as it turns out, is uncertain and inconsistent in her feelings for the brothers, and so their respective decisions in relation to her appear increasingly and, as it turns out, tragically unfounded as the play's action advances.

The ironic aspects of the play's initiating situation, when aligned with the extremity of their effects upon Rob in particular, not only prompt but also sustain the tragic momentum and overall trajectory of action. O'Neill emphasizes the ties of the Mayo family to nature, the farm and the land, as well as the innate, or "natural," aspects of the brothers' original intentions. Once these fundamental courses are reversed, though, there is no help for the situation and no way to set things right. Even when it appears that Andy, who enjoys business success during his travels, will be home in time to assist Rob and Ruth and in all likelihood rescue the farm, he is called away for a business opportunity that cannot be resisted. The spectrum of ironies in *Beyond the Horizon* is broad, indeed. Andy prospers even while disliking the foreign lands where he travels; Rob, who once dreamed of the chance to discover such locales for himself, sickens and endures a steadily worsening poverty and misery, including the death of his cherished daughter, Mary. He is too prideful to ask for the sort of assistance that his brother would have offered immediately, had Andy but realized the awfulness of his brother's plight. The brothers love one another deeply, yet still contribute directly if unintentionally to one another's suffering. The desperate situation in which Rob and Ruth find themselves is attributed to bad luck among other failings, yet it is good fortune for Andy that worsens their situation. Many missed chances, and a malign factor in the timing of events generally, contribute to the play's ironic turnabouts and to the consistent deterioration of Rob and Ruth's circumstances.

O'Neill is characteristically unsubtle in this early play, and the emotional pitch of its interactions tends toward the florid, with a style of expressiveness that at times can seem overwrought. Still, and beginning precisely with the reversed destinies of the Mayo brothers, the playwright succeeds in dramatizing a chain of occurrences that, with its peculiarly intrinsic qualities, has an ancestry in the enduring motifs of tragedy. When Andy determines early on that because of Rob and Ruth's feelings for one another he must leave the farm for the sea, thus abandoning the Mayo tradition for that of the Scotts (the mother's side of the family), the intensity of James Mayo's rage is such that Andy is denied by his father and disowned. Questioning his brother's decision, Rob protests that the "whole affair is so senseless – and tragic" (39). In fact, a particular combination of sense (the logic of the developing circumstances) and what appears to make no sense at all contributes strongly to the play's inherently tragic aspect. In this context, a powerful irony is evident in the apposition of how catastrophic (and "senseless") the events become, but at the same time how they arise naturally, even inevitably, within the star-crossed circumstances. Rob's deepening misfortune is variously attributed, together with his lack of farming skills, to "bad luck" as well as to divine punishment, but O'Neill fashions his tragedy primarily from an initial turn of fate that, in its full range of built-in implications, stands for an irreparable disruption of the natural order.

O'Neill's vision in *Beyond the Horizon* is widely embracing in aspiration and scope. The play is relentless in examining the characters' suffering and in probing what, if any, remedy can be located in circumstances that appear so dire and also unchangeable. O'Neill is painstaking in his dramatization of Rob Mayo's absolution, as well as complicity, with respect to what befalls him and his family. The causes of the Mayo family tragedy, a complex interweaving of immediate conditions and qualities of character, are played out in an arena of philosophical and religious inquiry that includes an opposition of the atheistical James Mayo and the faith of Sarah Atkins, Ruth's mother. With reference to the play's affinities with the ancestral heritage of tragedy, Joseph Wood Krutch commented, six years after its initial production: "Divesting himself of every trace of faith in the permanent value of love and presenting it as merely one of the subtlest of those traps by which Nature snares Man, O'Neill turns a play which might have been merely ironic into an indictment not only of chance or fate but of that whole universe which sets itself up against man's desires and conquers them" (Gelb 412–413).[1] In truth, the ironic aspect in *Beyond the Horizon* is linked inextricably with the ways in which chance and timing play out in this drama, with how the relationships and attitudes develop and alter among Rob, Ruth, and Andy over time, and, ultimately, with the intrinsic mechanisms and outcomes of an unstoppable tragic action.

Arthur Miller's *A View from the Bridge* (1955) is another American play in which the action is aligned consciously with the ancestry of tragic dramaturgy. Eddie Carbone is a Brooklyn longshoreman who, despite the admonitions of his wife Beatrice and lawyer Alfieri, continues on a disastrous course that arises from his refusal to acknowledge the nature of his feelings for his young niece, Catherine. The core irony in Miller's play results not from a crossing of character destinies, as in *Beyond the Horizon*, but rather from something closely akin to what Aristotle refers to in the *Poetics* as hamartia, in this instance a blindness to the truth of circumstances.[2] Hamartia is, in fact, a naturally ironic component of tragic drama, and one that corresponds directly to the more familiar dramatic and Sophoclean types of irony. That is, a character's unawareness of his or her mistake or frailty is nonetheless recognized by the audience, who also can perceive the potential for catastrophe. Hamartia is not, of course, a term ordinarily associated with modern stage characters, but Miller himself provides the context for such an association through his choral figure, the lawyer Alfieri, and from the clear references in the play to ancient tragedy. As Eddie makes his first entrance, Alfieri says that, "every few years there is still a case, and as the parties tell me what the trouble is, the flat air in my office suddenly washes in with the green scent of the sea, the dust in this air is blown away and the thought comes that in some Caesar's year, in Calabria perhaps or on the cliff at Syracuse, another lawyer, quite differently dressed, heard the same complaint and sat there as powerless as I, and watched it run its bloody course" (5).

Early in the play it becomes clear that Eddie has, as Alfieri says, "a destiny" (29). While Alfieri does the best he can to spell out the situation – "there is too much love for the daughter, there is too much love for the niece" (45) – Eddie won't hear. Indeed, he is unable to hear. He will never, no matter the provocation, recognize his own emotional complicity in the situation. The ironic disparities among what Alfieri and Beatrice can see, what Catherine comes to realize, and what Eddie cannot admit are finally what prompt the play's catastrophic end. Eddie, believing that he is doing all that he can to protect Catherine from the attentions of Rodolpho, one of the undocumented Italian immigrants the neighborhood is sheltering, turns him and his brother Marco in to immigration authorities. A personal as well as social code is thereby violated, and even though Alfieri warns Marco against retaliation – "Only God makes justice" (80) – the destiny that Alfieri prophesied is now assured. Eddie shouts his refutation of Marco's accusations publicly to the neighborhood residents, and demands that Marco set things right – "I want my name, Marco. Now gimme my name and we go together to the wedding" (84) – but when Eddie draws a knife, Marco grabs Eddie's arm and with his own strength turns the blade back into him. Eddie dies in Beatrice's arms as Alfieri, again in the role of tragic chorus, pays final homage to a man who "allowed himself to be wholly known" (86). Again, the ironic component in Eddie Carbone's tragedy is based in hamartia, and even at the play's end, even when Beatrice screams that he cannot have what he truly desires, Eddie refuses to be understood that way: "That's what you think of me – that I would have such a thought?" (84). While hamartia is, from one perspective, the counterpart of anagnorisis, Eddie's blindness is so severe that even his own passion can never be recognized and certainly not admitted.[3]

The historical connection of irony to tragedy is, of course, far from unusual. In fact, the ironic mode has been fundamental in tragic drama in ways that date to ancient drama's relations of a character's personal stature and qualities with external circumstances – at times to a cosmic realm typically associated with deities or with supersensory impressions more generally. Within the historical cosmos of tragedy, or in the collective lexicon of what is called the tragic vision, irony is typically associated with dramatic characters in relation to the powers that be or with the particular way in which events progress – that is, with fate, destiny, fortune, or operation of chance that may pertain to the aleatory yet also to an enigmatic guiding principle. Irony may reside in a hamartia/anagnorisis relation, as in *A View from the Bridge*, or, as in the case of *Beyond the Horizon*, in the connection of what may be "senseless and tragic" yet, from another perspective, be utterly logical in the circumstances.

Tragic irony is, however, not typically the American style. Despite the notable exceptions of O'Neill and Miller, the use of irony for an authentically tragic purpose is rare in the American theatre. O'Neill employs it elsewhere to magnificent effect, most searingly in *Long Day's Journey into Night*, where the Tyrone family spends the entire four acts of the drama acting out a deeply ironic and ever-worsening double bind: the more they endeavor to hide their anguish in whiskey (James, Edmund, Jamie) or morphine (Mary), the more the truth of their past betrayals, guilts, and recriminations emerges. The Tyrones yearn for unconsciousness, yet awareness prevails – and does so at their own unintentional insistence. For Miller, Eddie Carbone is a figure of modern tragedy in ways relatable to the playwright's other "common" men, Willy Loman and Joe Keller. However, the ancestrally tragic aspects of these plays are unusual indeed. Even Tennessee Williams, arguably the playwright closest in sensibility and vision – as well as renown – to O'Neill and Miller, does not rely on irony to particularly tragic ends. This is not to say that Williams's heroines are not portrayed under fiercely ironized personal circumstances. Maggie ("the Cat") Pollitt is a vital and passionate woman married to a man who pays her no romantic mind; Blanche DuBois fancies her precious refinements in the context of scarcely controllable lusts; Amanda Wingfield means well and drives her children crazy; Alma Winemiller's "doppelganger" stands for the modesty of a preacher's daughter knotted with desire for the doctor who may understand anatomy but knows little of delicate hearts. Yet still, and despite the regretful circumstances that may attend these women at their respective final curtains, Williams is not fundamentally a writer of tragic drama, and his ironic configurations, while potent in relation to individual figures, are not tragic in the ways that Miller's and O'Neill's are.[4]

From the ancestral perspective, the debt of O'Neill and Miller to European dramatists, and especially the modernist tradition in tragic drama, is widely known. O'Neill's portrait of Ruth Atkins, including her effect upon the Mayo brothers, the marriage to Rob, and the reversal of events in *Beyond the Horizon*, owes in part to the playwright's reading of August Strindberg.[5] Miller wrote his own adaptation of *An Enemy of the People*, and the influence of Henrik Ibsen upon his dramaturgy, including structural and stylistic elements along with the tragic influence per se, is pronounced. With respect to the connection of the ironic and the tragic modes, these affinities are critical, particularly in distinguishing a European ancestry from an American sensibility but also in defining some key differences in the dramaturgy of O'Neill and Miller by comparison with most other American dramatists. In the sphere of tragedy, the ironic factor often contributes powerfully to an impression of magnitude, cosmos, and philosophical implication, primarily through representations of destiny and fatality, sense versus no-sense, awareness and blindness, a dialectic of what is unintended yet intrinsic. Factors such as these, which have been vital in tragedy's composition and vision over centuries, have not been reflective lately of an American self-image or philosophy, perhaps especially in relation to a collective or societal view of what life's potentials ought to be. By contrast, there is a generalized resistance in the American psyche to the notion that destiny is inherited or dictated from past circumstances, that personal fallibility can be enduring as well as catastrophic, that elaborate social structures and codes mask a latent chaos or senselessness, that doom can be simply in the cards as well as in one's own personal makeup.

Irony endures, however, with a presence that is in fact quite marked in the American theatre, albeit in a non-tragic and possibly more diluted state. Apart from the rarity of the tragic mode per se, the potential scope of irony has been constrained in recent American drama, in part by an increased emphasis on cultural referentiality. Also, the fact that contemporary cultural trends elapse quickly can have the effect of underscoring what is ephemeral, often with a resulting sacrifice of resonance, depth of implication, or magnitude. Indeed, today's culturally reflective irony is often dependent upon the transient aspect, and frequently it is the ephemeral aspect that provides its basis. Contemporary irony is, in the theatre, fundamentally comparative as opposed to existential; and in cases when superficiality results, that too is part of the ironic commentary. Two American plays, Wendy Wasserstein's *The Heidi Chronicles* and Tony Kushner's *Angels in America Part I: Millennium Approaches*, are exemplary of a non-tragic yet seriously intentioned employment of irony in the contexts of cultural and historical referentiality. As such, they provide useful contemporary markers of irony's potentials, and of its scope and resonance when examined apart from the dialectical, tragic, and postmodern modes per se.

The Heidi Chronicles

Heidi Holland is a professor of art history at Columbia University, with a specialization in women painters such as Italian Mannerist Sofonisba Anguissola (c. 1532–1625), the subject of a lecture which, with illustrative slides, opens the play. As a relatively subtle irony, Wasserstein initiates the action on the topic of a historically authentic Renaissance woman, introduced here by a woman with her own catholic proclivities. Less subtle are the ways in which Professor Holland proclaims herself an ironist, first with reference to Sofonisba: "There is no trace of her, or any other woman artist prior to the twentieth century, in your current art history textbook. Of course, in my day this same standard text mentioned no women 'from the dawn of history to the present.' Are you with me? Okay" (160). Then, with reference to one of her slides: "This portrait can be perceived as a meditation on the brevity of youth, beauty, and life. But what can't?" (161). Her commentary provides wittiness and personality in combination with historical allusion; it also introduces the speaker's own past ("in my day") and, correspondingly, the aspect of time set in ratio to one's awareness and appreciation of it.

From this perspective, a series of flashback scenes begins, beginning with a high school dance in 1965, when Heidi is sixteen.

The characters of Peter Patrone, whom Heidi meets at the dance, and Scoop Rosenbaum, who is introduced in the following scene (a dance and rally for Eugene McCarthy, 1968) are Heidi's closest friends, desultory soul mates or romantic partners as the case may be, and fellow ironists. Neither of the males has the performative showmanship of, say, a Septimus Hodge – and they lack that degree of ancestral connection to the epigrammatic style of a Wilde or Shaw – but each has command of a requisite ironic code that exalts as it demeans but most importantly places the speaker within an ethos of privilege, hipness, and (especially) self-conscious brilliance. When Heidi first meets Scoop, he is editing the "Liberated Earth News," and later on he becomes the flashily successful editor of the trendy, significantly titled *Boomer* magazine. At the high school dance, Heidi and Peter sing along to "The Shoop Shoop Song," all the while improvising a conversation that incorporates or conflates knowing references to fiction and cinema – including Peter's prophetic, "I want to know you all my life. If we can't marry let's be great friends" (167). Christopher Bigsby, in his *Contemporary American Playwrights*, comments on the special combination of self-awareness and irony in these exchanges, noting that "Heidi has a self consciously ironic conversation with ... Peter Patrone, who becomes a key figure as the play continues, irony emerging as her principal mode" (347). Irony is, as noted, a characteristic mode for Septimus Hodge as well, and yet Wasserstein's verbal or conversational irony is not Stoppard's, especially in terms of its more immediate and specific, rather than inclusive or universalized, range of implication and portent.

At the McCarthy rally, Scoop and Heidi enact one of the play's signature ironic gambits, the playing off of mutually recognized cultural markers against actual or imagined circumstances. Heidi asks Scoop why a well-educated woman should "waste her life making you and your children tuna-fish sandwiches" (173).

SCOOP: I told you. You're a serious good person. And I'm honored. Maybe you'll think fondly of all this in some Proustian haze when you're thirty-five and picking your daughter up from Ethical

Culture School to escort her to cello class before dinner with Dad,
the noted psychiatrist and Miró poster collector.

HEIDI: No. I'll be busy torching lingerie.

SCOOP: Maybe I'll remember it one day when I'm thirty-five and
watching my son's performance as Johnny Appleseed. Maybe I'll
look at my wife, who puts up with me, and flash on when I was
editor of a crackpot liberal newspaper and thought I could fall in
love with Heidi Holland, the canvassing art historian that first
snowy night in Manchester, New Hampshire, 1968.

(174)

Here, as with Heidi and Peter at the earlier dance, the irony in
Scoop's tongue-in-cheek forecast is, for him, unintentionally significant. Scoop will indeed marry, but his wife will not be Heidi, even
though the two of them would seem to be one another's prime candi-
dates to wed. Scoop may be "obnoxious, sexist, and arrogant," as Jan
Balakian claims, but he is also Heidi's closest match, the smartest and
most able sparring partner she meets over time ("Chill" 95). Or, as
Heidi herself declares, Scoop may be a creep, but he's "a charismatic
creep" (181).[6]

A scenic progression that marks time, from 1965 through 1989,
taken together with an emphasis assigned to particular historical phenomena and related alterations in the attitudes of her characters, provides
Wasserstein with a continuing source for ironic appositions. There are
distinctive differences, for example, in how historical occasions and trends
are depicted, and in how the characters respond to them, in the first by
contrast to the second act of the play. Whereas the sequence of scenes in
act one includes Heidi's visit to a meeting of the "Huron Street Ann Arbor
Consciousness-Raising Rap Group" (1970) and a vociferous demonstration (coinciding with the resignation of Richard Nixon) for "Women in
Art" outside the Chicago Art Institute (1974), act two dramatizes the
extremity of cultural turnabout through a television interview with
Scoop, Peter, and Heidi on prominent "boomer" topics (1982), a "power"
lunch in a restaurant-of-the-moment (1984), and an event at New York's
Plaza Hotel where Heidi speaks to the alumni of Miss Crain's School on
the topic, "Women, Where Are We Going?" (1986). Complementing this

order of events, the theatre audience is witness to the progressive and finally extreme visual contrasts between the settings and interactions of Heidi's youth and her later environs and relationships. Each of the play's acts ends with an encounter between Heidi and Scoop, and both are consistently ironic in tone as well as in situation. Act one concludes as Scoop is marrying Lisa but nonetheless tells Heidi (as "their" song, Sam Cooke's "You Send Me," plays) that he loves her. Act two culminates with Scoop's visit to Heidi's apartment, a situation ripe for ironic commentary. Scoop is introduced to Heidi's newly adopted baby girl, alludes to a possible run for office on his part (no more *Boomer*), and, at the same time, recalls their first meeting at the Eugene McCarthy rally, "that first snowy night in New Hampshire." Their longstanding relationship is thus telescoped, with future along with past perspectives, but implicit throughout the encounter is the fact that neither Heidi nor Scoop has found a successful romantic relationship, above all with one another.

Wasserstein's play tracks a steady progression of change, not only in her characters' lives or in the cultural transformations they confront, but also in the individuated tones of their responses to events over time. With respect to the connection among relationships, historical fluctuation, and alteration in the characters' perspectives, Bigsby notes that, "beyond creating a comedy of manners, beyond offering an ironic account of male-female relationships, [Wasserstein] is concerned, in this play, with chronicling ... the changing attitudes and values of a society in which personal and public priorities are constantly in a state of flux." For Heidi, in fact, the difference between personal and public becomes increasingly apparent, especially late in the play as her own priorities become more and more estranged from those of a culture from which she is surprised to find herself at a remove. In this vein, Bigsby remarks that, "the different time scales enable [Wasserstein] to counterpose hopes to realizations, ambitions to achievements, as she dramatizes the impact of experience on those who set out on their journeys with a degree of innocence and naivety" (*Contemporary* 345). In fact, the successive changes in Heidi's perspective reveal a notable switch on her part from tonal irony as a mark of hip (if youthful) world-weariness to a caustic irony that signals the depth of her disenchantment. From this angle, the play is witness to a notable shift in Heidi's character, the hardening of an intentionally ironic and performative self-consciousness toward a self-protective defensiveness and pointed sarcasm.

The Heidi Chronicles relies upon a historically grounded and sequential pattern of cultural referentiality with a basis in irony. This type of irony – often with allusions to popular culture – arises not simply from the characters' wit, power of observation, or social codes, but from the play's structural and thematic combinations. The individual scenes, each with its own date and location, are ironized in comparison with one another as Heidi grows older, and they become so collectively within the frame of the play's present-day setting, as represented by Heidi's art lectures that introduce each act. Her status in present time (that is, 1989) is viewed consistently, therefore, in combination with the perspectives of each of the other individual years that are represented. As noted, the events of the second act are made ironic beside those of the first, and the play emphasizes the tonal shifts between scenes such as the church basement in Ann Arbor where the Huron Street Rap Group meets ("...either you shave your legs or you don't" 178) and the television studio where the host, April, manages to demean her interviewees even while ostensibly celebrating their accomplishments. Denise, April's assistant at the studio (and Lisa's sister), preps Heidi and her friends before the taping:

> Some of the topics April wants to cover today are the sixties, social conscience, relationships, Reaganomics, money, careers, approaching the big 4–0; Scoop: opinions, trends; Heidi: women in art, the death of ERA, your book; Peter: the new medicine, kids today; and April says the further out you can take your sexuality, the better. Our audiences enjoy a little controversy with their coffee.
>
> (215)

As a widening gap is dramatized between the idealistic intentions and current realities of the characters, Wasserstein's ironic vision sharpens into what Bigsby calls, in Modern American Drama, "an irony generated out of failed aspirations" (343). The Heidi Chronicles concludes on a note that is ostensibly promising, with Heidi's adoption of Judy. However, and as an irony likely unforeseen by the playwright, the years since the play's first performances have placed Heidi's concluding moments at a lengthening remove, thereby widening the disparity between what Heidi values or perceives and the social changes that an audience knows are yet to come.

A key means of marking changes in societal moods and historical tempos is Wasserstein's consistent and typically ironic use of popular music, mostly rock or rhythm and blues. Her choice of music for given scenes is appropriate to, and even emblematic of, their particular time and place, yet it also serves to comment, often wryly, on the action at hand. In the first scene (1965), the music at the dance includes, along with "The Shoop Shoop Song (It's In His Kiss)" by Betty Everett, two songs by the Rolling Stones, "Satisfaction" and "Play With Fire." Heidi and Peter have a splendid time dancing and singing along to Betty Everett, but "his kiss" is something that will never pertain to the two of them, no matter how close their friendship. At the McCarthy dance, the background music to Scoop and Heidi's first meeting is "Take Another Little Piece of My Heart" by Janis Joplin (with the band, Big Brother and the Holding Company), which signals exactly what the two of them will do to each other on several occasions over coming years. In the Ann Arbor church basement, Heidi, Susan, and the other women in attendance chime in with Aretha Franklin's "Respect," which underscores their mutually held desire for sisterhood but also the fact that "respect" seems curiously elusive, individually or socially. "You Send Me" is the music that Scoop and Heidi dance to at his wedding, an aptly ironic choice of accompaniment, as Helene Keyssar rightly points out (142). Heidi and Scoop may have both rated Sam Cooke an "A+" (203), but the intimacy of the song, and their closeness in this scene, is precisely what neither of them will be able to achieve in any lasting way. In the second act, Lisa's baby shower is accompanied by John Lennon's "Imagine," which refers on the one hand to his murder but also to an idealistic vision that appears increasingly out of reach for Heidi. As Keyssar notes, Wasserstein's selection of music speaks to the play's audience as well as its characters, in historical as well as cultural senses: "Although the key songs of the sixties, seventies, and eighties locate each scene, they also remind characters and spectators of the changes going on during the period of the play" (143). In this relation, too, the years since the play was first performed have further ironized the action. Wasserstein's musical score, comprised as it is of "classic rock" (i.e., oldies) simultaneously invokes, distances, and even alienates the play's past moments and departed feelings.

In *The Heidi Chronicles*, the irony of cultural referentiality – including the allusions to pop culture – bears a necessary connection to historical period, with consequent limitations in terms of shelf life. Simply in the context of theatrical spectacle, Wasserstein illustrates the quickly changing times – and changes in appearance among her characters – in part through the visually transitory aspect of fashion, as at the McCarthy dance (I, 2) where "A hippie in a Sergeant Pepper jacket smokes a joint" (168), or Lisa's baby shower (II, 1), in which Denise wears "a suit, tie, and sneakers" and Susan has found "a new look, with pants, heels and silk blouse" (206). In this latter scene, the idea that Scoop has to be in Princeton for "one of those 'looking forward to the eighties, looking back on the seventies' panels" (210), sounds increasingly quaint with distance, never mind that Scoop is not in Princeton but has rather been spotted with his new girlfriend, in Central Park at the John Lennon memorial. Through Heidi's experiences and observations, especially in act two, Wasserstein sustains a sharp dialectic of seriousness and superficiality, but the changes in societal and personal values that the play records turn the emphasis strongly toward the latter. Bigsby observes that, "Though the characters were always to some degree an expression of particular social and historically locatable attitudes, as the play progresses into the 1980s so Wasserstein deals more in caricature and cartoon, reflecting what seems to be a thinning out of personality, a surrender of fact to image" (*Contemporary* 352). Indeed, Wasserstein's scenic progression is designed so that cultural referentiality is inherently ironic, due in part to the built-in commentary of one sequence upon another but also to a successive displacement of what is held as valuable by what appears trivial. The "boomer" narrative is itself codified and ironized, as in April's generic reference to "members of the baby boom generation, the kids who grew up in the fifties, protested in the sixties, were the 'me's' of the seventies, and the parents of the eighties" (216). As inclusive as April's précis may be, however, it applies only obliquely to Heidi, who, though a boomer, fits in with few of the generational clichés.

Heidi refers, in her second lecture on painting, to the art critic or scholar as "being neither the painter nor the casual observer, but a highly informed spectator" (206), and here it would seem that she is speaking autobiographically, and not only in her scholarly persona. Throughout *The Heidi Chronicles*, the title character is frequently cast as the audience's surrogate, an informed spectator on the scene. With the rap group in Ann Arbor, the gathering at Lisa's baby shower, or the television studio taping, Heidi is more observer than participant, and as the discrepancies between her ideals and current realities broaden, she is ever more detached. Her speech to the alumni of Miss Crain's School ("Women, Where Are We Going?") begins as a wry anecdote on the peculiar notions of women she has lately observed but ends with a confession of feeling "stranded," and of her surprise at being so – "I thought the whole point was that we were all in this together" (229).

Heidi is emblematic, in one sense, of a generation that would "have it all," and she is also an individual who finds compromise, or even a change of course, difficult. Balakian notes the particular double bind: "Ironically, it is only when women have the opportunity to achieve their full potential that they will feel a sense of worthlessness" ("Chill" 98–99).[7] Wasserstein portrays Heidi, in fact, as being continually foiled in "having at all," except perhaps in the sense of career. Early in the play, as the friends signal their kinships through knowing references to appropriate professions, colleges, and lifestyle choices, there is a tacit assumption that all will be well for those who are privileged enough to believe in such notions. But Heidi's best friend Susan, moving along with the times in a way that Heidi cannot, abandons the causes that brought her to a consciousness-raising rap group in the first place, and neither Peter, who is gay, nor Scoop can ever be available for marriage, although Heidi loves them both. When, in their final scene, Scoop refers to Heidi's "caustic side" (245), his reference is to a tone of protective sarcasm that was at one time a spirited, if ironical, wittiness. In a way, it is Heidi's own self-image, including her own excellence, that has backfired. Bigsby describes her as "a woman who took pride in never fully committing herself, in seeing the ironies which undercut the seriousness of every cause" (*Contemporary* 351). And yet, the cultural trends and social changes are such that the ironies finally undercut

Heidi, leaving her in a state that, apart from her adoption, is close to solitude.

Heidi, Scoop, and Peter – the threesome at the play's center – re-enforce one another's expectations and points of view, even as they applaud each other's wit and ostensible worldliness. As Peter remarks, "According to my mental health friends, we're heading into a decade of self-obsession. I'm simply at the forefront of the movement" (187). In verbal performance, the ironic style of choice for all three is to juxtapose a current reference with a cultural stereotype that it takes hipness, someone in the know, or a select insider, to recognize.[8] When Scoop hears (appropriately, at his own wedding) that Heidi is living with someone, he demands to know exactly where that person went to college ("You're sort of living with an editor who went to Trinity College, Hartford?") and where is he a book editor – Knopf, Simon and Schuster, Harper and Row? (199–200). This is how, for Scoop, Heidi's friend can be "graded" as well as categorized. However, as the circumstances of the characters themselves gravitate further from mainstream cultural trends, their irony turns bitter – or, for Peter as well as Heidi, "caustic."[9] Moreover, the use of irony as a code of understanding among the select can occasionally have an opposite, unintended, effect. For Scoop and Heidi, irony provides a bond for intellect and humor, but it doesn't always clarify their positions and is at times a deflective shield.[10] For Heidi, indeed, Scoop is nearly impossible to pin down, despite the characteristic vividness of his presence. Identifying one of the core ironies in the play's action and its outcome, Keyssar notes that, "Despite changes in age, education, occupation, and responsibilities to others (i.e., family, lovers, friends) as well as themselves, no character in *The Heidi Chronicles* transforms herself or himself or 'the world'" (143). And, according to Bigsby, it is to some degree Heidi's perspective on her male friends that generates her "irony and humour, that makes her an ideal lens through which to view historical process. It is also what leaves her alone and unhappy" (*Contemporary* 354). The irony that is so fundamental to Heidi's world-view as well as to her relationships is also, and by its very mechanisms, isolating. Here once again, Wasserstein's verbal irony might be contrasted meaningfully with Stoppard's, especially in the sense of what becomes more individuated or solitary, as in Heidi's case, or consistently social, as with Septimus – at least prior to his self-exile. In Richard Rorty's view, "Irony seems inherently a private matter. On my definition, an ironist cannot get along without the contrast between the final vocabulary she inherited and the one she is trying to create for herself. Irony is, if not intrinsically resentful, at least reactive. Ironists have to have something to have doubts about, something from which to be alienated" (87–88). From this perspective, Heidi Holland is irony embodied – the fervent "spectator" who stands too much apart from the game to ever successfully join in.

Angels in America Part I: Millennium Approaches

Tony Kushner's play, like Wendy Wasserstein's, casts the changing situations of its characters against a flow of events in recent American history. *Angels in America Part I* is also strongly dependent upon a framework of cultural referentiality, and, as in the case of *The Heidi Chronicles*, the years since its debut have introduced an aspect of estrangement, a heightened ephemerality that results from the increasing distance in time. From the vantage point of the early 1990s, when the play was written, what occurred in the 1980s (including the Reagan administration and the onset of the AIDS crisis) was immediate. Since that time, the play's situations, as well as its historical figures and references, naturally have become more remote, with a corresponding diminishment in the ironic relations of incident and cultural framework. More so than Wasserstein, however, Kushner is interested in the ironies of societal appositions over individual mannerisms of behavior, thought, and speech. Whereas *The Heidi Chronicles* relies for its wry and ironic expressiveness upon the wittiness of its title character and her friends, *Angels in America* situates the several crises in its characters' lives and relationships against a panorama of intense social disruption, producing a series of sharply ironic cultural disparities. The extremity of circumstances that Louis and Prior, as well as Joe and Harper, confront is brought in this fashion into a vivid, if highly ironized, relief against a spectrum of political, historical, and religious points of reference.

David Savran notes the play's "insistent tendency to ironize," and locates the source of Kushner's ironic strategy in the playwright's consistent reliance upon a pattern of duality – "binary oppositions" (212) – that is manifested in conflict, contradiction, and finally ambivalence. In Savran's words, "The opposite of nearly everything you say about *Angels in America* will also hold true." He suggests, in fact, that one "might well rebuke the play as Belize does Louis: 'you're ambivalent about everything.' And so it is" (208–209). This ambivalence, in itself symptomatic of the play's dualistic scheme, underlies what Savran refers to as the play's "ironic/comic tone," that which enables Kushner's characters to speak gravely in comedic terms, as in act one, scene four, when Prior shows Louis his Kapusi's sarcoma, a signature symptom of AIDS:

> PRIOR: K. S., baby. Lesion number one. Lookit. The wine-dark kiss of the angel of death.
>
> LOUIS: (*Very softly, holding Prior's arm*): Oh please . . .
>
> PRIOR: I'm a lesionnaire. The Foreign Lesion. The American Lesion. Lesionnair's disease.
>
> LOUIS: Stop.
>
> PRIOR: My troubles are lesion.
>
> LOUIS: Will you *stop*.
>
> PRIOR: Don't you think I'm handling this well? I'm going to die.
>
> (21)

Of all Kushner's characters in *Angels*, Louis is the one most torn by ambivalence, unable as he is to love Prior and still face up to Prior's disease, guilty as he is about the seeming abandonment of his partner for another. In addition, however, Louis is situated centrally in the play's political vortex, what Savran calls its air of "political disputation," which centers mostly on Louis, "the unmistakably ambivalent, ironic Jew, who invariably sets the level of discussion and determines the tenor of the argument." Savran's idea is that Louis, with "all of his contradictions," becomes "by default the spokesperson for liberal pluralism, with all *its* contradictions" (222). In scene seven of act two, Louis inquires, with respect to the incumbent First Family:

> What's it like to be the child of the Zeitgeist? To have the American Animus as your dad? It's not really a *family*, the Reagans, I read *People*, there aren't any connections there, no love, they don't even speak to each other except through their

agents. So what it like to be Reagan's kid? Enquiring minds
want to know.

(71)

Kushner assigns Louis a pattern of associations – and by extension a set
of cultural reference points – with a tonal quality that is in fact more
germane than the ostensible topic at hand, the Reagan family, including
Patty and Ron. Louis's deliberately ironic tone allows him to mock the
very source of his understanding ("I read *People*") even as he lays claim to
that understanding. Moreover, he is able to debase the real subject – the
nature and importance of family relations, one of *Angels in America*'s key
motifs – by closing his question with a quippy allusion to curiosity of a
National Enquirer variety.

Along with Louis, the other main characters (Prior, Harper, Joe,
and Roy) also enact and embody the drama's ironic and ambivalent interplay among ideological oppositions. As the focus of the play alternates
continually between these figures, and as the depiction of the cultural
contexts shifts, so too do the characters evince and stand for a series of
ironic reversals. As Natalie Meisner points out: "The protagonist Prior,
a gay man who in other circumstances might be condemned by the
Christian right for his sexual choice, becomes a prophet; Roy Cohn, a
rabidly anti-gay crusader, is himself suddenly thrust out of the closet"
(177).[11] The fact, of course, that Roy will not admit to being a gay man
only adds to the pathetic irony, not only of his own health but also how
he comports and represents himself with Joe in addition to his physician.
As a personality *in extremis*, though, it is Harper who acts out, if not
the horror of terminal illness (as in the case of Prior and Roy), then the
intensified anxiety that comes of her truly apocalyptic terror. Although
Kushner does not open his play with Harper, it is her speech in act one,
scene three that sets the millenarian tone:

> HARPER: I'm undecided. I feel ... that something's going to give.
> It's 1985. Fifteen years till the third millennium. Maybe Christ
> will come again. Maybe seeds will be planted, maybe there'll be
> harvests then, maybe early figs to eat, maybe new life, maybe
> fresh blood, maybe companionship and love and protection,
> safety from what's outside, maybe the door will hold, or maybe ...

maybe the troubles will come, and the end will come, and the sky
will collapse and there will be terrible rains and showers of poison
light, or maybe my life is really fine, maybe Joe loves me and I'm
only crazy thinking otherwise, or maybe not, maybe it's even
worse than I know, maybe ... I want to know, maybe I don't. The
suspense, Mr. Lies, it's killing me.

MR. LIES: I suggest a vacation.

(18)

Just as Louis alludes, albeit through his negative model of the Reagans, to
an ideal of family, Harper is obsessed with a paragon of safety, a multi-
form security that she fears can no longer be possible, for herself or for
the world at large. How can there be safety when the cataclysm looms
so close, in intimate as well as national and global terms? In this sense,
Harper's outcry stands for the collective angst of a world still waiting for
what the turn of the millennium would bring (again, a question importantly changed since the play's initial performances). Stanton Garner
describes Harper's terror as reflective of the global nightmare:

> Like the apocalyptic allusions elsewhere in Kushner's play,
> Harper's imagery reflects eschatological anxieties particular to
> this century's end: global warming, nuclear war, and AIDS. Her
> concern with holes in the ozone layer – "Over Antarctica. Skin
> burns, birds go blind, icebergs melt. The world's coming to an
> end" (I: 28) – embodies the nightmare of eco-catastrophe, while
> her obsession with "systems of defense giving way" conflates the
> Cold War anxiety over atmospheric nuclear attack (Star Wars
> paranoia) with the image of a body's immune system collapsing.
>
> (177)

Each of the individuals in *Angels in America* enacts a variation on
Harper's relation of global horror and personal perception, what Bigsby,
in *Contemporary American Playwrights*, calls the play's linkage
"between public issues and private pain" (109). Faced collectively with
an array of terrors, and largely without the sorts of families, support
systems, or intimacies they would choose, the characters do what they
can to postpone catastrophe, or deflect it with affected cheer, mockery,

and most of all, irony. As in the case of *The Heidi Chronicles*, Kushner's characters are adroit at calling upon a full range of cultural touchstones, with plays, movies, and works of literature included along with the many political and religious allusions. Just as the play is catholic in its depiction of politics and also pan-religious (Mormon, Jewish, and Christian, primarily), so too is it culturally homogeneous with respect to the recognition by the several characters of their mutually held sign systems. Prior and Belize quote Tennessee Williams – "Stella for star" (*A Streetcar Named Desire*) and "You're just a Christian martyr" (*The Glass Menagerie*), and a Katherine Hepburn rendition from both characters ("Men are beasts" / "The absolute lowest") is appropriately included (59, 61). Another gay playwright, William Inge, is also referenced:

> PRIOR: I warned you, Louis. Names are important. Call an animal "Little Sheba" and you can't expect it to stick around. Besides, it's a dog's name.
> LOUIS: I wanted a dog in the first place, not a cat. He sprayed my books.
> PRIOR: He was a female cat.
>
> (19)

When Harper vanishes, in act one, scene seven, the mutual dream sequence with Prior, he reacts with a line of Dorothy's from *The Wizard of Oz*: "People come and go so quickly here" (33), and in scene five Joe and Harper refer to the movies "Rosemary's Baby" and "The Exorcist" as having locations with devils, by comparison with their "creepy" apartment (24). In act three, Prior's nightmare includes his singing from *My Fair Lady* – "All I want is a room somewhere, Far away from the cold night air" (88). Among the gay characters in particular, familiar (and often clichéd) references are code for both mutuality and apartness, for establishing gender demarcations while at the same time denoting them as "other." As Meisner points out, "girl talk" and "ironic distancing" are part of the "pastiching of Belize and Prior" (180). Both of these characters, Meisner asserts, are able to "harness ironic self knowledge in order to perform their gender identities" (187).

What Savran calls the play's "binary" structure, and what Bigsby (*Contemporary*) calls its "dualisms," are both productive of dramaturgical patterns that are conducive to ironic apposition, in terms of scenic structure as well as the characters' individual situations.[12] Kushner adds to this effect by dramatizing several encounters with a split-scene effect, so that, as in act one, scene eight, the audience watches Joe and Harper at home and, concurrently, Louis and Prior in bed. Later, in act three, scene two, Louis and Belize argue about race and politics while Prior, in the hospital, painfully endures having his lesions examined by Emily. Along with such marked separations, however, there is a manifest, if at times unspoken, effort toward transcendence and unification, or at least toward a breakdown of the categories that create the sorts of rifts or divisions that ensure duality. In this context, Bigsby notes that, "Variety, heterogeneity, unpredictability, transformations, pluralisms, ambiguities, anarchic gestures are contrasted with the arbitrary codes, legalisms, fixities of a society which works by exclusion" (*Modern* 421). As Savran puts it, *Angels in America* dramatizes a "utopia/dystopia coupling," a constant ironic tension, played out in several arenas, between the idealized and the dysfunctional (212).[13]

Kushner fashions a time sequence in which, as in *The Heidi Chronicles*, individual experiences are matched continually with collective ones, and subjective emotional states are, of necessity, paired with historical incident, often to jarring effect. The present-day situation of *Angels* is, again, one that is increasingly distant, a "now" that James Fisher describes as associated with "selfishness, faithlessness, and isolation, as typified by the era itself, by archconservative politician Roy Cohn, and by a perceived decline of compassion in American society at the end of the twentieth century" (55). The play's "now" is, of course, millenarian, and in that context implicitly apocalyptic. As Garner, writing near the end of a decade and of a millennium, characterizes the 1990s: "As the twentieth century confronts its own 'last days,' millenarianism and apocalypticism have come to constitute a nexus where high culture and low, belief and behavior, meet and overlap" (174). Such an atmosphere is well suited to what has been called Kushner's dramaturgical "promiscuity" – the consistent pastiche, the mixing of components at will, the disregard for standardized boundaries and the success at crossing them, and what Garner aptly calls the "present's problematic relationship to its historical contexts" (179).[14]

The historical "now" that provides the setting for both Kushner's and Wasserstein's plays also marks the onset of a particular cultural nexus with respect to irony, especially in regard to its social meanings and effects. In this connection, notably, the repercussions have extended well beyond the time frame of the respective plays' actions as well as their debut dates. *Angels in America* is particularly symptomatic of a tension in the contemporary concept of irony, particularly in relation to societal discourse, and serves therefore as an indicator of dispute over the uses as well as the nature of an ironic standpoint. The characters in *Angels*, as in *The Heidi Chronicles*, rely upon irony as a natural language, falling into its referential patterns as if by default. In this sense, they have in common not only a style of phrasing but also a shared existential status and world-view. With respect to the pervasiveness of irony in contemporary culture, Alan Wilde suggests that, "in the twentieth century the ironic vision of life so overwhelms the arts that by now we perhaps take for granted its almost ubiquitous presence" (13). Indeed, it is the readiness with which one can assume this situation that enables these characters to refer with such alacrity and confidence to so broad an ironic framework. For Wilde, and with his emphasis, "modern art (modernist and postmodernist) *is* overwhelmingly ironic" (29).

Irony, in the contemporary as well as postmodern senses, typically connotes not merely duality or juxtaposition, but fracture – the appearance of what is related and yet disassociated, concurrently. When confronted as a matter of course with such incongruence, the natural response can be ironic in the sense of compensatory. In this connection, Alan Wilde refers to the "understanding of irony as a mode of consciousness, a perceptual response to a world without unity or cohesion" (2). Both of these attributes of an ironic sensibility are apparent in *Angels*, as characters such as Louis and Prior fall naturally into ironized speech as a means of self-defensive compensation for what lacks unity and, moreover, in response to what is immediately threatening in their circumstances. However, as one can tell from Harper's apocalyptic visions, *everything* is potentially threatening. Wilde identifies a form of "disjunctive" irony as well as a "suspensive" form, and each of his types can be aligned with the pervasive disunity that *Angels* dramatizes and to which its characters respond. For Wilde, "disjunctive irony (the characteristic form of modernism) strives, however reluctantly, toward a condition of paradox. The ironist, far more basically adrift, confronts a world that appears inherently disconnected and fragmented. At its extreme or 'absolute' point ... disjunctive irony both recognizes the disconnections and seeks to control them" (10). The struggle for control, in this relation, comes across in the characters' behavior as an effort to establish mutually held frameworks of reference, generally through ironic means. "Suspensive" irony, by contrast, is a "yet more radical vision of multiplicity, randomness, contingency, and even absurdity" which, for Wilde, "abandons the quest for paradise altogether – the world in all its disorder is simply (or not so simply) accepted" (10). Here, in effect, is the universe (or multiverse) of *Angels in America* as described by Bigsby, with all of its variation, "heterogeneity, unpredictability, transformation, pluralisms, ambiguities" (*Modern* 421).

Together with the omnipresence of fracture and disruption, however, there is a coincident effort, existing alongside the threat, nightmare, and apocalypse in *Angels*, toward unification, healing, and community. Here also, the nature and positioning of the ironic mode are critical, perhaps especially so in regard to a shifting cultural awareness of what irony can portend. Jedediah Purdy's book, *For Common Things: Irony, Trust, and Commitment in America Today*, is a messianic call to transcend the cynically ironic default of contemporary culture and to relocate an irony of surprise, discovery, and reverence (203). This book, its author announces, is "a response to an ironic time," and the terms of its rebellion are set forth immediately in the Preface:

> Irony has become our marker of worldliness and maturity. The ironic individual practices a style of speech and behavior that avoids all appearance of naivete – of naïve devotion, belief, or hope. He subtly protests the inadequacy of the things he says, the gestures he makes, the acts he performs. By the inflection of his voice, the expression of his face, and the motion of his body, he signals that he is aware of all the ways he may be thought silly or jejune, and that he might even think so himself. His

wariness becomes a mistrust of language itself. He disowns
his own words.

(xi)

Though Purdy is not referring here to characters in drama, his description
is nonetheless utterly performative. Irony, for "the ironic individual," is
enacted; it is not merely spoken, but is performed through movement,
gesture, and facial expressiveness. In short, irony is *acted*, and it is
performed self-consciously and with total awareness of context. This is
the irony, if not of Prior or Louis in *Angels in America*, then certainly of
Scoop Rosenbaum in *The Heidi Chronicles*, and perhaps of Heidi herself.
For Purdy, there is "something fearful" in "today's ironic manner":

> It is a fear of betrayal, disappointment, and humiliation, and a
> suspicion that believing, hoping, or caring too much will open us
> to these. Irony is a way of refusing to rely on such treacherous
> things. However, there is also something perceptive about irony,
> and sometimes we must consider whether the ironist is right. The
> ironist expresses a perception that the world has grown old, flat,
> and sterile, and that we are rightly weary of it. There is nothing to
> delight, move, inspire, or horrify us. Nothing will ever surprise us.
> Everything we encounter is a remake, a rerelease, a ripoff, or a
> rerun. We know it all before we see it, because we have seen it all
> already.
>
> (xi–xii)

Or, as Prior says to Harper in act one, scene seven: "It's something you
learn after your second surprise party. It's All Been Done Before" (33).
Prior's tone is archly ironic, reflecting in its way Purdy's theory of
ironic imitation: "Irony is powered by a suspicion that everything is
derivative" (14).

And yet (ironically), the characters refuse to settle for the very
condition that provokes their ironic self-awareness and comportment,
and so *The Heidi Chronicles* is idealistic in the face of disillusionment
while *Angels in America* is utopian despite the threat, or fact, of
calamity. Bigsby refers to the play's "utopian pluralism," and remarks
that Kushner, "who seems to throw out so many challenges to

American values, sees himself as squarely in the American grain, accepting its utopian ambitions, celebrating its potential for genuine democracy" (*Contemporary* 110–111). In Bigsby's view, the play's "barely controlled exuberance, its pluralism of voices, stylistic hybridity, promiscuous mixing of genres, races, ideologies, its faith, ultimately in the moral and spiritual resources of the individual and the will to connect, are a manifesto for a utopia which is not a programmatic structure and does not lie in some distant time and place, but is within the grasp of those who understand its necessities" (*Modern* 424). For the characters in *Angels*, even as they face crises and catastrophes, together as well as individually, the future remains to be changed and the "great work" is still to be done.

"I do not believe," writes Purdy, "that, even where it is strongest, irony has convinced us that nothing is real, true, or ours" (xv). The reference here, again, is to an irony typed as a peculiarly contemporary method of transaction and self-presentation that contains an implicit world-view based on what is perceived as transitory, ephemeral, or indefinable. The characters in *Angels* as well as in *The Heidi Chronicles* deploy or fall back upon this sort of irony, but their seeming nonchalance is deceptive, as is their apparent success with ironic self-defensiveness. Heidi will adopt, Scoop will run for office, and Louis will pursue his political convictions. Garner points to the "refusal of closure" in *Angels* (parts one and two) which "allows an opening into the play's peculiarly late-Shakespearean world of unexpected opportunities, temporary reprieves, and second chances" (178). The crises in the lives of Prior and Louis, Joe and Harper, are not presented, in themselves, as ironic, nor are they held at arm's length, despite the characters' regular attempts at comic deflection.

Purdy argues: "In lighter moments [the ironist] revels in cliché, creating the oft-reported impression that today's youthful conversation is little more than an amalgam of pop-culture references, snatches of old song lyrics and bursts of laughter at what would otherwise seem the most solemn moments" (13–14). Yet still, for the characters in *The Heidi Chronicles* and to a lesser degree *Angels in America*, the song lyrics and pop references are not used simply for ironic badinage, but are the valued and necessary touchstones for a culture at particular moments in time. The characters may affect a tone of archness, mockery, or comedic deflection, but that does not detract necessarily from what is needful in their points of reference, be it "The Shoop Shoop Song" that Heidi and Peter dance to or Prior's many references to plays and movies. Purdy says: "Refusing to place its trust in the world, irony helps to make a world that is the more likely to be worthy of despair" (20). With respect to these two plays, however, the situation is considerably more complicated, and the characters' use of irony can be as much for mutual recognition, community, and a critique of values as for self-defense or for questioning the legitimacy of received truth or meaning.

On those occasions when irony is, indeed, equated only with what is derivative, quoted, deprived of meaning, or proceeding from disenchantment, the trope is diminished inaccurately, categorized according to understandings that are overly restrictive, and cheated of its more profound breadth of scope and magnitude. "Our contemporary irony," says Purdy, "shrugs off, doubts, and reassembles significance to drain words of evocation, beauty and moral weight. It discovers behind the appearance of meaning the fact of insignificance. It is a static irony, a way of staying unmoved by our neighbors, the world, ourselves" (203). Here again, neither *Angels in America* nor *The Heidi Chronicles* bear this out, if for no other reason than the ties of friendship and the need for community among the characters are too strong – the characters in both plays may be modishly ironic, but not one of them is "unmoved." Purdy declares that, "Angelic spirituality is also a way of defying the weariness of an ironic culture" (23–24), which contrasts neatly with Savran's assertion that *Angels* "demonstrates that there are angels in America, that America is in essence a utopian and theological construction, a nation with a divine mission. Politics is by no means banished insofar as it provides a crucial way in which the nation is imagined. But it is subordinated to utopian fantasies of harmony in diversity, one nation under a derelict God" (222–223).

Both *Angels in America* and *The Heidi Chronicles* premiered well in advance of the terrorist attacks of September 11, 2001, which is noteworthy here to the extent that a contemporary and American concept of irony has been altered by this along with other post-millennial events and circumstances. More pointedly, a changing conception of irony and of ironic cultural referentiality has been reflected, in popular terms at least, before and then following the events of 9/11/01. In October 1999, for example, Joel Stein's "In Defense of Irony" appeared in *Time* magazine. The author acknowledged his admiration for Jedediah Purdy's book but also registered some modest disagreement, as in: "skepticism without irony is unfun. It leads to folk songs" (42). In July 2000, James Poniewozik's "Irony is Dead, Long Live Irony (On the Web)" appeared in *Time*, including the author's assertion that irony is alive and well in spite of a media columnist's contention that the world wide web is "an irony-free zone" (74). In both of these instances, the "irony" referred to is of a tepid variety, akin to sarcasm, cynicism, or witty ridicule rather than to the ironic as, potentially, a vision of experience or a trope of philosophical dialectic and discovery.

By late September 2001 – that is, soon after the attacks in New York and Washington D. C. – the popular discourse on this topic had changed markedly. In "The Age of Irony Comes to an End" (also in *Time*) Roger Rosenblatt's argument resembles Purdy's in its rejection of contemporary irony's alleged dodge against the real and true: "For some thirty years – roughly as long as the Twin Towers were upright – the good folks in charge of America's intellectual life have insisted that nothing was to be believed in or taken seriously. Nothing was real." For Rosenblatt, the stark reality of grief, the fact of how people aided one another in distress, and "the preciousness of ordinary living" dispel the ironic (79). However, to cast irony in opposition to the "real," even on such urgent terms or in the context of national catastrophe, is to severely and misguidedly detract from its range of meaning and potency, deny its larger capabilities, and constrain its humanism. Contemporary irony of the popular variety may be diluted significantly by American culture's fascination with itself, or by a corresponding tendency toward the derivative, quoting what has already been to the exclusion of what is or has yet to come. And, of course, the very fact of a diminishment in verbal or situational irony's range of import or status may itself be symptomatic of cultural depletion – or be related to post-9/11 historic events including the wars in Iraq or Afghanistan and a world financial crisis. American drama, however, can still employ and reference irony to considerable, and also immediate, humanistic effect. Both *Angels in America* and *The Heidi Chronicles* may lose to the transience and ephemerality of the cultural and historical trends they mark or predate, but their idealism, utopianism, and especially humanism are framed and qualified, but not finally negated, by a shared ironic spirit.

8   Irony's theatre

Irony, to be sure, does not belong solely to the theatre or only to modernity. Its connections with language and speech alone, not to mention the several philosophical contexts and perspectives, are so fundamental as to insure an ironic presence in discourse generally as well as in literary and theatrical artistry. Still, theatre and drama incorporate irony in notably singular ways, and the settings of modernism and of the contemporary stage have provided exemplary occasions, not only for the ironic mode to be usefully employed but also for it to be reassessed with regard to its notable tendencies and strengths as well as potential immediacy of application. Irony in the theatre is, of course, an ancient as well as transhistorical phenomenon. What, again, could be more starkly ironic than Oedipus setting out to locate the cause of the plague on his city, complete with his self-description as "luck's child"? Oedipus, in his narrowing quest, enacts and also embodies an ironic fate: his personal role in events is built into his history, as is his blindness to the circumstances. In another epoch, the terrible irony of Lear's turning against his favorite child could scarcely produce a more cataclysmic outcome. And yet, irony in its modern iterations, and for characters in theatre more recently, is not the same as it was for Sophocles or Shakespeare.[1] Modernity has cast irony on its own terms, if not in its own image, since the late nineteenth century, and in this regard the theatre continues to reconfigure both the capabilities and limitations of the ironic, referring to this "master" trope in ways that, perhaps ironically, have a tendency to interrogate its own versatility and power of application or allusion.

As one noteworthy figure of embodied irony, Halvard Solness is, like Oedipus, associated closely with a factor of "luck." And, as a fellow character in tragedy, he too is implicated in part by a vision of cosmos. Yet the very suggestion of the cosmic, which would pertain in the case of Sophoclean drama to a pantheon of divinities and daimonic powers, has a distinctly ironic connotation for Henrik Ibsen and, by extension, for his master builder. In one sense, the ineffable disparity between the will or moods of ancient gods and the cognizance of mortals is a profoundly religious, as well as tragic, reading of humankind's relation to divinity or the transcendent. For Solness, on the other hand, the contrast between his own fate and his reading of divine intent is best understood as an ironic schism, underscored by the related and equally ironic agency of Hilda Wangel. Thus, *The Master Builder* is "religious" on highly restricted and skeptical terms, with the powers that affect Solness ("Him," "helpers and servers," the "impossible") less decipherable as distinct entities or universalized forces than as ironized extensions of the builder's own prescience, vainglory, or paranoia.

Even so, Ibsen's drama can be read as supersensory and, in its way, profoundly cosmic in scope, with the latter characteristic arising primarily from ironic patterns and associations that strengthen the impression of an overmastering component of sense or balance in the play's universe. Within this realm, the singular appropriateness and magnitude of Barthes's acme, together with Ibsen's dramaturgy of finely apposed arrivals and departures, powerfully conveys the contours of a meaningful order. Concurrently, however, such an orderliness is undermined in ironic terms by the wild card of uncertainty that arises to a notable degree from the mercurial and thus unreliable nature of Solness himself. For Ibsen, in this instance, irony functions as a signifier for what is systematic but also as a compromising agent regarding any ultimate or reified apprehension of cosmos. Even as *The Master Builder* seems to invoke and even celebrate the transcendent, it finally calls it to question, with the closing image of Solness falling – and of Hilda's ecstatic reaction – casting doubt on any coherent participation of "Him" in the master builder's life or final destiny.

Ibsen's versatile irony is delivered most forcefully through a vivid theatrical vocabulary and use of stage imagery as well as in literary terms – and he is by no means alone in this regard among modern dramatists. The individual character, or figure of irony personified, is in the theatre an agent for what is demonstrated rather than described, embodied instead of narrated. Indeed, the sensory nature of theatrical character can be, in itself, a powerful agency of ironic perspective and expressiveness. A character in a play may or may not be aware of his or her ironic circumstances, but in most cases it is an embodied performance and demonstration of irony, rather than a statement or description, that results. Lopakhin grows intensely aware of how ironic his changed circumstances have become on Lyubov's estate, and the Father has a finely developed philosophical notion of how ironic disparities define his existence, appropriately, as both a representative figure and an illusory figment in the theatre. By contrast, Candida Morell's husband has scant notion of his status as an ironized figure of fun, and Septimus, despite the promptness of his wit, has no cognizance of how ironically dire his historical circumstances will become. Septimus exists, in fact, within an aesthetic double bind: he is able at once to observe circumstances with ironic humor but at the same time be trapped within the ironic momentums of Stoppard's play and the torque of its events. Whatever their differences, however, it is always the individuated characters in drama that must live the irony, experience it, convey and stand for it. In body, language, and deeds, they comprise irony's manifest theatrical presence; they are the agents of its workings and its spectrum of significance.

Different stage figures will, certainly, mediate the ironic in varied ways, with given ironic behaviors evinced more verbally, as with Scoop Rosenbaum, or more linked to situational factors, as in Lopakhin's interrelations, or consciously philosophic, as in the case of Vershinin. Just as Solness is symbolic as a personification of irony, Lopakhin represents the trope's more performative aspects and capacities. Indeed, Lopakhin's link to the mastering irony in *The Cherry Orchard* is direct and personal. His single utterance ("I bought it.") condenses the entire reversal of his circumstances – and that of Lyubov's family, including its own reflection of a more sweeping historical change – into a single phrase. Lopakhin is not only aware of this turnabout, he cannot help but glory in it, despite the catastrophic outcome for those that he admires most and even loves. But Lopakhin's performance of the ironic is more exacting than even the play's core irony would suggest. Irony, for him, resides also in the details of a habitual glance at his watch, as if marking time until August 22, the day of the estate auction. When Lopakhin intrudes quickly into the conversation between Anya and Varya to "moo," it is a precisely articulated instance of Chekhovian juxtaposition but also a mini-performance of an ironic sensibility. In this perspective, then, Lopakhin can be understood as embodying irony, just as Solness or Reverend Morell also can, but in his case the connection of the ironic to the business of theatrical performance is more pronounced, and also more finely detailed.

The figure who embodies irony contains the trope within, and continually acts out its terms. The performance of irony is, by comparison, related often to the broader situations of a play, to the storytelling and to drama's structural principles and dramaturgical patterns. In varying degrees, this combination applies to many of the characters discussed in these chapters, in that theatrical figures share the obvious trait of being tied inextricably to the overall dramatic actions they engage in, illustrate, and help to advance. Nonetheless, this very situation retains its particularity as well as centrality. The apparent autonomy or free will of any character in drama can always be viewed ironically, in that such independence is only an illusion created by the dramatist. The case is especially revelatory, however, for the figure who – with awareness or not – is snared in an ironic situation or progression of events: that is, the individual character who is synecdochic in relation to an overarching ironic pattern. In this way among others, a dramatic character can be the medium, or translation, of the possibly more abstract ironies of dialectic and philosophy. Mother Courage, for example, cannot *not* enact the core irony in Brecht's drama: the impulse to haggle and sell is too strong in her nature; the wagon will continue its journey with or without the children, and episode will follow episode.

The relation of characterization to dramaturgical structure has, of course, many intricacies, including the stipulation that, for the theatrical figure, irony is individual yet typically situational and shared among the dramatis personae, at once. Irony, phenomenally, is by nature partnered, in that ironic expression always requires the recognizable context or countering assertion. With reference again to Cleanth Brooks, irony is "the most general term that we have for the kind of qualification which the various elements in a context receive from the context" (209) – an assessment that may be applied to theatrical as well as literary genres.

This intrinsic quality of irony is akin, in fact, to what Northrop Frye recognizes as a pattern in literature: "The literary structure is ironic because 'what it says' is always different in kind or degree from 'what it means'" (*Anatomy* 81). In drama, the quality of irony arises in a structural context when the interrelation among events is neither innocent nor dispassionate but rather conveys its own tonal significance with regard to the appositions themselves. In *Arcadia*, for instance, the portrayal of daily life among the Coverlys in 1809 at Sidley Park is not reflective of any particular ironies, apart from Septimus Hodge's wry observations of conditions and, especially, his interpersonal relations on the estate. In the scenic alternation, however, and from the added perspective of the late twentieth century, events in both eras assume a notably ironic perspective – particularly so when Stoppard accentuates the comparison between ages (and the characters in each) through his continuing opposition of the time frames. The alternation is so powerfully ironic in this case that even a tortoise can be a messenger of irony, not to mention the figures in the present that endeavor so unsuccessfully to comprehend their predecessors. When acts of performative demonstration go hand in hand with an ironical structuring of the drama, the effect becomes even more accentuated, as in the case not only of Lopakhin or Septimus but also of Mother Courage. Indeed, the structure of Brecht's play is such that the episodes, as well as the more nuanced movements within them, make for an increasingly ironized succession, culminating in the death of Kattrin and in Courage's unenlightened continuation of the journey.[2] Within such a "progression" (ironic itself because of what is not learned) Brecht continually shows his title character in moments of performative irony, especially so in those instances when her demonstrative gestus of "mother" is positioned structurally in direct relation to that of haggler and ready supplier to those other than her children.

The directional quality of theatrical action is basic to what Langer calls the "mode of Destiny" in drama – as against the novelistic mode of "Memory" (307). By contrast with representation through literary narrative, events and circumstances that are depicted on the stage can have a kinetic aspect that purely non-theatrical forms do not necessarily share. Irony, in this particular relation to dramatic structure, can evince not only an element of sequence but also one of momentum. That is, the ironic too can progress toward a future – or, one might say, toward its own "Destiny." Such a future, in turn, is likely to represent the completed revelation of a master irony embodied in the collective experience of the characters, or of the one character, as in the case of Solness, the Father, or Mother Courage. Events, when seen as individual instances within such an ironic, or "destined" progression, may come across merely as happenstance or, at the opposite extreme, assume the character of Barthes's acme, where an apparently circumstantial quality gives way to ironic meaning, when "chance signifies" (192). Irony in the theatre can, of course, be verbal or situational; it can refer pointedly to a given state of affairs or simply involve a passing observation, just as in a novel. With respect to structural considerations, though, theatrical irony tends to assume the shape of a process in flux in relation to plot. From this perspective, including the fact that drama must demonstrate rather than describe, the ratios of cause and effect can take on a particularly ironic aspect, complementing the tendency of dramatic action to advance in accord with innate and opposing stresses. A play may feature a single event that has a notable aspect of irony or that portends an ironic outcome – the appearance of Hilda, the arrival of Marchbanks at the Morell household, the visit of the Father to Madame Pace's establishment – but a play's total ironic pattern will also include the dramatic outcomes of these occasions, the ironically "destined" consequences of a precipitating event that contains, in effect, the very qualities that will play out in the ensuing drama. Theatrical action, especially in regard to this kinetic and forward-directed quality, can enforce an ironic impression as effectively as the dramaturgical structure per se.

Here, the emphasis that Burke, and then States, place upon the instance – or, more likely, *instances* – of peripeteia in dramatic action is especially germane regarding the ironic trope in relation to plot structures. That dramatic action has what States refers to as a "principle of curvature" is directly reflective of an order of stage events that acquires its own ironic shape (*Irony* 27). As opposed to the traditional "arc," a contour of developing action toward denouement, States's principle refers to a configuration marked by successive fluctuation, a series of turns from given conditions toward their opposites – a process of reversal, in other words, rather than an acute instance of peripety.

Again, as Burke stipulates in *A Grammar of Motives*, the "ironic formula" indicates that, "what goes forth as A returns as non-A" (517). States, refining this theorem somewhat by arguing for the necessity of complete opposition, clarifies: "What goes forth as A must inevitably return as non-A, not simply as *other than* A" (*Irony* 13).

Importantly, the Burkean conjecture indicates an agency, a "what" that advances from point to point, and that also "goes forth" in a sequential theatrical action containing a mechanism of change. Marchbanks "goes forth" as Morell's pet project, and ends up shaking the preacher's self-image and marriage. Vershinin and Tusenbach would seem to bring a promise of change for Masha and Irina, yet the regiment's departure leaves the sisters desolate. "English" is the motif that goes forth as Mr. and Mrs. Smith begin their evening, and babel is the result. In each instance, there is an advancing ironic operation that turns the one condition in the direction of its opposite. Yet even within such steady movement there can be sharply distinguished moments of peripeteia, at times accompanied in Aristotelian fashion by anagnorisis, as in the case of Heidi Holland's realization – "I thought the point was that we were all in this together" (232) – which is both a culmination and a turning point as she shifts on this axis from a more social inclination in the direction of greater isolation.

To the extent that irony in the theatre is conveyed through speech along with performative detail and scenic imagery, the ironic is an aurally theatrical as well as linguistic behavior. Even when the dialogue does not belong to a demonstrative ironist such as Septimus Hodge or Scoop Rosenbaum, this attribute of the ironic in relation to the stage can be especially marked. Theatrical speech is framed generally by no qualifying description or narrative context; further, the dialogue exists as interchange among the characters, for themselves and for the audience to hear rather than to read as text. The spoken ironic voice is as old as the theatre, by design or not. When Agamemnon, upon returning from war, insists upon his autonomy to Clytemnestra, he is quite possibly the only one, on the orchestra stage or in the theatron, who believes that to be the case. Jason's patronizing assurances to his wife, in *Medea*, or the expressive guile of Dionysus toward Pentheus, in the *Bacchae*, serve also as ancestral exemplars of irony theatricalized by spoken as well as scenic means.

Yet here again, modernity brings a different perspective to the deployments and resonances of ironic language and referentiality. As Ernst Behler asserts, "Irony is inseparable from the evolution of the modern consciousness"; and for him, irony is "a decisive mark of literary modernity" (73). In addition, ironic language is peculiarly elastic in this situation: it may aid in communication, yet also hinder or even render it impossible. In each case, however, it is language itself that makes the difference. "The ironic manner of expression," writes Behler, "can be described as attempting to transcend the restrictions of normal discourse and straightforward speech by making the ineffable articulate, at least indirectly, through a great number of verbal strategies, and accomplishing what lies beyond the reach of direct communication" (111). One is reminded here, perhaps, of Stoppard as "ironist first-class" or of Septimus, whose linguistic skills allow for finely calibrated levels of communication with the theatre audience – and also for his own entertainment and self-satisfaction, even while bypassing those on stage with whom he is ostensibly conversing. For Stoppard, this variety of spoken irony allows for a greatly expanded range of inference and tonality. Even so, modern ironic speech can obfuscate, and do so intrinsically, with the vagaries and susceptibilities of language perceived as culpable. As Behler suggests:

> Characteristically enough, the ironic discourse itself, because of its highly self-reflective character, practices critical, deprecating observations of a self-referential nature as a constantly recurring technique. It has a particular predilection for toying with antinomies and self-contradictions imposed upon us by our being inscribed in language, by the subterranean determination imposed upon us through language.
>
> (112)

For the Smiths and the Martins, "English" turns dramatically and progressively into a highly orchestrated, contrapuntal "anti" symphony of nonsense. But modern theatrical speech has, in innumerable instances and not only after Ionesco, been exemplary of an ironic questioning of spoken dialogue's efficacy, at least when it comes to any attempt at accuracy, authenticity, or understanding among characters. As Behler says, there is an "implicit critique of reason and rationality in ironic communication" (111). Yet still, and in further irony, the fallibilities and slippages of language in the modern or postmodern view – and, in turn, of dialogue for the theatre – have proven on occasion to be eminently allusive, suspenseful, and performatively expressive, as notably in the plays of Samuel Beckett or Harold Pinter.

Factors of performance, dramatic structure, and theatrical dialogue not only affect the particular composition and linguistic presentation of irony but can define a context for the trope's philosophic dimensions as well. On the modernist stage and since, such philosophical emphasis has been directed often toward existential conundrums or crises with an ironic spin, as in *Six Characters in Search of an Author*, or toward the playing out of an interactive and dialectical configuration among ideas, as in *Candida* (or virtually any of Shaw's social plays). In these instances, too, theatrical and performative elements serve not only to deliver an ironic perspective but also to contribute in significant measure to a probing and revelation of irony's capabilities. Irony by its own contradictory nature may resist categorical definition, but its power and range of application can arise from this very multifariousness. With reference to irony as a "semantic farrago" (10), Morton Gurewitch also identifies the trope's dialectical application:

> Ambiguity, duplicity, multiplicity, paradox, disjunctiveness, complexity, elusiveness, provisionality, incertitude, indeterminism – these are only a few of irony's linkages. Irony also suggests an equilibrium of opposed forces or at least a condition of suspension between contrary powers.
>
> (15)

Implicit in Gurewitch's formulation is a notion of irony as dramatic: that is, as related intrinsically not only to an "equilibrium" of opposition but also to antagonistic terms in suspenseful conflict with one another.

Theatrical dialectic may be ideologically or philosophically based, but a set of dialectical oppositions, with a basis in conflicting premises, must of necessity locate the antithetical voices through dramatic character and situation. Again, one might recall Burke's equation among fundamental terms, in his outline of "Four Master Tropes," with "dialectic" corresponding to "irony" as well as to "dramatic" – particularly in the relation of ideas to agents of action (*Grammar* 503, 511–512). Burke does not mention, however, that what is dramatic in the equation may also be theatrical. That is, a dialectic or its double, the mastered irony, may be apprehended in terms of spectacle as well as through the appositions of argument or the points of view of characters. Put differently, and apart from the extrapolation from Burke, dialectic in the theatre is likely to be sensory; it may be seen as well as heard, a factor that distinguishes it sharply from ways in which the dialectical might operate in, say, a literary narrative. Irony and dialectic may, as States has it, be "fellow travelers" (*Irony* 3), but so are the dramatic and the theatrical, with each term containing its own potential relationships to what is dialectical or ironic.

In *Candida*, Eugene Marchbanks's status as intruder in the Morell household provides Shaw with multiple opportunities for cogent, visual images of his play's dialectical antagonisms. In physique as well as in behaviors, of course, Marchbanks is the picture of extreme contrast as well as vocal opposition to the way Morell appears and to what the preacher stands for. To the extent that Shaw's dialectical configuration in *Candida* centers on matters of maternal, marital, and romantic relations as well as who may be the "best" man for the title character, the irony in these dialectics can be vivid in visual terms when any two of the triangle of characters – Morell, Candida, Marchbanks – are together, or when all three share the stage at once. Morell's arrival home in the third act is particularly indicative as he walks in upon his wife and Marchbanks together by the fireside, the young poet with his head in her lap. Even as Candida and Marchbanks are quick to speak, there is an instant when nothing need be said: the spectacle alone conveys the intersection of Morell's newfound discomfort and mistrust with what he perceives as a genuinely romantic scene (an impression which Candida and her young admirer have done little to prevent). Marital, maternal, and romantic relations thus collide pictorially, together with the rivalry of the husband and self-styled suitor, and Shaw's mise-en-scène is all that is necessary for a clarified gestus of the play's dialectical movements.

In *Mrs. Warren's Profession*, the title character is symbolic of another sort of Shavian dialectic, in this instance centering on economic survival as against capitalistic exploitation, or "way of life" more generally; she stands, too, in colorful contrast to the New Woman personified by her daughter Vivie. Yet Mrs. Warren also embodies the playwright's fondness for tweaking his audience's response to such oppositions through theatrical spectacle and, often, through force of a character's personality in addition to manner of speech and rhetoric. In Mrs. Warren, Shaw portrays a character who, purely as a theatrical presence, exhibits considerable warmth and benevolence of spirit. She can be forthright, apparently guileless, and casually engaging in her no-nonsense volubility. Her daughter, by contrast, is cool (not to say cold), businesslike, and mathematical. Vivie may be correct in her convictions, and may have Shaw's ideological sympathy, but the dramatist opts for painting her as consistently priggish in contrast to her mother's easy-going humaneness. In the second act, Mrs. Warren arrives at one of the play's key questions: "My God, what kind of woman are you?" Vivie responds: "The sort the world is mostly made of, I should hope. Otherwise I don't understand how it gets its business done." The confrontation continues, Mrs. Warren retaliating with, "You! You've no heart" – and, concluding her castigation: "Shame on you for a bad daughter and a stuck-up prude!" (192). In the play's final tableau, Mrs. Warren leaves Vivie alone in the chambers of Honoria Fraser in Chancery Lane, having failed utterly in her project of gaining either sympathy or daughterly affection. Vivie, for her part, is absorbed contentedly with her figures and tables. Here as elsewhere, Shaw cagily uses a stage picture in ironic counterpoint to the qualities and behaviors of his characters to complicate or, indeed, reinforce a play's dialectics. Who is "right" in the end, the New Woman with "no heart" or the personable yet entrepreneurial madam? Shaw's ironies here, as in *Candida*, are theatrical as well as rhetorical, and his audience is witness to stage images that may have quite different and possibly opposing appeals to the eye and for the intellect.

Would Shaw have been amused, were he given the opportunity, at the unity of theatrical spectacle and dialectic in Caryl Churchill's *Cloud 9?* On this one can only speculate, but Churchill's combination of colonial Victorian and modern settings, not to mention her spin on marital, romantic, familial, gender, and class relations in a politicized context would certainly seem amenable to Shavian humor and sensibility. In this play, Churchill relies upon the unexpected stage picture, and in particular the inversions regarding gender roles, to underscore situational ironies along with the play's sexual and political dialectics. In the first act, which takes place in British colonial Africa, the marriage of Clive and Betty (played by a man), the relation of Clive to his black servant Joshua (played by a white man), or to his son Edward (played by a woman) or daughter Victoria (signified by a doll) provide a continually arresting visual counterpoint to expected deeds and conventional household relations. For act two, in the modern setting, all the characters save one are played by actors of a corresponding race and gender, with the greater familiarity or predictability now ironized and made more impactive because of the profundity of difference from what has come before.

The union of irony with stage spectacle need not, however, be so pronounced as in *Cloud 9* nor does it need to characterize an entire play's scheme of visual presentation. The arrival of Hilda Wangel and the entrance of Lopakhin following the estate auction are each highly dependent upon stage picture as well as a finely calibrated moment in the playwright's dramaturgy. Without the foretold, yet abrupt, visual image of "youth" as presented by Hilda at the master builder's door, and without the awaited, then fully realized, image of Lopakhin making his announcement, the full ironic impression afforded by theatre is necessarily lessened. For Brecht, the sustained, gestic image of Mother Courage with her wagon and family members – either singly or together – makes for a constant pictorial reminder of the play's core ironic appositions. In the closing sequences of *Arcadia*, when Stoppard brings his contemporary characters together on stage with those in the past, as Septimus and Thomasina waltz with Valentine and Hannah beside them unseen, the theatre audience alone is afforded the privileged viewpoint, one of uncommon ironic import.

And yet, it is *Six Characters in Search of an Author* that provides the most arresting and complex model of modern irony's partnership with theatrical imagery. With the stage itself as the setting, Pirandello can play deliberately on the apparent contradiction of depicting actors in rehearsal, an occasion with no audience, while at the same time underscoring the spectacle of actors interacting with "characters" before the live theatrical audience that beholds not a rehearsal but the play itself. For the Actors and the Characters, and within the context of

Pirandellian ironies that are connected so intimately with the playwright's metatheatrics and mise-en-scène, the consistent pictorial motif of *Six Characters* is that of an irremediable, existential fracture among actor, character, and "real" personage – not to mention what has "happened" in the Characters' story by contrast to the play's present stage action. In this sense, the Scene – the encounter of the Father and Stepdaughter at Madame Pace's, enacted in alternation by the Characters and Actors and observed by the Director – delivers an intensely aural as well as visual gestus.

> STEPDAUGHTER: It's still ringing in my ears. It drove me mad, that scream! – You can have me acted as you wish, sir – it doesn't matter. Even dressed. As long as my arms – only my arms – are bare.

And further:

> Scream! Scream, Mama! (*She buries her head in the Father's chest and with her shoulders hunched as if to fend off the scream, she goes on in a voice of stifled pain*). Scream the way you screamed then!
> MOTHER: (*hurling herself on them to separate them*). No, my darling! My darling daughter! (*And after having separated her from him*) You brute! Brute! She's my daughter! Don't you see she's my daughter?
> DIRECTOR: (*retreating at the scream, down to the footlights, amid the dismay of the Actors*). Wonderful! Yes, wonderful! And then the curtain.
>
> (Caputi 245)

The Actors cannot possibly capture the encounter in any way that will meet the Characters' standard of authenticity. Yet with the Characters' own reality – that is, the constituent terms of their story – in dispute among themselves, the project of enacting the "truth" can be delivered imagistically by Pirandello as an impossible divide among all the performers, Actors and Characters. Here the Pirandellian principle of opposition, the *sentimento del contraria*, is framed as a theatrically vivid as well as ideological phenomenon. Indeed, what *Six Characters* presents visually – and as running complement to its philosophical dialectic between Director and the Father primarily – is the continuing spectacle, in tandem with argument, of the profound ontological incongruities at the center of Pirandello's drama.

Irony, once again, is eminently capacious as well as notoriously contradictory. In its philosophical dimension and by the nature of its versatility, the ironic is able to incorporate theatrical and dramatic representation and, at the same time, emphasize factors of dialectic, paradox, reversal, apposition, and linguistic counterpoint – to mention several of its more noteworthy and elastic capabilities. Irony's adaptability is also broadly situational, particularly so in relation to cultural and historical settings as well as to the dramaturgical arrangements of given works. Irony for Chekhov is not the same as, say, for Pirandello, Ionesco, or Stoppard, not only because the respective dramatic situations and characterizations are different but so too are the audiences and modes of theatrical communication at various times. To abbreviate States's claim, the trope requires someone who "gets the irony," a notion that, in the transhistoric view, might well apply to theatre audiences as well as to stage characters.

Even so, there is plenty that persists in the nature of irony to vouch for a transhistorical aspect alongside the versatility. Eric Gans not only sponsors this idea, which in his view has its own ironic twist, but also argues for the trope's fundamental status: "Irony is built into the formal representation-relation that is the basis of human culture. In this sense, it is truly a transhistorical phenomenon, one that annuls its own historicity in the very act of producing it" (74). The basic affiliation of irony, language, and speech enforces this universality. As Gans argues: "Irony attends us everywhere, always gifted with prestige . . . No mere figure of speech, irony is central to all thought, for the use of language as such is essentially ironic" (64). On the matter of irony and its representation in art, Gans identifies a key aesthetic ratio with respect to a dialectic of form and content:

> It is because the esthetic effect is the direct experience of irony
> that the greatest artworks are the most ironic. The oscillatory
> structure of esthetic experience, ever circulating between form

and content, realizes the same paradox that the ironist enacts in speech. Esthetic form dissolves as the mere revelation of content, but content can possess significance only by recalling the form in which it is revealed.

(70)

Along these lines, then, irony is fundamental and also constant, basic not only to language and artistic representation but also to aesthetic effect. The ironic double bind to which Gans refers is, in fact, an essence of art.

Still, the universalized, or cosmic, potential that may belong to irony's nature and ancestry can be delimited by epoch and by situational variables, in social and historical as well as dramaturgical contexts. Can theatrical irony in a contemporary or postmodernist context recall or deliver the breadth of vision that belongs to the ironic heritage and repertoire of an earlier modernist drama? Or, is it rather the case that what Gans calls "our meta-ironic post-modern culture" will inevitably, and by definition, deny the trope such an embracing import (68)? The behaviors and the impact of irony in the theatre are by no means constant, and there is continual alteration in accord with the sensibilities of those who would employ or apprehend it in widely varying dramatic situations. Irony can portend an inclusive, if inscrutable, atmosphere of sense, reciprocity, or meaningfulness, as in *The Master Builder*; it can intimate the relation of character to time as both a quotidian present and an eternity, as in the plays of Chekhov; it can denote a progressive and paradoxical gravitation toward the negative, to self-cancellation, as in *Six Characters in Search of an Author*; through speech itself, ironically, it can embrace the failure of language as in *The Bald Soprano*. From so wide-ranging a perspective, in fact, theatrical irony can be understood as barometric, not only in relation to cultural tempers but also to the adaptable capabilities of dramaturgy that speak to differing eras and attitudes.

Morton Gurewitch traces irony's inclusive adaptability from a basis in discourse to a cosmic inquiry:

Irony, once a Socratic midwifery, is also associated with demystification and unmasking, with a smilingly skeptical

222

qualification of conviction and faith, and intelligent
disenslavement from ideology. But irony also invokes striking
discrepancies, startling juxtapositions, the shock of unexpectedly
altered circumstance. Irony points to a reader's (or spectator's)
superior awareness, indeed to anyone's superior awareness.
Yet irony also invokes oddities of fate and mysteries and
iniquities of the cosmos.

(15)

Irony's cosmic trait is, arguably, among its more exalted qualities; it is
also among its rarest manifestations, particularly so in recent times.
The cosmic, or universalized, factor in irony signifies a breadth of
vision and a richness of implication that, while possibly enigmatic (as
with Ibsen or Chekhov), connotes nonetheless a frame of understanding that ranges well beyond the immediate or quotidian. The cosmic
dimension allows for abstract time along with past or present circumstance; it bespeaks the eternal dialectic of sense and no-sense, typically
with the ironic voice itself as arbiter. And yet, more fundamentally,
irony can point simply to natural occurrence and progression, to the
way of the world, to the cosmic joke, to the familiar but strange "oddities" or appositions that achieve their breadth of application precisely
because of a quirky rightness, symmetry, or unexpected determinacy.

Theatrical irony is supremely potent yet vulnerable to constraint,
at once. Muecke quotes Thomas Mann, who characterized the "problem
of irony" as "without exception the profoundest and most fascinating in
the world." As Muecke has it, continuing, the "history of irony is also
the history of both comic and tragic awareness. In the last two hundred
years, irony has enabled men to confront both the death of God and the
discovery that the world was not made with them particularly in mind;
and here nothing less is involved than the defeat of 'cosmic' hope and
despair" (*Irony* 80–81). Irony of late, or in the postmodern context, is
more localized, more constrained, and more skeptical of so embracing a
view, its referentiality narrowed at times to merely a sly quotation. In
"The Moviegoer," David Denby's appreciation of Susan Sontag following
her death, the early 1960s are characterized as a "last earnest moment
in American culture." At that time, Denby writes, "Irony was a mode of

aggression that separated the knowing from the saps, not a weak-backed accommodation to the undermining proliferation of media images and the leveling of cultural values" (91–92). And yet, when a culture reads differently, where there is openness to a wider-ranging, and even cosmic depth of implication, the ironic sensibility retains the broadest of resonances and its theatrical voice endures powerfully. Irony is fundamental to theatre, in much the same way that drama, in Muecke's phrasing, is "essentially ironigenic, that is, productive of irony" (*Ironic* 71). The inborn versatility and dependency of the ironic trope upon situational variables will, by necessity and over time, vary the terms of its expressiveness as well as its reception and appreciation. Yet the great ironies of the modernist stage will assuredly abide, if at times perilously, in accord with the barometers of other times, in different theatres, and before new audiences.

Notes

Irony personified: Ibsen and *The Master Builder*

1. Frye writes: "Irony is naturally a sophisticated mode, and the chief difference between sophisticated and naïve irony is that the naïve ironist calls attention to the fact that he is being ironic, whereas sophisticated irony merely states, and lets the reader add the ironic tone himself" (*Anatomy* 41).

2. Shaw has this comment on Solness in his review of *The Master Builder* (1892): "Also he is daimonic, not sham daimonic like Molvik in *The Wild Duck*, but really daimonic, with luck, a star, and mystic 'helpers and servers' who find the way though the maze of life for him. In short, a very fascinating man, whom nobody, himself least of all, could suspect of having shot his bolt and being already dead" (*Quintessence of Ibsenism* 120). For discussion of the implications of daimon in the tragic context see, for example, my own *After Dionysus: A Theory of the Tragic.*

3. Compare Brustein's argument ("The Crack in the Chimney") that Solness's discovery of the fire's actual source suggests a deliberate disrupton, on Ibsen's part, of the conventions of naturalistic logic (143).

4. Ewbank identifies a pattern in Ibsen's later plays, which "begin at a breaking-point and follow a structural pattern where an arrival – Hilde Wangel, the Rat Wife (and Asta), Ella (and Mrs. Wilton), Irene – forces a crisis condition into an active crisis" (140).

5. Both Clurman and Templeton refer to Hilda's entrance in this way, although Clurman describes the *coup de théâtre* as "typical" (173) whereas Templeton refers to how "Solness's personification takes on literal life in Hilda's famous knock" (266).

6. Clurman distinguishes the catalytic factor from Ibsen's primary subject of inquiry: "Hilda is the play's catalyst, she is not its center" (171).

7. Meyer writes that, in 1906, "George Brandes published a series of letters which Ibsen had written between October 1889 and December 1890 (i.e., eighteen to twelve months before he began *The Master Builder*) to a

young Austrian girl named Emilie Bardach. These revealed that, in the summer of 1889, when Ibsen was sixty-one and Emilie was eighteen, they had met at Gossensass in the Austrian Tyrol and that some kind of infatuation had resulted; whether mutual or one-sided was not quite clear. They had corresponded for over a year, and then Ibsen, gently but firmly, had told her not to write to him any more" ("Introduction" 122). Translated texts of several of the letters are included in the "Introduction" as well as in Meyer's *Ibsen: A Biography.*

8. Regarding the character's connection to *The Lady from the Sea,* Templeton asserts: "The most important model for Hilda Wangel was herself as a young girl" (263). And further: "In a striking example of literal, linear intertextuality unique in Ibsen's plays, Hilda Wangel is the only major character to appear twice; it is the Hilda of *The Lady from the Sea* whom master builder Solness met when he came to her town ten years ago" (264).

9. For Templeton, "Ibsen's letters show overwhelmingly that his feelings for Emilie Bardach were those of a man as well as a writer; his insistence on her physical loveliness and his nostalgia for the happiness they had shared are not the expressions of a man who was interested in a woman primarily as poetic inspiration. Ibsen had fallen in love" (246). See Templeton (256–257) for a viewpoint that disputes both Meyer and Koht on Ibsen's relationships with the three women.

10. For Meyer (*Biography*): "The character of Solness was the nearest thing to a deliberate self-portrait that Ibsen had yet attempted" (697). Meyer calls this work the "most personal and revealing of all his plays" (691). In Koht's view, "Many of the problems that had filled [Ibsen's] mind in the last few years are concentrated in *The Master Builder.* There is much talk of mysterious forces, of a variety of 'demons' within, of unexpressed wishes translating themselves into action, of unconscious thoughts that have a life of their own, of the power of one spirit over another – Hilde has power over Solness, he over Kaja Fosli" (435). Compare also Archer: "Of all his writings, [*The Master Builder*] is probably the most original, the most individual, the most unlike any other drama by any other writer ... *The Master Builder* had no model and has no parallel. It shows no slightest vestige of outside influence. It is Ibsen, and nothing but Ibsen" (240–241).

11. States argues: "In this essential sense, then, irony is the drama's principle of curvature; it is the force to which all of the clear moments of reversal we can confidently call peripeties, and all of the smaller things we call ironies of speech, bear a vital synecdochic relationship" (*Irony* 27).

The character of irony in Chekhov

1. Translations of *The Cherry Orchard* and *Three Sisters* to which I refer are, unless otherwise indicated, Ann Dunnigan's.

2. In *The Real Chekhov* (187–196), Magarshack refers to letters written by the playwright, 1903–1904, to company members of the Moscow Art Theatre, many of which refer to the qualities of individual characters in *The Cherry Orchard*.

3. Compare Gilman, who interprets Lopakhin's "moo" as a "reflection of his easy position vis-à-vis the household and a rather clumsy attempt to display it" (*Plays* 218). For Richard Peace, "a certain lack of seriousness in Lopakhin's relationship to Varya" is betrayed in this scene (150).

4. In Dunnigan's translation, and in Ronald Hingley's, the stage direction is "ironically," whereas in Stark Young's it is "sarcastically." For one discussion of verbal irony in Chekhov, see Adamantova and Williamson.

5. For discussion of Chekhov's health during the writing of *The Cherry Orchard*, see for example Troyat (*Chekhov*) or Valency (*String*).

6. Compare Peace, who describes a present time that "looks two ways" and is symbolized by the "contrasting dresses" of Masha and Irina who wear black and white respectively (76).

7. States refers to this type of simple irony as "the so-called Sophoclean or dramatic irony: we know; he doesn't. Or, more likely, we know, and he only *suspects*," a construction that derives from the Oedipus plot (*Pleasure* 89).

8. Compare Styan's reference, regarding *The Cherry Orchard*, to "an embracing structure of comi-tragic ambivalence" (198).

9. Corrigan's idea, especially if understood in the context of juxtaposition, can be compared with Styan's: "Chekhov knows that by reversing a current of feeling, muting a climax, toppling a character's dignity, contradicting one statement by another, juxtaposing one impression with its opposite, he is training his audience to see the truth of the total situation" (198).

10. For Stark Young, as for Dunnigan, the translation of the two words is "nonsense" and "consensus," whereas in Hingley's version, Chebutykin's line is, "Stuff and nonsense. Bunki, bunko, bunko" (252).

Irony and dialectic: Shaw's *Candida*

1. Irvine argues that Shaw is careful not to present Candida with a true choice: "Eugene could have been twenty-eight, he is eighteen. He could have been Jovian and red-bearded, like Jack Tanner; he is 'slight, effeminate, with a delicate childish voice'" (174).

2. Berst agrees with Irvine's assessment, finding Marchbanks "unsatisfactory as a psychological portrayal." Yet the poet is still, in Berst's view, "effective dramatically" (41). Marchbanks's qualities as poet and genius are controversial, as is the character's psychological rendering more generally. Berst writes that Marchbanks "has certain attributes of genius, but he is as yet only an incipient poet" (57), while Bentley argues that Shaw does not "make us believe in the poet's poetry" ("Making" 306).

3. Burke writes: "A human role (such as we get in drama) may be summed up in certain slogans, or formulae, or epigrams, or 'ideas' that characterize the agent's situation or strategy. The role involves properties both intrinsic to the agent and developed with relation to the scene and to other agents. And the 'summings-up' ('ideas') similarly possess properties derived both from the agent and from the various factors with which the agent is in relationship. Where the ideas are in action, we have drama; where the agents are in ideation, we have dialectic" (*Grammar* 511–512).

4. States provides a historical context for this interrelation or triad: "... it is understandable why *irony* came to be equated with *dialectic* in the late eighteenth century and why these terms, in turn, became descriptive, if haphazard, equivalents of the term *dramatic*. For it was at this time that critics, following modern developments in philosophy and science, began to interpret literary works as the inter*action* of ideas, and thus a set of terms was needed that would transpose the mute mimetic order of action into concepts, or dialectic" (*Irony* 8–9).

5. Langer contrasts the dramatic and narrative modes: the "literary mode is the mode of Memory; the dramatic is the mode of Destiny" (307). Compare States: "Whereas we think of irony as the agency of discovery of opposition and contradiction in the 'infinity of possibles' and dialectic as the ideological struggle waged by the possibles (dialectic equals irony explained), we would be most apt to use the word drama, or dramatic, when the struggle involves human action, or what Miss Langer would call Destiny (drama is irony acted out, or, if you wish, dialectic personified)" (*Irony* 23).

6. All quotations from *Candida* are from Shaw, *Selected Plays*.

7. Finney writes: "For together with those features that recall the Virgin, Candida possesses qualities of a very different literary type, that of the New Woman. This combination produces a hybrid uncommon not only in Shaw's oeuvre but in turn-of-the-century literature in general" (193).

8. See Dukore (56). Irvine disputes that emphasis on this connection: "The stage directions and the symbolism of the play indicate that she is to be regarded primarily as the mother-woman. Her maternal indulgence

toward the adult male infant is stressed to the point of objectionable omniscience. Granted that she is predominantly maternal in outward manner and psychological attitude; that the maternal manner, in a beautiful and intelligent woman, is charming to most men – and indeed it is often simply a reassuringly innocent disguise for sex – nevertheless, Candida is much more than a schematization of the mother-instinct" (175–176).

9. Shaw wrote, in a letter to the *Evening Standard*, that "in the real typical doll's house it is the man who is the doll" (Dukore 54). The range of dialectical associations between the two plays is complemented by the fact that Janet Achurch played the role of Nora Helmer as well as that of Candida.

10. See for example, Nethercot's "Preface on Ventriloquism" (*Men and Supermen* ix–x). Dukore's assessment is that Shaw did not "believe in disembodied ideas. On the contrary, he felt it was impossible to give audiences intellectual satisfaction unless ideas were embodied in real people whose problems were interesting" (11). Compare Brustein's comment on Shaw the polemicist apart from the plays: when the dramatist "opens his mouth for an extradramatic utterance, he invariably manages to diminish his stature as a dialectical artist by reducing his complex perceptions to uniformitarian dogma" (*Revolt* 184).

11. Gainor finds "ironic parallels" between the myth of Proserpine/Persephone and the actual conditions of Prossy, and suggests that Prossy's complaint "seems an ironic version of the illnesses suffered by New Women in Victorian fiction" (26, 31–32).

12. Compare Bentley, in *Life of the Drama*: "On the face of it, Bernard Shaw may seem simply to be identified with the ironists, and by placing them at the center of his compositions to have reversed the traditional structure of comedy, which had a knave or fool at its center. But at least several of Shaw's comedies, and those among the best, turn out to be traditional in the end, as the ironist proves to be an imposter. Bluntschli, in *Arms and the Man*, is an example" (131).

13. For Gilman, Natasha's "act of usurpation is carried out in an extremely oblique manner, behind everyone's back, we might say, in the interstices of other activity, with nothing directly said about it as a process and nothing consciously acknowledged by anyone except for one hermetic outburst by Masha" (*Plays* 151).

14. Holroyd argues that, "The crisis between Candida and Marchbanks comes early in the third act when Candida offers herself ('Do you want anything more?') to Marchbanks. We have been prepared for this and

told how to interpret it in her conversation with Morell in the previous act – and the words and situation were as much as the Examiner of Plays would allow" (316). Compare Berst on the fireplace scene: "This is their most intimate point of contact, the climax of their relationship, and it is bogus, surrogate, and incomplete, since they are existing on two different levels" (51).

15. Holroyd recounts Shaw's trip to Italy in October, 1884, when he saw "the Renaissance sculpture at the Bargello in Florence, particularly admired Raphael's pictures in the Uffizi and the Palazzo Pitti as well as a Botticelli Virgin and Child in Milan." *Candida* was, for Shaw, his "modern pre-Raphaelite play." Titian's *Virgin of the Assumption* as well as Correggio's were also influential in inspiring, for the dramatist, a "Cockney Candida" (314).

16. From the often-cited letter from Shaw to James Huneker, 1904, quoted here in Nethercot (15).

17. Irvine sets forth the terms of "misunderstanding": "In her too confident superiority and her present subservience to Eugene's thought, [Candida] has missed all the storm signals. She does not dream that James cannot grasp her combination of steadfast affection with clear-sighted detachment, that he has understood every word in a personal, emotional context. Morell, on the other hand, is convinced that she cannot love him, since she does not love him for his reasons. The misunderstanding is complete" (176–177).

18. Compare Dukore: "At the resolution of *Candida*, the wife chooses her husband, but though their marriage is saved, he does not understand why she chose him rather than his rival, and he realizes how little comprehension of himself and his wife he has ever had" (60). Or, in Bentley's assessment, "now that the scales have fallen from Morell's eyes, the marriage can never be the same again. It is not easy to be *re*illusioned" (*Thinker* 134–135).

19. On the unresolved factor, compare Bentley (*Thinker*): "Although we have always been told that Shaw is so much a propagandist that all his characters are merely trumpets of Shavian good or anti-Shavian evil, in actual fact Shaw attains to an astonishing, many-sided objectivity. As skillfully as any other dramatic dialectician who has ever written, he can do full justice to thesis and antithesis alike. That is why people find him contradictory and seldom look for a Shavian synthesis" (135).

20. Berst's thesis is that, "Although the play offers a threefold perspective in terms of its three major characters, Morell is at its most significant dramatic and dialectic epicenter. Candida with her charm and Marchbanks with his vigor tend to divert attention toward themselves,

but it is Morell and his values which undergo the most sustained attack
and analysis, and it is as a result of this attack that Candida's mother-
woman role is revealed as egocentric and philistine, and Marchbanks's
poetic vision, so acutely critical, is revealed as myopically romantic"
(65). Regarding the Shavian pattern of diverse standpoints, Berst
concludes that, "Shaw's greatest accomplishment is that he has given
vital illumination to several divergent views – Candida's domestic
vision, warm and maternal on one hand, but narrow and egocentric on
the other; Marchbanks's poetic vision, incisive and iconoclastic, but
irresponsible and romantic; and Morell's social vision, kindly and
humanitarian, but rhetorical and melodramatic" (74).

Pirandello's "Father" – and Brecht's "Mother"

1. All quotations from *Six Characters in Search of an Author* are, unless
   indicated otherwise, from Anthony Caputi's translation.
2. Compare States, who remarks on the tragic associations of a *"total
   irony"* that is "not nihilistic but apocalyptic" (*Irony* 34).
3. Compare Lewis, in *The Contemporary Theatre*: "The audience is one
   reality; the rehearsing actors another, with the stage as the instrument
   for transforming appearance into a different illusion of reality; and
   lastly, the characters created in fiction, who now want to know how
   their lives will end – all three interchanging their respective concepts"
   (*Contemporary* 134–135).
4. In his "Preface" to *Six Characters*, Pirandello recalls his first image of a
   family of characters, and describes the image of the Father first (363). In
   Walter Starkie's view, "The father and the stepdaughter were evidently
   those that struck the author's mind with the first flush of inspiration,
   and so they are very nearly completely realized." He contrasts these two
   with the other four characters, who are "on different planes" (208).
5. Kennedy also emphasizes the Father's manner of speech; his
   "articulateness in the open situation marks a central disproportion; an
   excess of words trying to eke out what he feels as a constricting pittance
   of words in his fixed scene" (187).
6. For Bentley, the mask is the "outward form," while the face is "the
   suffering creature" (*Thinker* 150).
7. Brustein notes the Father's status as "Pirandello's philosophical
   raisonneur" (*Revolt* 311).
8. States qualifies such a view, noting occasions when "irony rises above
   its own negative tendency in the hands of a great tragic poet" (*Irony* 35).
9. All quotations from *Mother Courage and Her Children* are from Eric
   Bentley's translation.

10. See Gilman's discussion of the play's full title and its implications (*Making* 223–224), and also Bentley on "courage" and cowardice (*Commentaries* 158).
11. Compare Lyons: "There is an irony in the fact that the little human community of Fierling's family is, to a strong degree, seen by Mother Courage as objects which belong to her. They seem to exist for her as commodities. Certainly she has strong feeling for them; yet they seem to her to be things which she owns more than individual and unique beings" (97).
12. It is not my purpose here to enter into the longstanding debate on Mother Courage's possibly empathetic qualities in relation to the performance style of epic theatre. See, for a representative example, Martin Esslin's discussion of Brecht's own response to the character, and the adjustments made in order to discourage more affective responses (*Brecht* 230–232).

Absurdist irony: Ionesco's "anti-play"

1. In "Why Do I Write?," Ionesco identifies contradiction with his own experience and its application to his drama: "I don't have the feeling that I have said things that are new, but rather that I experienced intensely two contradictory apprehensions: the world is at once marvelous and atrocious, a miracle and hell, and these antithetical feelings, these two obvious truths, constitute the backdrop of my personal existence and my oeuvre" (13).
2. Lamont elaborates: "Ionesco's irony is close to the Socratic undermining of existence, that 'infinitely bottomless, invisible, and indivisible spiritual state' diagnosed by Kierkegaard in *The Concept of Irony*. This process of derision must be situated in a zone one might call 'the between,' an 'empty space,' a 'nothingness' that conceals what is perhaps most important" (*Imperatives* 5).
3. All quotations from *The Bald Soprano* are from Donald M. Allen's translation.
4. In his introduction to *The Theatre of the Absurd*, Esslin identifies a "sense of metaphysical anguish at the absurdity of the human condition" as characteristic of the work of Ionesco along with Beckett and others (xix).
5. Compare Lane, who identifies the "saucy maid" among stereotyped characters including "the randy Fire Chief" and "the bourgeois English couple" in reference to Ionesco's use of genre conventions (37).
6. Pronko suggests: "The Smiths and the Martins, whose evening of chatter we witness, are gross exaggerations of types we know – and even

of ourselves, for one of the characteristics of Ionesco's theater is that we may recognize ourselves, or elements of ourselves, in people, situations, and language which are pushed beyond credibility until they explode in a kind of dramatic paroxysm" (6).

7. I refer to Emile Zola's "Naturalism in the Theatre" and August Strindberg's "Preface" to *Miss Julie*, and to the emphasis in both documents on naturalistic elements such as environment, ancestry, and physiology, as well as psychological factors.

8. Compare Esslin, in *The Theatre of the Absurd*, who describes the dramaturgy of absurdist plays generally, and notes that "if a good play is judged by subtlety of characterization and motivation, these are often without recognizable characters and present the audience with almost mechanical puppets" (xvii).

9. See also Hayman's characterization of a clock that "joins in the confusion by striking seven and immediately contradicting itself by striking three" (19). Near the end of the play, Ionesco's stage direction describes the strokes of the clock as "more nervous" (39).

10. Compare Grossvogel, who sees Ionesco's theatre generally as "consistently derived from the confrontation with language" (79), and McDermott, who refers to the phrase "bald soprano" as one that "served Ionesco's purpose well in signaling the final collapse of the *word* – sound without meaning, without significance – the way of the world" (41).

11. Saussure clarifies that, "The word 'arbitrary' also calls for comment. The term should not imply that the choice of the signifier is left entirely to the speaker ... I mean rather that it is unmotivated, i.e. arbitrary in that it actually has no natural connection with the signified" (69).

12. Compare Derrida's assertion that "as soon as one seeks to demonstrate in this way that there is no transcendental or privileged signified and that the domain or play of signification henceforth has no limit, one must reject even the concept and the word 'sign' itself – which is precisely what cannot be done. For the signification 'sign' has always been understood and determined, in its meaning, as sign-of, a signifier referring to a signified, a signifier different from its signified. If one erases the radical difference between signifier and signified, it is the word 'signifier' itself which must be abandoned as a metaphysical concept" (281).

"Ironist First Class": Stoppard's *Arcadia*

1. The "First Class" characterization is John Lahr's, from his review of a revival of Stoppard's *Jumpers* ("Stalkers" 101).

2. Schiff writes that "the unsettled nature of a superb joke – or its relatives, a superb paradox or a superb tautology – is for Stoppard a kind of paradigm of beauty; it's the atom of his art, irreducible, alive, complete in itself and yet forever sending out ripples" (215).

3. Brassell observes "how well Stoppard catches the measure of Wilde's idiom" in *Travesties*, and remarks on "how his wit can at times rival Wilde's own" (150). Stoppard's fondness for literary and historical allusions has not always met with approval. Kenneth Tynan noted (in 1977) that, "People sometimes say that Stoppard, for all his brilliance, is fundamentally a leech, drawing the lifeblood of his work from the inventions of others. In 'Rosencrantz and Guildenstern,' he battens on Shakespeare, in 'Inspector Hound' on Christie, in 'Jumpers' on the logical positivists, in 'Travesties' on Wilde, James Joyce, and Lenin" (79).

4. All references to the text of *Arcadia* are from the Faber and Faber edition (1993).

5. Alwes argues that, with regard to *Arcadia*'s split time frame, the play "confers an almost transcendentally privileged perspective on the audience by freeing them from the constraints of time to which his characters are so thoroughly (and self-consciously) subjected, and the effect is ultimately one of consolation" (392).

6. Regarding the factor of communication between characters in the different eras, Sternlieb and Selleck suggest that, "One of *Arcadia*'s more trenchant ironies is that, in the nineteenth century, a thirteen-year-old and her tutor were better equipped to converse than two adult academics in the twentieth" (483).

7. In Alan Reynolds Thompson's phrasing, "The seeming simpleton in Old Comedy who got the laugh on the boastful antagonist was an eiron." Thompson notes that the Greek audience did not understand the concept of irony in the way that it developed later (4).

8. Compare Edwards: "The truth, the emotional core of this madness, left typically unstated by Stoppard, but all the more poignant for that reason, is that by the eve of Thomasina's seventeenth birthday, Septimus and she are in love, though they are not even aware of it themselves. The pain of her irrecoverable loss in the fire must be at the root of the hermit's desperate attempts to restore hope 'through good English algebra'" (182).

9. On the issue of motive for Septimus's computations, compare Wheatley, who argues that, as a response to Thomasina's death, he "assumes the proof of her mathematical theory as his life's work and adopts the role of hermit she had 'created' in his presence, when she drew in a figure of a hermit on Noakes's sketch of the uninhabited hermitage planned for the garden" (175). See also Melbourne: "Septimus's philosophy of knowledge

is that 'nothing can be lost,' a view which might indeed have led him to a frenzied attempt to save the world" (567).

10. See also Hunter: "Thomasina now offers him a permission: 'You may.' But Septimus does not have the permission of his own conscience: 'I may not.' Finally in what has been ironically a little like a tutorial on auxiliary verbs, the pupil's 'you must' sounds like an assertion of determinism, whereas the tutor's last refusal is an assertion of free will: 'I will not.' With free will goes the obligation of moral choice" (199–200).

11. Compare Melbourne's reference to the "human warmth" of Septimus's feelings for Thomasina, "the only sort of 'heat energy' which need not grow cold over time. The Sidley Park hermit is thus at once scholar and lover, another symbol uniting *Arcadia*'s themes of intellectual and carnal knowledge" (571).

12. John Fleming (191–192), Michael Vanden Heuvel (225), and Susanne Vees-Gulani discuss the dramaturgy of *Arcadia* as analogous to the science. As Vees-Gulani notes, *Arcadia*'s "structural organization reflects back on the content itself, revealing how it forms a self-similar structure. In this manner Stoppard's play can be seen as a dynamic process, again pointing to chaos theory, which is often understood as a science of becoming rather than being" (423).

13. See Vanden Heuvel's discussion of *Travesties* as a "postmodern pastiche" and in relation to irony (220–221), and Fleming's reference to Stoppard's "conscious intertextuality" (49).

14. Compare Hutcheon on the "seriousness" of irony in the postmodern context: "Many of the foes of postmodernism see irony as fundamentally anti-serious, but this is to mistake and misconstrue the critical power of double-voicing. As Umberto Eco has said, about both his own historiographic metafiction and his semiotic theorizing, the 'game of irony' is intricately involved in seriousness of purpose and theme. In fact irony may be the only way we *can* be serious today. There is no innocence in our world, he suggests. We cannot ignore the discourses that precede and contextualize everything we say and do, and it is through ironic parody that we signal our awareness of this inescapable fact. The 'already-said' must be reconsidered and can be reconsidered only in an ironic way" (39).

15. Vanden Heuvel aligns Stoppard's emphasis on order and disorder, as well as the science of thermodynamics, with the play's affinities with postmodernity: "The principles of thermodynamics underlying the content and the structure of the play mimic brilliantly in scientific terms the postmodern notion of what Heiner Muller has called the 'entropy of discourse,' that is, the manner by which signification

assumes a kind of structure of presence, intentionality and interpretability, only to disperse into absence and randomness. The shadow of entropy allows Stoppard to propose various kinds of structure in the world of both the present and past Derbyshire households he depicts, as well as in the structure of his own play, even as such organization and taxonomies are breaking down – literally turning his theatrical apparatus into a steam engine surrendering useful, orderly heat to its environment" (225).

16. Booth observes, comparing plays and other works, that, "Dramatic irony . . . is of course by no means confined to plays, and it does not depend on the convention of soliloquies. It occurs whenever an author deliberately asks us to compare what two or more characters say of each other, or what a character says now with what he says or does later. Any plain discrepancy will do, though it is true that conventions like the soliloquy or the epistolary technique in novels are especially useful because especially sure" (63). In *Arcadia*, such discrepancy is seen particularly in the observations of Hannah Jarvis by comparison with the actions of Septimus and Thomasina, as witnessed by the audience. With reference to drama specifically, Muecke notes that irony's connection with theatre arises in part because "it is the audience that sees and the dramatis personae who are seen, who are unaware of being observed, blind to the fact of being watched," a situation that has a redoubled effect in *Arcadia* because of the twin time frames in which characters in one era observe those in another, even as all are watched by the audience. Muecke continues: "The stage is a place where something is about to happen or be revealed. Since the audience feels this but the dramatis personae generally do not, there is a basic potential for irony inherent in drama. Moreover, what is about to happen is something that is going to happen to the unsuspecting dramatis personae. Their blindness therefore has reference to the future as well as to the present" (*Ironic* 66–67).

American ironies: Wasserstein and Kushner

1. See also Shaeffer's commentary on O'Neill's kinship with tragedy – "at last an American tragedy, viable and persuasive" – and point of view on the play's shortcomings as well as aspirations (419).
2. Hamartia, which is mentioned briefly in Chapter 13 of Aristotle's *Poetics*, is commonly understood in relation to error or miscalculation on the part of a given character. See Hardison and also Vernant on the association with blindness as opposed to error; as the latter writes: "Hamartia means, in its proper sense, blindness" (285).

3. Else, for example, describes a connection between hamartia and recognition in relation to the Aristotelian concept of plot (384–385).
4. Compare Raymond Williams, who briefly situates Tennessee Williams in the following context: "The human condition is tragic because of the entry of mind on the fierce, and in itself tragic, animal struggle of sex and death. The purpose of the drama is then to cut through these mental illusions to the actual primary rhythms. This is, in a literal sense, drama on a hot tin roof" (147–148).
5. Gelb makes several references to O'Neill's admiration for, and influence by, Strindberg, including the Nobel speech where he notes "the debt my work owes to that greatest genius of all modern dramatists, your August Strindberg" (814). O'Neill's *Welded*, among his several works that depict marital relations, is modeled to some degree on Strindbergian drama and attitudes (517–518). See also Shaeffer on Strindberg's influence on *Beyond the Horizon* in particular: "As a disciple of Strindberg, O'Neill was intent on depicting love as a trap and marriage as a prison, especially for the male." Yet also: "At the same time it is too narrow a view to regard *Beyond the Horizon* as simply O'Neill's variations on a theme by Strindberg; the play also dramatizes the unhappy fate of two men who were false to their essential natures" (420).
6. Wasserstein comments: "It was interesting for me in *The Heidi Chronicles* to write Scoop Rosenbaum; I got to be the smart Jewish boy who tormented me all my life. I thought, 'now I get to be you,' and it was fabulous; it was like revenge of the nerds" (Bryer 272).
7. Balakian states, in another context, that Wasserstein's "characters have a metaphysical angst as they try to figure out how to live their lives in the face of so many options" ("Feminist" 215).
8. Stringfellow refers, in this relation, to the "original" statement and its ironic expression (4).
9. Bigsby comments on Peter's changing "his confident tone for a caustic irony" (*Contemporary* 352).
10. Scoop, in particular, might fit with Stringfellow's observation that certain people "resort to irony characteristically, invariably, even neurotically; we have all encountered the person who is not free not to speak ironically. It is in such individuals that we see how deeply rooted irony can be in character and, therefore, how intimate the connection is between irony and the unconscious determinants of character" (1).
11. Compare Bigsby (*Contemporary*) on *Angels* as a play that "deliberately stages the physical reality no less than the social and political implications of gay love. But this is one of the ironies floating in the background, for the very conservative forces for whom scatological

language is offensive (Joe asks his boss, Roy Cohn, to moderate his language) are happy to endorse judicial corruption. Those who are distressed by open displays of love are all too happy to remain blind to its lethal consequences. Those who celebrate American values seem oblivious to the extent to which they daily betray them" (112).

12. Bigsby remarks that, "Intellectually, Kushner is constantly drawn to dualisms, to the tension that he sees as defining the nature of identity, but more significantly is committed to the transcendence of those dualisms" (*Contemporary* 88).

13. For Savran, Kushner's "binary oppositions" include "heaven/hell, forgiveness/retribution, communitarianism/individualism, spirit/flesh, pleasure/pain, beauty/decay, future/past, homosexuality/ heterosexuality, rationalism/indeterminacy, migration/staying put, progress/stasis, life/death" (212).

14. Savran calls *Angels* a "promiscuously complicated play that is very difficult to categorize generically" (209), while Fisher remarks on Kushner's "particular skill for bringing together wildly disparate plot lines, political theorems, and aesthetic motifs in original and satisfying ways" (59).

Irony's theatre

1. The observation concerning Oedipus and "luck" is qualified, of course, by a modern as opposed to ancient viewpoint on irony. See again Thompson's assertion that the Greeks did not apprehend irony in ways that characterize subsequent epochs (4).

2. Regarding Brecht's ordering of events and emphasis on juxtaposition, see also his directive on sequence in staging as "one thing after another" (*Couragemodell*), in Jones (87).

Works cited

Adamantova, Vera, and Rodney Williamson. "Chekhovian Irony and Satire and the Translator's Art: Visions and Versions of Personal Worlds." In Clayton, 211–224.

Alwes, Derek. "Oh, Phooey to Death!: Boethian Consolation in Tom Stoppard's *Arcadia*." *Papers on Language and Literature* 36:4 (Fall 2000): 392–404.

Andreev, Leonid. "Letters on the Theatre." In Senelick, 223–272.

Archer, William, intro. *The Works of Henrik Ibsen*, Volume x. New York: Charles Scribner's Sons, 1912.

Attar, Samar. *The Intruder in Modern Drama*. Frankfurt: Peter D. Lang, 1981.

Balakian, Jan. "*The Heidi Chronicles*: The Big Chill of Feminism." *South Atlantic Review* 60:2 (May 1995): 93–102.

   "Wendy Wasserstein: A Feminist from the Seventies to the Present." In Murphy, 213–231.

Barnett, Claudia, ed. *Wendy Wasserstein: A Casebook*. New York: Garland Publishing, 1999.

Barricelli, Jean-Pierre, ed. *Chekhov's Great Plays: A Critical Anthology*. New York: New York University Press, 1981.

Barthes, Roland. "Structure of the *Fait-Divers*." *Critical Essays* (1964). Evanston, Ill.: Northwestern University Press, 1972.

Bassnett-McGuire, Susan. *Luigi Pirandello*. New York: Grove Press, 1983.

Behler, Ernst. *Irony and the Discourse of Modernity*. Seattle: University of Washington Press, 1990.

Bely, Andrey. "The Cherry Orchard." In Senelick, 89–92.

Bentley, Eric. *The Brecht Commentaries 1943–1980*. New York: Grove Press, 1981.

    "Father's Day." *The Drama Review*. 1:13 (Fall 1968): 57–72.

    The Life of the Drama. New York: Atheneum, 1972.

    "The Making of a Dramatist (1892–1903)." In Bogard and Oliver, 290–312.

    The Playwright as Thinker: A Study of Drama in Modern Times. New York: Harcourt, Brace, and World, 1946.

Bentley, Eric, ed. *Naked Masks: Five Plays*. By Luigi Pirandello. New York: Dutton, 1952.

Berst, Charles A. *Bernard Shaw and the Art of Drama*. Urbana: University of Illinois Press, 1973.

Bigsby, Christopher. *Contemporary American Playwrights*. Cambridge: Cambridge University Press, 1999.

    Modern American Drama 1945–2000. Cambridge: Cambridge University Press, 2000.

Bogard, Travis, and William I. Oliver, eds. *Modern Drama: Essays in Criticism*. Oxford: Oxford University Press, 1965.

Booth, Wayne C. *A Rhetoric of Irony*. Chicago: University of Chicago Press, 1974.

Brassell, Tim. *Tom Stoppard: An Assessment*. London: Macmillan Press, 1985.

Brecht, Bertolt. *Brecht on Theatre*. Ed. and trans. John Willett. New York: Hill and Wang, 1957.

    "*Couragemodell 1949*." In Jones, 78–137.

    Mother Courage and Her Children. Trans. Eric Bentley. New York: Grove, 1955.

Brooks, Cleanth. "Irony as a Principle of Structure." In Zabel, 729–741.

    The Well-Wrought Urn: Studies in the Structure of Poetry. New York: Harcourt, Brace, Jovanovich, 1947.

Brustein, Robert. "The Crack in the Chimney: Reflections on Contemporary American Playwriting." In Edelstein, 141–157.

    The Theatre of Revolt: An Approach to the Modern Drama. Boston: Little Brown, 1962.

Bryer, Jackson R. *The Playwright's Art: Conversations with Contemporary American Dramatists.* New Brunswick: Rutgers University Press, 1995.

Burke, Kenneth. *A Grammar of Motives (1945).* Berkeley: University of California Press, 1969.

    "Othello: An Essay to Illustrate a Method." *Perspectives by Incongruity.* Ed. Stanley Edgar Hyman. Bloomington: Indiana University Press, 1964. 152–195.

    The Philosophy of Literary Form: Studies in Symbolic Action. Berkeley: University of California Press, 1941.

Cambon, Glauco, ed. *Pirandello: A Collection of Critical Essays.* Englewood Cliffs, N. J.: Prentice-Hall, 1967.

Caputi, Anthony, ed. and trans. *Six Characters in Search of an Author. Eight Modern Plays.* New York: W. W. Norton, 1991.

Chekhov, Anton. *Best Plays by Chekhov.* Trans. and intro. Stark Young. New York: Modern Library, 1956.

    Chekhov: The Major Plays. Trans. Ann Dunnigan. New York: Penguin/Signet, 1964.

    The Oxford Chekhov, Volume III. Trans. and ed. Ronald Hingley. London: Oxford University Press, 1964.

Clayton, J. Douglas, ed. *Chekhov Then and Now: The Perception of Chekhov in World Culture.* New York: Peter Lang, 1997.

Clurman, Harold. *Ibsen.* New York: Da Capo, 1977.

Coe, Richard N. *Eugene Ionesco.* New York: Grove, 1961.

Colebrook, Claire. *Irony.* London: Routledge, 2004.

Corrigan, Robert. "The Drama of Anton Chekhov." In Bogard and Oliver, 73–98.

Culler, Jonathan. *Structuralist Poetics.* Ithaca, N.Y.: Cornell University Press, 1975.

Demetz, Peter, ed. *Brecht: A Collection of Critical Essays.* Englewood Cliffs, N. J.: Prentice-Hall, 1962.

Denby, David. "The Moviegoer." *New Yorker* (September 12, 2005): 90–97.

Derrida, Jacques. *Writing and Difference.* Trans. and intro. Alan Bass. Chicago: University of Chicago Press, 1978.

Dukore, Bernard F. *Bernard Shaw, Playwright: Aspects of Shavian Drama.* Columbia: University of Missouri Press, 1973.

Works cited

Edelstein, Arthur, ed. *Images and Ideas in American Culture: Essays in Memory of Philip Rahv.* Hanover, N. H.: Brandeis University Press, 1979.

Edwards, Paul. "Science in *Hapgood* and *Arcadia.*" In Kelly, 171–184.

Eekman, Thomas A., ed. *Critical Essays on Anton Chekhov.* Boston: G. K. Hall and Company, 1989.

Egan, Michael, ed. *Ibsen: The Critical Heritage.* London: Routledge and Kegan Paul, 1972.

Else, Gerald A. *Aristotle's Poetics: The Argument.* Cambridge, Mass.: Harvard University Press, 1957.

Empson, William. *Seven Types of Ambiguity.* New York: New Directions, 1947.

Esslin, Martin. *Brecht: The Man and His Work.* New York: Doubleday, 1960.

⠀⠀⠀⠀⠀*The Theatre of the Absurd.* Garden City, N. Y.: Doubleday, 1961.

Ewbank, Inga-Stina. "The Last Plays." In McFarlane, 126–154.

Fergusson, Francis. "*The Cherry Orchard*: A Theater-Poem of the Suffering of Change." In Jackson, 147–160.

⠀⠀⠀⠀⠀*The Idea of a Theatre.* Princeton, N.J.: Princeton University Press, 1949.

Finney, Gail. *Women in Modern Drama: Freud, Feminism, and European Theater at the Turn of the Century.* Ithaca, N.Y.: Cornell University Press, 1989.

Fisher, James. *The Theater of Tony Kushner: Living Past Hope.* New York: Routledge, 2001.

Fjelde, Rolf, ed. *Ibsen: A Collection of Critical Essays.* Englewood Cliffs, N. J.: Prentice-Hall, 1965.

Fleming, John. *Stoppard's Theatre: Finding Order Amid Chaos.* Austin: University of Texas Press, 2001.

Frye, Northrop. *Anatomy of Criticism.* Princeton, N.J.: Princeton University Press, 1957.

⠀⠀⠀⠀⠀*Fools of Time.* Toronto: University of Toronto Press, 1967.

Gainor, J. Ellen. *Shaw's Daughters: Dramatic and Narrative Constructions of Gender.* Ann Arbor: University of Michigan Press, 1991.

Gans, Eric. *Signs of Paradox: Irony, Resentment, and Other Mimetic Structures*. Stanford, Calif.: Stanford University Press, 1997.

Garner, Stanton B., Jr. "*Angels in America*: The Millennium and Postmodern Memory." In Geis and Kruger, 173–184.

Geis, Deborah, and Steven F. Kruger. *Approaching the Millennium: Essays on "Angels in America."* Ann Arbor: University of Michigan Press, 1997.

Gelb, Arthur, and Barbara Gelb. *O'Neill*. New York: Harper & Brothers, 1962.

Gilman, Richard. *Chekhov's Plays: An Opening Into Eternity*. New Haven, Conn.: Yale University Press, 1995.

        The Making of Modern Drama. New York: Farrar, Straus, and Giroux, 1972.

Gosse, Edmund. *Henrik Ibsen*. New York: Charles Scribner's Sons, 1908.

Grene, David. *Reality and the Heroic Pattern: Last Plays of Ibsen, Shakespeare, and Sophocles*. Chicago: University of Chicago Press, 1967.

Grossvogel, David I. *Four Playwrights and a Postscript: Brecht, Ionesco, Beckett, Genet*. Ithaca, N.Y.: Cornell University Press, 1962.

Gurewitch, Morton. *The Ironic Temper and the Comic Imagination*. Detroi, Mich.: Wayne State University Press, 1994.

Hardison, O. B., and Leon Golden, trans. *Aristotle's Poetics: A Translation and Commentary for Students of Literature*. Tallahassee: Florida State University Press, 1981.

Hayman, Ronald. *Eugene Ionesco*. New York: Frederick Unger, 1976.

Hingley, Ronald. *Chekhov: A Biographical and Critical Study*. New York: Barnes and Noble, 1950.

Holroyd, Michael. *Bernard Shaw: A Biography*, Volume I: *The Search for Love*. New York: Random House, 1988.

Hunter, Jim. *Tom Stoppard: "Rosencrantz and Guildenstern Are Dead," "Jumpers," "Travesties," "Arcadia"*. London: Faber and Faber, 2000.

Hutcheon, Linda. *A Poetics of Postmodernism: History, Theory, Fiction*. London: Routledge, 1988.

Hynes, Joseph. "Tom Stoppard's Lighted March." *Virginia Quarterly Review: A National Journal of Literature and Discussion* 71:4 (Autumn 1995): 642–55.

Works cited

Ibsen, Henrik. *Ibsen: The Complete Major Prose Plays*. Trans. and intro. Rolf Fjelde. New York: Penguin, 1965.
  "When We Dead Awaken" and Three Other Plays. Trans. Michael Meyer. Garden City: Doubleday, 1960.
Ionesco, Eugène. *"The Bald Soprano" and Other Plays*. Trans. Donald M. Allen. New York: Grove Press, 1958.
  Notes and Counter Notes: Writings on the Theatre. New York: Grove Press, 1964.
  "The World of Ionesco." *International Theatre Annual* 2 (1957). Qtd. in Weiss, 480–481.
  "Why Do I Write? A Summing Up." In Lamont and Friedman, 5–19.
Irvine, William. *The Universe of G.B.S.* New York: McGraw-Hill, 1949.
Jackson, Robert Louis, ed. *Chekhov: A Collection of Critical Essays*. Englewood Cliffs, N. J.: Prentice-Hall, 1967.
James, Henry. "Ibsen's New Play." *Pall Mall Gazette* (February 17, 1893). In Egan, 266–269.
Jernigan, Daniel. "Tom Stoppard and 'Postmodern Science': Normalizing Radical Epistemologies in *Hapgood* and *Arcadia*." *Comparative Drama* 37:1 (Spring 2003): 3–35.
Johnston, Brian. *The Ibsen Cycle: The Design of the Plays from "Pillars of Society" to "When We Dead Awaken."* University Park: Pennsylvania State University Press, 1992.
Jones, David Richard. *Great Directors at Work*. Berkeley: University of California Press, 1986.
Kaufmann, R. J., ed. *G. B. Shaw: A Collection of Critical Essays*. Englewood Cliffs, N. J.: Prentice-Hall, 1965.
Kelly, Katherine E., ed. *The Cambridge Companion to Tom Stoppard*. Cambridge: Cambridge University Press, 2001.
Kennedy, Andrew K. "*Six Characters*: Pirandello's Last Tape." In Marker and Innes, 181–190.
Kern, Stephen. *A Cultural History of Causality*. Princeton, N.J.: Princeton University Press, 2004.
Keyssar, Helene. "When Wendy Isn't Trendy: Wendy Wasserstein's *The Heidi Chronicles* and *An American Daughter*." In Barnett, 133–160.

Kierkegaard, Søren. *The Concept of Irony*. Trans. and intro. Lee M. Capel. Bloomington: Indiana University Press, 1965.

Koht, Halvdan. *Life of Ibsen*. Trans. and ed. Einar Haugen and A. E. Santaniello. New York: Benjamin Blom, 1971.

Kramer, Jeffrey, and Prapassaree Kramer. "Stoppard's *Arcadia*: Research, Time, Loss." *Modern Drama* 40:1 (Spring 1997): 1–10.

Krutch, Joseph Wood. *Modernism in Modern Drama: A Definition, and an Estimate*. Ithaca, N. Y.: Cornell University Press, 1953.

Kushner, Tony. *Angels in America Part I: Millennium Approaches*. New York: Theatre Communications Group, 1995.

Lahr, John. "*Stalkers and Talkers*" (Review of *Jumpers*). *New Yorker* (May 3, 2004): 101.

    "*Talking Terror*" (Review of *The Coast of Utopia*). *New Yorker* (September 23, 2002): 95.

Lamont, Rosette C. *Ionesco's Imperatives*. Ann Arbor: University of Michigan Press, 1993.

Lamont, Rosette C., ed., *Ionesco: A Collection of Critical Essays*. Englewood Cliffs, N. J.: Prentice-Hall, 1973.

Lamont, Rosette C., and Melvin J. Friedman, eds. *The Two Faces of Ionesco*. Troy: Whitson Publishing Company, 1978.

Lane, Nancy. *Understanding Ionesco*. Columbia: University of South Carolina Press, 1994.

Langer, Susanne. *Feeling and Form: A Theory of Art*. New York: Charles Scribner's Sons, 1953.

Leach, Robert. "Mother Courage and Her Children." In Thomson, 128–138.

Lewis, Allan. *The Contemporary Theatre: The Significant Playwrights of Our Time*. New York: Crown, 1971.

    Ionesco. New York: Twayne, 1972.

Lyons, Charles R. *Bertolt Brecht: The Despair and the Polemic*. Carbondale: Southern Illinois University Press, 1968.

McFarlane, James, ed. *The Cambridge Companion to Ibsen*. Cambridge: Cambridge University Press, 1994.

Magarshack, David. *Chekhov the Dramatist*. New York: Hill and Wang, 1960.

The Real Chekhov: An Introduction to Chekhov's Last Plays. New York: Barnes and Noble, 1972.

Marker, Frederick J., and Christopher Innes, eds. Modernism in European Drama: Ibsen, Strindberg, Pirandello, Beckett; Essays from "Modern Drama." Toronto: University of Toronto Press, 1998.

McDermott, John V. "Ionesco's The Bald Soprano." The Explicator 55:1 (Fall 1996): 40–41.

McDonald, David. "Derrida and Pirandello's Six Characters." Modern Drama 20:4 (December 1977): 421–436.

Meisel, Martin. Shaw and the Nineteenth-Century Theater. Princeton, N.J.: Princeton University Press, 1963.

Meisner, Natalie. "Messing with the Idyllic: The Performance of Femininity in Kushner's Angels in America." The Yale Journal of Criticism 16:1 (2003): 177–189.

Melbourne, Lucy. "Plotting the Apple of Knowledge: Tom Stoppard's Arcadia as Iterated Theatrical Algorithm." Modern Drama 41:4 (Winter 1998): 557–572.

Mennemeier, Franz Norbert. "Mother Courage and Her Children." In Demetz, 138–150.

Meyer, Michael. Ibsen: A Biography. Garden City, N.Y.: Doubleday, 1971.
    "Introduction" to The Master Builder. In "When We Dead Awaken" and Three Other Plays. Garden City, N.Y.: Doubleday, 1960. 111–128. Reprint, "Ibsen and Emilie Bardach." In Weiss, 46–55.

Miller, Arthur. A View from the Bridge (1955). New York: Penguin, 1977.

Muecke, D. C. The Compass of Irony. London: Methuen, 1969.
    Irony. The Critical Idiom 13. London: Methuen, 1970.
    Irony and the Ironic. The Critical Idiom 13. London: Methuen, 1982.

Murphy, Brenda, ed. The Cambridge Companion to American Women Playwrights. Cambridge: Cambridge University Press, 1999.

Nethercot, Arthur H. Men and Supermen: The Shavian Portrait Gallery. Cambridge, Mass.: Harvard University Press, 1954.

Ohmann, Richard M. "Born to Set it Right: The Roots of Shaw's Style." In Kaufmann, 26–41.

Oliver, Roger W. Dreams of Passion: The Theater of Luigi Pirandello. New York: New York University Press, 1979.

O'Neill, Eugene. *Beyond the Horizon (1920). Four Plays by Eugene O'Neill.* New York: Penguin/Signet, 1998.

Paolucci, Anne. "Comedy and Paradox in Pirandello's Plays (An Hegelian Perspective)." *Modern Drama* 20:4 (December 1977): 321–340.

    Pirandello's Theater: The Recovery of the Modern Stage for Dramatic Art. Carbondale: Southern Illinois University Press, 1974.

Peace, Richard. *Chekhov: A Study of the Four Major Plays.* New Haven, Conn.: Yale University Press, 1983.

Pirandello, Luigi. "Preface" to *Six Characters in Search of an Author* (1925). In Bentley, ed., *Naked Masks*, 363–375.

    Short Stories. Trans. and intro. Frederick May. London: Oxford University Press, 1965.

    Six Characters in Search of an Author. Trans. and intro. Eric Bentley. New York: Signet, 1970 (rep. 1998).

Poniewozik, James. "Irony is Dead, Long Live Irony." *Time* (July 17, 2000): 74.

Pronko, Leonard. *Eugene Ionesco.* New York: Columbia University Press, 1965.

Purdy, Jedediah. *For Common Things: Irony, Trust, and Commitment in America Today.* New York: Knopf, 1999.

Reid, John. "Matter and Spirit in *The Seagull.*" *Modern Drama* 41:4 (Winter 1998): 607–622.

Richards, I. A. *Principles of Literary Criticism.* New York: Harcourt, Brace, Jovanovich, 1925.

Risso, Richard D. "Chekhov: A View of the Basic Ironic Structures." In Barricelli, 181–188.

Rorty, Richard. *Contingency, Irony, and Solidarity.* Cambridge: Cambridge University Press, 1989.

Rosenberg, Marvin. "Pirandello's Mirror." In Marker and Innes, 127–141.

Rosenblatt, Roger. "The Age of Irony Comes to an End." *Time* (September 24, 2001): 79.

Saussure, Ferdinand. *Course in General Linguistics* (1915). Ed. Charles Bally and Albert Sechehaye, trans. and intro. Wade Baskin. New York: McGraw-Hill, 1966.

Works cited

Savran, David. "Ambivalence, Utopia, and a Queer Sort of Materialism: How *Angels in America* Reconstructs the Nation." *Theatre Journal* 47:2 (May 1995): 207–227.

Schechner, Richard. "*The Bald Soprano* and *The Lesson*: An Inquiry into Play Structure." In Lamont, ed., *Collection*, 21–37.

    "The Unexpected Visitor in Ibsen's Late Plays." In Fjelde, 158–168.

Schiff, Stephen. "Full Stoppard." *Vanity Fair* (May 1989): 153–156, 214–215.

Schoeps, Karl H. *Bertolt Brecht*. New York: Frederick Unger Publishing Co., 1977.

Senelick, Laurence, ed. and trans. *Russian Dramatic Theory from Pushkin to the Symbolists: An Anthology*. Austin: University of Texas Press, 1981.

Shaeffer, Louis. *O'Neill: Son and Playwright*. Boston: Little, Brown, and Company, 1968.

Shaw, Bernard. *Mrs. Warren's Profession*. London: Constable, 1905.

    Plays by George Bernard Shaw. Foreword by Eric Bentley. New York: Penguin/Signet, 1960.

    The Quintessence of Ibsenism. London: Hill and Wang, 1913.

    Selected Plays. New York: Dodd, Mead, and Company, 1981.

    Shaw on Theatre. Ed. E. J. West. New York: Hill and Wang, 1958.

Sinicropi, Giovanni. "The Metaphysical Dimension and Pirandello's Theatre." *Modern Drama* 20:4 (December 1977): 353–380.

Skaftymov, A. "Principles of Structure in Chekhov's Plays." In Jackson, 69–87.

Slonim, Marc. *From Chekhov to the Revolution: Russian Literature 1900–1917*. New York: Oxford University Press, 1953.

Speirs, Ronald. *Bertolt Brecht*. London: Macmillan, 1987.

Starkie, Walter. *Luigi Pirandello, 1867–1936*. Berkeley: University of California Press, 1965.

States, Bert O. *Great Reckonings in Little Rooms: On the Phenomenology of Theatre*. Berkeley: University of California Press, 1985.

    Irony and Drama. Ithaca, N.Y.: Cornell University Press, 1971.

The Pleasure of the Play. Ithaca, N.Y.: Cornell University Press, 1994.

Stein, Joel. "In Defense of Irony." *Time* (October 4, 1999): 42.

Sternlieb, Lisa, and Nancy Selleck. "'What Is Carnal Embrace?': Learning to Converse in Stoppard's *Arcadia*." *Modern Drama* 46:3 (Fall 2003): 482–502.

Stoppard, Tom. *Arcadia*. London: Faber and Faber, 1993.

Storm, William. *After Dionysus: A Theory of the Tragic*. Ithaca, N.Y.: Cornell University Press, 1998.

Stringfellow, Frank, Jr. *The Meaning of Irony: A Psychoanalytic Investigation*. Albany, N.Y.: State University of New York Press, 1994.

Styan, John L. "The Cherry Orchard." In Eekman, 192–200.

"Pirandellian Theatre Games." In Marker and Innes, 142–150.

Sypher, Wylie. "Cubist Drama." In Cambon, 67–71.

Templeton, Joan. *Ibsen's Women*. Cambridge: Cambridge University Press, 1997.

Thomson, Peter, ed. *The Cambridge Companion to Brecht*. Cambridge: Cambridge University Press, 1994.

Thompson, Alan Reynolds. *The Dry Mock: A Study of Irony in Drama*. Berkeley: University of California Press, 1948.

Troyat, Henri. *Chekhov*. Trans. Michael Heim. New York: Ballantine, 1988.

Tynan, Kenneth. "Withdrawing With Style from the Chaos" (Profiles). *New Yorker* (December 19, 1977): 41–111.

Valency, Maurice. *The Breaking String*. Oxford: Oxford University Press, 1966.

The End of the World: An Introduction to Contemporary Drama. New York: Oxford University Press, 1980.

Vanden Heuvel, Michael. "'Is Postmodernism?' Stoppard Among/Against the Postmoderns." In Kelly, 213–228.

Vees-Gulani, Susanne. "Hidden Order in the 'Stoppard Set': Chaos Theory in the Content and Structure of Tom Stoppard's *Arcadia*." *Modern Drama* 42:3 (Fall 1999): 411–426.

Vernant, Jean-Pierre. "Greek Tragedy: Problems of Interpretation." In Richard Macksey and Eugenio Donato, eds., *The Structuralist*

Works cited

Controversy: The Languages of Criticism and the Sciences of Man. Baltimore, Md.: Johns Hopkins University Press, 1972. 273–295.

Vittorini, Domenico. The Drama of Luigi Pirandello. New York: Dover, 1957.

Wasserstein, Wendy. "The Heidi Chronicles" and Other Plays. New York: Random House, 1991.

Weiss, Samuel A., ed. Drama in the Modern World: Plays and Essays (Alternate Edition). Lexington, Mass.: D. C. Heath and Company, 1974.

Wheatley, Alison. "Aesthetic Consolation and the Genius of the Place in Stoppard's Arcadia." Mosaic: A Journal for the Interdisciplinary Study of Literature 37:3 (2004): 171–184.

White, Hayden. Metahistory: The Historical Imagination in Nineteenth-Century Europe. Baltimore, Md.: Johns Hopkins University Press, 1973.

Wilde, Alan. Horizons of Assent: Modernism, Postmodernism, and the Ironic Imagination. Baltimore, Md.: Johns Hopkins University Press, 1981.

Wilde, Oscar. "The Importance of Being Earnest" and Other Plays. New York: Penguin/Signet, 1985.

Williams, Raymond. Modern Tragedy (1966). Toronto: Broadview, 2006.

Zabel, Morton Dauwen, ed. Literary Opinion in America: Essays Illustrating the Status, Methods, and Problems of Criticism in the United States in the Twentieth Century. New York: Harper and Brothers, 1937, rev. edn. 1951.

Index

Index

DATE DUE

Demco, Inc. 38-293